"From years of friendship, conversation, shared burdens, mutual intercession, and the same vision of our great God, I trust Sam's biblical faithfulness. He brings a keen eye and a wakened soul to God's Word. The overflow for us is fresh insight and strong feeling. I thank God for Sam Storms. My life is sweeter because of the seasoning he brings."

—**John Piper**, Pastor for Preaching and Vision,
Bethlehem Baptist Church, Minneapolis, Minnesota

"Many devotional books lack biblical and theological depth. Storms's work is a striking exception. His meditations on Colossians faithfully communicate the message of the letter so that readers are enriched both biblically and theologically. Moreover, the meaning of Colossians is applied with wisdom and power so that I found myself encouraged, convicted, and challenged. Here is evangelical theology at its best."

—**Thomas R. Schreiner**, James Buchanan Harrison
Professor of New Testament Interpretation,
The Southern Baptist Theological Seminary

# the HOPE of Glory

**Crossway books by Sam Storms:**

*Signs of the Spirit: An Interpretation of Jonathan Edwards's "Religious Affections"*

*Chosen for Life: The Case for Divine Election*

*the*
# HOPE
## of
# *Glory*

*100 Meditations on Colossians*

SAM STORMS

CROSSWAY BOOKS
WHEATON, ILLINOIS

The Hope of Glory: 100 Meditations on Colossians
Copyright © 2007 by Sam Storms
Published by Crossway Books
      a publishing ministry of Good News Publishers
      1300 Crescent Street
      Wheaton, Illinois 60187

All rights reserved. No part of this publication may be reproduced, stored in a retrieval system, or transmitted in any form or by any means, electronic, mechanical, photocopy, recording, or otherwise, without the prior permission of the publisher, except as provided for by USA copyright law.

Cover design: Jessie McGrath
Cover illustration: IStock
First printing 2007
Printed in the United States of America

Unless otherwise indicated, Scripture quotations are from *The Holy Bible, English Standard Version*®, copyright © 2001 by Crossway Bibles, a publishing ministry of Good News Publishers. Used by permission. All rights reserved.
Scripture quotations marked NASB are from *The New American Standard Bible.*® Copyright © The Lockman Foundation 1960, 1962, 1963, 1968, 1971, 1972, 1973, 1975, 1977, 1995. Used by permission.

Scripture references marked NIV are from *The Holy Bible: New International Version.*® Copyright ©1973, 1978, 1984 by International Bible Society. Used by permission of Zondervan Publishing House. All rights reserved.
    The "NIV" and "New International Version" trademarks are registered in the United States Patent and Trademark Office by International Bible Society. Use of either trademark requires the permission of International Bible Society.

Scripture quotations marked KJV are from the King James Version of the Bible.

All emphases in Scripture quotations have been added by the author.
ISBN 978-1-58134-931-3

**Library of Congress Cataloging-in-Publication Data**
    Storms, C. Samuel, 1951–
    The hope of glory : 100 daily meditations on Colossians / Sam Storms.
      p. cm.
    ISBN 978-1-58134-931-3 (tpb)
    1. Bible. N.T. Colossians—Meditations. I. Title.

BS2715.54.S76 2007
227'.706—dc22
                                                  2007040782

| VP | | | 18 | 17 | 16 | 15 | 14 | 13 | 12 | 11 | 10 | 07 | 08 |
|----|----|----|----|----|----|----|----|----|----|----|----|----|----|
| 15 | 14 | 13 | 12 | 11 | 10 | 9 | 8 | 7 | 6 | 5 | 4 | 3 | 2 | 1 |

Lovingly dedicated
to
Mike and Betty Jane Cawley

In heartfelt appreciation for your constant encouragement
and your generous support of Enjoying God Ministries

# Contents

| | |
|---|---|
| Introduction | 11 |

**Part 1: Colossians 1:1–29**

| | |
|---|---|
| 1. By the Will of God (1:1a) | 17 |
| 2. Our Dual Identity (1:2a) | 20 |
| 3. Grace *to* You, Grace *with* You (1:2b) | 23 |
| 4. And Peace from God (1:2b) | 25 |
| 5. Why Thank God? (1:3–4) | 27 |
| 6. Faith and Love: Visible Virtues (1:4) | 29 |
| 7. Hope: The Fountain of Faith and Love (1) (1:4–5a) | 32 |
| 8. Hope: The Fountain of Faith and Love (2) (1:4–5) | 36 |
| 9. The Word of Truth (1:5b–6) | 39 |
| 10. In the Spirit (1:8) | 42 |
| 11. A Remarkable Man (1:7–8; 4:12–13) | 45 |
| 12. Intercession: Why, for Whom, and How Often? (1:9a) | 48 |
| 13. Intercession: What Should We Ask For? (1:9b) | 51 |
| 14. Fruitless Knowledge? (1:10) | 54 |
| 15. Worthy of the Lord/Pleasing to the Lord (1:10) | 57 |
| 16. Power and Perseverance (1:11) | 60 |
| 17. Glad-hearted Gratitude! (1:12a) | 63 |
| 18. Qualified in Christ (1:12) | 66 |
| 19. Delivered from Darkness (1:13) | 68 |
| 20. Forever Forgiven (1:14) | 71 |
| 21. Who Is This Man? (1:15–20) | 75 |
| 22. Seeing the Father in the Son (1:15) | 79 |
| 23. Praising Christ with Prepositions (1:16) | 82 |
| 24. Shaken, but Safe in Him (1:17) | 85 |
| 25. Preeminent in All Things (1:18) | 88 |
| 26. Wholly God (1) (1:19; 2:9) | 91 |

| | |
|---|---:|
| 27. Wholly God (2) (1:19; 2:9) | 94 |
| 28. Wholly God (3) (1:19; 2:9) | 97 |
| 29. Will Everyone Be Saved? (1) (1:20) | 100 |
| 30. Will Everyone Be Saved? (2) (1:20) | 103 |
| 31. Before (1:21) | 107 |
| 32. But Now (1:22) | 110 |
| 33. After (1:22) | 113 |
| 34. No Continuation, No Presentation (1:23) | 116 |
| 35. Joy in Suffering? (1:24) | 120 |
| 36. Filling Up the Afflictions of Christ (1:24) | 123 |
| 37. The Hope of Glory (1:25–27) | 127 |
| 38. Everyone for Everyone (1:28) | 130 |
| 39. His Power Divine (1) (1:29) | 133 |
| 40. His Power Divine (2) (1:29) | 136 |

## Part 2: Colossians 2:1–23

| | |
|---|---:|
| 41. A Most Fervent Wrestle with the Lord (2:1–3) | 143 |
| 42. The Anatomy of a Prayer (2:1–3) | 146 |
| 43. Defeating Doubt (2:1–3) | 149 |
| 44. Treasuring Christ (2:1–3) | 152 |
| 45. How's Your Faith? (2:4–5) | 155 |
| 46. Thanks, I Needed That! (2:6–7) | 158 |
| 47. Fullness for Life (2:8–10) | 161 |
| 48. Glorious Truths in Gruesome Terms (2:11) | 165 |
| 49. Why I Am a Baptist (2:12) | 168 |
| 50. Faith in What? (2:12) | 172 |
| 51. Alive in Him! (2:13–14) | 175 |
| 52. Jesus Paid It All (2:13–14) | 178 |
| 53. Demons: Disarmed, Displayed, Defeated (1) (2:15) | 181 |
| 54. Demons: Disarmed, Displayed, Defeated (2) (2:15) | 184 |
| 55. Legalism Can Be Lethal (2:16–23) | 189 |
| 56. Don't Let Them Judge You (2:16–17) | 192 |
| 57. Don't Let Them Disqualify You (2:18–19) | 196 |
| 58. Don't Let Them Enslave You (2:20–23) | 201 |

## Part 3: Colossians 3:1–25

| | |
|---|---:|
| 59. Fighting Pleasure with Pleasure (3:1–4) | 207 |
| 60. Celebrating Christocentricity! (3:1–4) | 210 |

| | |
|---|---|
| 61. Was Paul (Am I, Are You) a Gnostic? (3:1–4) | 213 |
| 62. Hidden in Him (3:1–4) | 218 |
| 63. Glorified in Him (3:1–4) | 222 |
| 64. Ruthless or Reckless? (3:5–11) | 226 |
| 65. Sexual Impurity: A Warning (3:5) | 230 |
| 66. Idolatry without Idols (3:5) | 234 |
| 67. Is a God without Wrath a Good God? (3:6) | 237 |
| 68. Changing Clothes (3:8) | 241 |
| 69. The Destructive Power of Deception (3:9a) | 245 |
| 70. "To Life" versus "From Life" (3:9–10) | 248 |
| 71. To Be Like Jesus (3:10) | 251 |
| 72. "All That Matters Is You, O Lord!" (3:11) | 254 |
| 73. Changed by His Choice (3:12) | 257 |
| 74. The Seamless Garment of Christian Godliness (3:12) | 260 |
| 75. Forgive, as the Lord Has Forgiven You (1) (3:13) | 263 |
| 76. Forgive, as the Lord Has Forgiven You (2) (3:13) | 267 |
| 77. The Crowning Glory of Christian Godliness (3:14) | 271 |
| 78. The Peace of Christ (3:15) | 274 |
| 79. How Rich the Word of Christ! (3:16) | 277 |
| 80. Singing Truth (3:16) | 281 |
| 81. Wholehearted Worship (3:16) | 285 |
| 82. Comprehensive Christianity, or, Doing All in the Name of Christ (3:17) | 288 |
| 83. Wives Who Submit to Their Husbands (3:18) | 292 |
| 84. Husbands Who Lovingly Lead Their Wives (3:19) | 297 |
| 85. Focus on the Family (3:20–21) | 300 |
| 86. Is All Scripture Profitable? (3:22–4:1) | 304 |

### *Part 4: Colossians 4:1–18*

| | |
|---|---|
| 87. You Are Serving the Lord Christ! (3:22–4:1) | 309 |
| 88. The Easiest Thing about Prayer (4:2) | 312 |
| 89. Pray Thankfully! (4:2) | 315 |
| 90. Just Do It! (4:3–4) | 318 |
| 91. Open Doors for the Gospel (4:3–4) | 322 |
| 92. Human Setbacks or Divine Setups? (4:3–4) | 325 |
| 93. "Salty" Speech and the Salvation of Souls (4:5–6) | 329 |
| 94. When Christians Clash (1) (4:10, 14) | 333 |
| 95. When Christians Clash (2) (4:10, 14) | 338 |

## Contents

| | | |
|---|---|---|
| 96. | When Christians Clash (3) (4:10, 14) | 342 |
| 97. | Superstar-less Christianity (4:7–17) | 345 |
| 98. | Women on the Front Lines (4:15) | 348 |
| 99. | The Public Reading of "Lost" Scripture (4:16) | 351 |
| 100. | Remember My Chains (4:18) | 355 |
| | Notes | 358 |

# *Introduction*

The existence of this book of meditations on Paul's letter to the Colossians can be explained by something Jonathan Edwards said in a sermon he preached in November 1739. The message was titled, "The Importance and Advantage of a Thorough Knowledge of Divine Truth." As is the case with much of what Edwards wrote, the prose is not what we in the twenty-first century are accustomed to reading, but don't let that deter you from the truth of what he said:

> Be assiduous in reading the holy Scriptures. This is the fountain whence all knowledge in divinity must be derived. Therefore let not this treasure lie by you neglected. Every man of common understanding who can read, may, if he please, become well acquainted with the Scriptures. And what an excellent attainment would this be![1]

"Be assiduous." I trust that Edwards had in mind the definition we commonly employ today: "assiduous: marked by careful unremitting attention or persistent application."[2]

Most Christians would give assent to the title of Edwards's message: "Yes, of course it's *important* that we read and understand God's Word. There is great *advantage* in the pursuit of a *thorough knowledge* of divine truth. We must be *careful* and *unremitting* in the *attention* we give to it." But the fervency of that assertion, I regret to say, is rarely met with a proportionate devotion to actually *doing* it.

Why? Could it be that we simply don't believe that Scripture, to use Edwards's words, is a fountain, a treasure, the knowledge of which is an excellent attainment? The energy behind his exhortation is the unshakable conviction that Scripture truly is a *fountain*, a free-flowing, never-ending flood of truth, wisdom, and encouragement. It is a *treasure*, "more to be desired . . . than gold, even much fine gold; sweeter also than honey and drippings of the honeycomb" (Ps. 19:10). It is an excellent attainment, for in keeping the Scriptures there is great reward (Ps. 19:11).

The truth that we gain from the Scriptures is wide-ranging, the treasure is multifaceted, and the reward is incalculable. But in the book of Colossians it can be reduced to one glorious reality: Jesus Christ. This is the apostle's point in Colossians 1:27, from which I've derived the title to this book. There he mentions the greatness of the riches of the glory of the mystery that God has made known to us: "Christ in you, the hope of glory."

We love the Scriptures because they lead us to Christ. We are assiduous in our reading of God's Word because therein we see the beauty of God revealed in his Son; therein we taste the soul-satisfying sweetness of his redemptive blessings, therein we experience the sin-slaying power of his indwelling presence. In him, says Paul, "are hidden all the treasures of wisdom and knowledge" (Col. 2:3). He is our exceeding great reward. Oh, what an excellent attainment there is in a thorough knowledge of divine truth!

**A Word about Structure and Style**

This book is not a technical commentary on Colossians. Such volumes are in abundant supply, a few of which I've noted in the notes to the text. Still, one can certainly gain a fairly thorough grasp of the argument and ideas of Paul by reading through all one hundred meditations. But my target audience isn't the scholarly community.

I've written for the average, educated Christian believer. Well, that's not entirely accurate. I'm assuming that, although "average," you are passionate to know Christ better, hungry to be filled with the knowledge of the truth, and desperate to see him lifted high and holy in your life and in the experience of the church as a whole. If that describes you, or what you wish were true of you, then this book was designed specifically with you in mind.

Each meditation is intentionally short, and most can be read in five to ten minutes. To help you keep the larger context in mind, you might want to try the following approach: each day, read the chapter from which the day's reading comes, and each week (perhaps on Sunday), read the entire book of Colossians once. At that rate, you will read Colossians 1 forty times, Colossians 2 eighteen times, Colossians 3 twenty-nine times, Colossians 4 thirteen times; and you will read the entire book (in one sitting) fifteen times! You may wish to study and meditate upon them as part of your daily devotional life. Or you may find them helpful in your more in-depth analysis of God's Word. Perhaps they can be used as a guide in your small group or Sunday school class.

In any case, I've labored to maintain a delicate, and often difficult, balance between stylistic simplicity on the one hand and theological substance on the other. I've not avoided the hard texts in Colossians, but in addressing them I've worked at making Paul's meaning accessible to any Christian with an inquiring mind and a hungry heart. Notes are kept to a minimum. Only rarely do I appeal to something in the Greek text, and even then I strive to make it intelligible to those who read only the English Bible.

As for the English Bible, I've chosen to use the English Standard Version (ESV). One of my goals is to persuade you to embrace the ESV as your primary translation for study and memorization. Although I occasionally appeal to other translations, such as the New American Standard Version (NASB) and the New International Version (NIV), I've grown to love and appreciate the ESV for its combination of literal translation and readable style. I can only hope that you come to share my convictions.

To assist you in your study, I've placed the relevant passage for each meditation at the top of the page. In many instances, the Scripture verses accompanying the meditation are set within the context of the broader Scripture passage, and where this occurs the particular verse(s) in focus appear(s) in bold type. However, I encourage you to read them with your own Bible open and your finger on the text.

Finally, there is good reason for my use of the word *meditation* in describing these one hundred studies. In Psalm 145:5, David declared: "On the glorious splendor of your majesty, and on your wondrous works, I will meditate." This is what Scripture ultimately was designed to do: point us to the glorious splendor of God's majesty and deepen our satisfaction in the wondrous work he has achieved in Christ. So, don't merely read these studies on Colossians: ruminate! Don't simply study: saturate! I believe that in this way, through concentrated meditation on the Christ-exalting Word of Paul's epistle to the Colossians, the Holy Spirit will awaken in your heart that joy in Jesus that Peter can only describe as "inexpressible and filled with glory" (1 Pet. 1:8).

Sam Storms<br>
September 2006

Part 1

# Colossians 1:1–29

# 1
# By the Will of God

## Colossians 1:1a

**Paul, an apostle of Christ Jesus by the will of God, and Timothy our brother**, to the saints and faithful brothers in Christ at Colossae: Grace to you and peace from God our Father.

One of the reasons we ignore certain statements in Scripture is our misguided belief that they simply don't apply to us. For example, when the apostle Paul introduces his epistles he typically describes himself as "an apostle of Christ Jesus by the will of God" (Col. 1:1a; cf. also Eph. 1:1; 2 Tim. 1:1; 1 Cor. 1:1; Gal. 1:1).

I'm not an apostle and I doubt that you are either. So what possible relevance does a statement like that have for you and me? Before I answer that, let's consider what Paul had in mind for himself.

In the first place, this was an expression of his entire theological perspective. He became a Christian "by the will of God." His authority as an apostle is "by the will of God." The power of his ministry, whether in teaching or healing the sick, is "by the will of God." It is only "by God's will" (Rom. 15:32) that he will eventually visit Rome. And whatever more he will achieve before he breathes his final breath is "by the will of God."

Second, he needed to make clear to the Colossians (and to us) that they (and we) are obligated to listen to him. The Colossians were being led astray by false teachers, and we are certainly in no short supply of them today. But it is Paul, not they, who speaks with divine authority and sanction. If it is "by the will of God" that Paul speaks in this letter, then it is "the will of God" that we heed and embrace all he says in it.

In sum, Paul didn't aspire to or ask or apply for the job (after all, until captured by the grace of God on the road to Damascus he was evidently content with and proud of his status as a revered Pharisee; see Phil. 3:4–6). His ministry as an apostle did not come by human nomination nor did he look for human confirmation. It was by divine initiation, preparation, and authentication, which is to say, "by the will of God."

So what does this have to do with you and me? Everything! Here is why. It isn't simply Paul's apostolic authority in the first century but all things in all our lives at every moment in the twenty-first century that must be attributed to the "will of God." Paul himself made this clear in Ephesians 1:11 when he described God as the one "who works all things according to the counsel of his will."

Did you see that: *all things*! Not just Paul's ministry but yours as well. Paul was an apostle "by the will of God" whereas some of you are school teachers "by the will of God." Others are housewives "by the will of God" while many are nurses, physicians, lawyers, factory workers, salesmen, athletes, or missionaries "by the will of God." God's will extends to your life and calling and career no less so than to Paul's. Yours may not entail the spiritual authority that his did, but it is no less an expression of God's enablement and calling than Paul's or Peter's or John's or anyone's to whom we attribute greatness.

Have you paused to ponder the fact that who you are is "by the will of God," as well as what you do, where you live, how much you own, whatever you accomplish? Needless to say, this excludes your sinful deeds and rebellious attitude and failure to obey the Scriptures. For example, if Scripture declares that "this is the will of God, your sanctification: that you abstain from sexual immorality" (1 Thess. 4:3), then we dare not say that sexual immorality (or any other violation of the Word) is "by the will of God."

I take away at least two things from knowing that my life and achievements and efforts and gifts and opportunities are "by the will of God." First, there is an element of *security* in knowing this. The security is in the realization that my life cannot extend beyond

God's grace or capacity to redeem all things for his glory and my good. If all is "by the will of God" then I can celebrate his presence in my life and his hand on all that I seek to do in obedience to his Word. God's "will" encompasses and permeates and infuses all that you and I will ever be or do or say or think.

This experience of security especially extends to times of trial and hardship. Suffering for righteousness' sake is also "by the will of God." In fact, Paul declares that "it has been granted" (i.e., graciously given) to us to suffer for his name's sake (Phil. 1:29). Knowing that such experiences are not serendipitous or chance happenings but are orchestrated "by the will of God" will alone sustain us in the hour of testing.

Second, knowing that God is working all things according to the counsel of his will imparts a *dignity* not only to Paul's apostleship but also to your life and ministry, as well as mine. God values who we are and what we do because it is the fruit of his will working and orchestrating all things for the glory and praise of his grace in Christ Jesus. There is no second-rate job or inferior ministry or meaningless endeavor when all is "by the will of God."

It's stunning to consider that my daughter changes the diapers of my grandsons "by the will of God," and that I'm typing these words "by the will of God," and that you are reading them "by the will of God," and that all of us are simultaneously breathing "by the will of God."

So, don't ever think that because you aren't an apostle or a pastor or a public figure with power and prestige you are any less the product of God's will or are somehow on the outside looking in on what he is doing in the pursuit of his redemptive purpose. Lay your hand on your heart and your mind and the fruit of your labors, and above all your salvation in Jesus Christ, and rejoice that it is all "by the will of God."

# 2

# Our Dual Identity

## Colossians 1:2a

Paul, an apostle of Christ Jesus by the will of God, and Timothy our brother, **to the saints and faithful brothers in Christ at Colossae**: Grace to you and peace from God our Father.

Following his standard practice, Paul addresses this letter to "the saints" in Christ at Colossae. As you know, *saints* is a precious word that has been sorely perverted. For many people it conjures up images of a painfully thin, sad-faced monastic sort of soul who looks as if he's been sucking on a lemon.

Most of you are aware, I hope, that the word translated "saints" was used primarily to describe people set apart or separated unto God, consecrated by his grace to be a unique and treasured possession. The Old Testament background for this terminology is found in Exodus 19:6. The focus is more on *separation* than *sanctity* (although the former should always lead to the latter). It has in view more one's *position* than *purity*.

It's important to know that the word *saint* (as with the word *priest*) is always found in the plural in the New Testament, with but one exception (Phil. 4:21); but even there, Paul refers to "every" saint! This does not bode well for the "solitary saint," the "Lone-Ranger Christian" so often seen in our highly individualized Western way of looking at the faith. I'll address this at more length in a subsequent lesson.

But what most intrigues me about Paul's description of these believers is that they are both "in Christ" and "at Colossae." They are simultaneously citizens of two kingdoms. They live at one and the same time in Christ and in the world of this ancient Roman city.

Note well the emphasis on both earthly *and* spiritual geography: they live in both Colossae and Christ. Klyne Snodgrass comments on this phenomenon in his commentary on Ephesians. I have taken the liberty of substituting "Colossae" for "Ephesus":

> To speak of Paul's sense of "geography" is an attempt to describe the "place" where he thought Christians live. In Paul's mind, just as these Christians live literally in the region near [Colossae], they also live in Christ. The terrain, climate, values, and history in which people grow up and live helps to define who they are. As really as this region near [Colossae] defines who they are, Christ defines who believers really are. He is the "sphere of influence" or "power field" in which they live and from which they benefit and are transformed. That is, his Spirit, values, character, history, and purposes shape their lives. People can live in other spheres (cf. 2:1–3), but Christians live in Christ. Jesus Christ must never be depersonalized by such language, but we will not understand Paul unless we learn to think of life as lived *in* Christ.[3]

Thus there are two levels of experience for believers, two kingdoms of which they are citizens, two perspectives from which we may view life. For me today, I am in Kansas City. In a real sense, that is *where* I am. But it cannot and must never exhaust *what* I am. We are more than citizens of an earthly city or state or country. Bishop Handley Moule put it this way:

> They moved about Colossae "in Christ." They worked, served, kept the house, followed the business, met the neighbors, entered into their sorrows and joys, . . . suffered their abuse and insults when such things came—all "in Christ." They carried about with them a private atmosphere, which was not of Asia but of heaven. To them Christ was the inner home, the dear invisible but real resting place. . . . And what a rich gain for poor Colossae, that they, being in Him, were in it.[4]

No matter where you are geographically and physically, what you are spiritually will never change. You may be *at* work, *at* play, *over*seas, *under* the weather, *out of* money, but you are always and unchangeably *in* Christ.

You may be *down* in the dumps, *over* the hill, or *beside* yourself, but you are always and unchangeably *in* Christ. You may be *at* paradise or *in* prison, *at* the movies or *in* Chicago, but you are always and unchangeably *in* Christ. Your geographical, earthly, physical location has no effect on your spiritual identity.

But the reverse is different. It is precisely because you are *in* Christ that wherever you live and work and play, you make an impact, you carry an influence, you make a difference. Your spiritual identity as one in Christ must control and characterize how you live, *wherever* you live.

And remember: it is *in* Kansas City or Chicago or Dallas or whatever geographical location you call home that you are *in* Christ. They are true simultaneously. You do not live in Christ only while you are at church, on your knees, or in a home group, then return to being simply in your city when you leave that more holy atmosphere. Your "in-Christness" is not simply a heavenly reality that obtains only somewhere up there. You are in Christ even when you are in sin, although the reality of the former ought to progressively diminish your experience of the latter!

What an indescribable privilege and joy: to be a *saint, in Christ, in Kansas City*!

# 3

# Grace to You, Grace with You

## Colossians 1:2b

Paul, an apostle of Christ Jesus by the will of God, and Timothy our brother, to the saints and faithful brothers in Christ at Colossae: **Grace to you and peace from God our Father**.

There is great and glorious encouragement in the fact that Paul begins his letters by blessing his readers with the grace of God. This reference to grace is more than a standard literary device by which letters were begun. It is a sincere prayer for the release of divine favor and power into the lives of those to whom he writes. It is also significant that at the beginning of Paul's letters he says, "Grace [be] *to* you," while the blessings at the end say, "Grace [be] *with* you." Why? John Piper suggests that

> at the beginning of his letters Paul has in mind that the letter itself is a channel of God's grace *to* the readers. Grace is about to flow "from God" through Paul's writing *to* the Christians. So he says, "Grace *to* you." That is, grace is now active and is about to flow from God through my inspired writing *to* you as you read—"grace [be] *to* you." But as the end of the letter approaches, Paul realizes that the reading is almost finished and the question rises, "What becomes of the grace that has been flowing to the readers through the reading of the inspired letter?" He answers with a blessing at the end of every letter: "Grace [be] *with* you." *With* you as you put the letter away and leave the church. *With* you as you go home to deal with a sick child and an unaffectionate spouse. *With* you as you go to work and face the temptations of anger and dishonesty and lust. *With* you as you muster courage to speak up for Christ over lunch. . . . [Thus] we learn that grace is ready to flow *to* us every time we take up

the inspired Scriptures to read them. And we learn that grace will abide *with* us when we lay the Bible down and go about our daily living.[5]

Let me add two additional comments to what Piper has said. First, this will all make sense only if we expand our understanding of what grace is. Divine grace is more than an attitude or disposition in the divine nature. It is surely that, but an examination of the usage of this word in Scripture reveals that grace, if thought of only as an abstract and static principle, is deprived of its deeper implications.

The grace of God, for example, is the power of God's Spirit converting the soul. It is the activity or movement of God whereby he saves and justifies the individual through faith (see especially Rom. 3:24; 5:15, 17). Therefore, grace is not something in which we merely believe; it is something we experience as well.

Grace, however, is not only the divine act by which God initiates our spiritual life, but also the very power by which we are sustained and nourished in, and proceed through, that life. The energizing and sanctifying work of the indwelling Spirit is the grace of God.

After Paul had prayed three times for God to deliver him from his thorn in the flesh, he received this answer: "My grace is sufficient for you, for my power is made perfect in weakness" (2 Cor. 12:9). Although Paul undoubtedly derived encouragement and strength to face his daily trials by reflecting on the magnificence of God's unmerited favor, in this text he appears to speak rather of an experiential reality of a more dynamic nature. It is the operative power of the indwelling Spirit to which Paul refers. That is the grace of God.

Second, if Piper is right and the grace of God comes to us and abides with us via the instrumentality of Holy Scripture and its inspired truths, then we see here yet another example of what theologians have called "the means of grace." Among the latter have often been mentioned the sacraments or ordinances of the church: the Eucharist and baptism. But the sanctifying, sin-killing, Christ-exalting, soul-satisfying presence of the Holy Spirit also comes to us by means of the written Word! There can be little if any expectation of triumphant Christian living apart from the grace that is mediated to us and diffused throughout our hearts and minds preeminently through the Scriptures. When the Word, by the power of the Spirit, is heard, embraced, and enjoyed, we are strengthened to resist the flesh and to savor the Son.

# 4

# And Peace from God

## Colossians 1:2b

Paul, an apostle of Christ Jesus by the will of God, and Timothy our brother, to the saints and faithful brothers in Christ at Colossae: **Grace to you and peace from God our Father**.

In the previous meditation we saw that the empowering and abiding presence of divine grace comes to us by means of the Scriptures. But let's not overlook the gift of "peace," which also flows to us "from God our Father" (1:2b).

When Paul refers to "peace," he is not talking about some superficial psychological giddiness that comes from reaping the material comforts of Western society (as justifiably grateful we may be for the latter). This is the kind of peace that, rather than being dependent on material and physical comfort, actually frees you from bondage to physical comforts and liberates you from dependence on worldly conveniences and appliances and whatever else money can buy.

The peace of Colossians 1:2 is different from, although clearly related to, what I would call the "objective" peace of Romans 5:1. There Paul declares that since we have been justified by faith "we have peace with God" through Jesus Christ. To have or to be at "peace with God" is a reference to the nature of our relationship with him now that his wrath has been exhausted in his Son on our behalf. The holy hostility and righteous indignation provoked by our sin has been forever satisfied in the sufferings of Christ Jesus.

But here in Colossians 1 Paul is describing a felt, tangible experience of mind and heart. The peace that, like grace, comes from our God and Father is a confident repose in the truth that what God has promised he will fulfill. It is that restful assurance and very real sensation that nothing can separate us from the love of Christ.

Perhaps the best way to describe this peace is by pointing to what it does for us in the midst of crisis, pain, and the disillusionment of life in a fallen world. Paul has in mind that glorious work of the Spirit in our hearts that says:

> "A sudden tsunami may sweep away my house and family, but my life is hidden with Christ in God" (see Col. 3:3).

> "A terrorist may separate my head from my body, but nothing can separate me from the love of God in Christ Jesus my Lord" (see Rom. 8:35).

> "An incurable disease may ravage my body, but God causes all things to work together for good to those that love God and are called according to his purpose" (see Rom. 8:28).

> "An unfaithful spouse may walk out, never to return, but God has promised never to leave me or forsake me" (see Heb. 13:5).

> "Enemies of the faith may persecute me and confiscate my property, but I can still rejoice because I have a better possession and an abiding one, an inheritance that is imperishable, undefiled, and unfading, kept in heaven for me" (see Heb. 10:34; 1 Pet. 1:4).

This is the abundant Christian life: a peace and joy and satisfaction in God so deep and unmovable and indelible that no amount of suffering can shake it or induce me to take offence at God.

# 5

# Why Thank God?

## *Colossians 1:3–4*

**We always thank God, the Father of our Lord Jesus Christ, when we pray for you, since we heard of your faith in Christ Jesus and of the love that you have for all the saints,** because of the hope laid up for you in heaven.

This past Christmas I received a red and white University of Oklahoma sweater-vest from my daughter and her husband. To say that I was profoundly grateful is an understatement. When it came time to express my gratitude, I didn't address my sentiments to my sister, although she has been extremely generous to me over the years. Nor did I turn to my wife and say, "Honey, this is a wonderful gift. Thank you so much!"

I hope you realize why. No one, at least no one in his or her right mind, says "thank you" to people who are not responsible for whatever gift or opportunity or blessing it is that one is considering. We express our gratitude to the person who purchased or produced or in some way is responsible for its now being ours. This is simple common sense that does not require much discussion.

So what are we to make of Paul's consistent practice of thanking God for the faith and love and obedience of the various believers to whom he addressed his many epistles? Colossians is no exception to this Pauline rule. We read in Colossians 1:3–4, "We always thank God, the Father of our Lord Jesus Christ, when we pray for you, since we heard of your faith in Christ Jesus and of the love that you have for all the saints."

If Paul believed that these Colossians were themselves ultimately responsible for the presence of faith and love in their hearts, why did he bother to thank God? Why didn't he simply congratulate the Colossians and get on to other matters? On the other hand, if Paul believed, and I believe he did, that God was ultimately the source for their trust in Jesus and their affection toward one another, it makes perfectly good sense for him to express his gratitude to God each time he prays for these Christians.

In his sermon on Ephesians 1:15–18, John Calvin makes much the same point. Paul again does "not cease to give thanks" for the Ephesians because he has heard of their "faith in the Lord Jesus" and their "love toward all the saints" (Eph. 1:15–16a). I've taken the liberty of quoting Calvin, substituting "Colossians" for "Ephesians." He writes:

> Now, with all this, he shows that faith and love are the very gifts of God and do not come from ourselves, as men always imagine through a devilish pride. I told you before that St. Paul did not play the hypocrite in giving thanks to God for the faith and love of the [Colossians]. If every man was able to believe and have faith of his own accord, or could get it by some power of his own, the praise for it ought not to be given to God. For it would be but mockery to acknowledge ourselves indebted to him for what we have obtained, not from him, but from elsewhere. But here St. Paul blesses God's name for enlightening the [Colossians] in the faith and for framing their hearts to make them loving. It is to be concluded, therefore, that everything comes from God.[6]

Do you find faith resident in your heart? Are you this moment believing in Jesus and trusting him for life and breath and all things? Do you feel a deep and abiding affection for the people of God? Do you delight in showing compassion and generosity towards those in the body of Christ? If so, do not reach around to pat yourself on the back. Rather, extend your hands toward heaven and say: "Thanks, God!"

# 6

# Faith and Love: Visible Virtues

## Colossians 1:4

We always thank God, the Father of our Lord Jesus Christ, when we pray for you, **since we heard of your faith in Christ Jesus and of the love that you have for all the saints**, because of the hope laid up for you in heaven.

There are four critically important things to remember about faith and love as they are described by Paul in Colossians 1:4. First, neither can exist independently of the other. Second, they are by God's design public virtues, visible expressions of a saving relationship with Jesus Christ. Third, faith is only as good as its object. Fourth, and finally, Christian love cannot be selective. Let me briefly explain what I mean.

First, love without faith is sloppy and insipid. It yields to compromise when truth is at stake. It lacks courage and is complicit in the sinner's slide toward a Christless eternity. Of what good is it, in the ultimate sense, to shower someone with affection in the absence of a robust confidence in Jesus and the courage to proclaim him as the sinner's only hope?

Likewise, faith without love is arid and pompous and eventually mean-spirited and unkind. How dare we say we believe and trust in Jesus and then turn a cold shoulder to the very people for whom he died?

I've often heard it said that most Christians will gravitate to one or the other, either to gentleness and tenderhearted compassion, on the one hand, or to unyielding faith and affirmation of theological truths on the other; but few, if any, can hold both with equal fervor in one's heart.

I don't buy it. Consider the case of Charles Spurgeon, surely the greatest expository preacher of the nineteenth century (and perhaps of any century). Dr. Joseph Parker, a neighboring minister, once said of Spurgeon:

> Mr. Spurgeon was absolutely destitute of intellectual benevolence. The only colors he recognized were black and white. With him you were either up or down, in or out, dead or alive. As for middle zones, graded lines, light compounding the shadow in a graceful exercise of give-and-take, he simply looked on them as heterodox. . . . On the other hand, who could compare with him in moral sympathy? Who so responsive to pain and need and helplessness? In this view Mr. Spurgeon was in very deed two men.[7]

Another of Spurgeon's contemporaries, James Douglas, concurs:

> The brain of this truly great man was of a giant order. . . . He did with ease, and spontaneously, mental feats which men of name and inordinate vanity, struggle in vain, even by elaboration, to accomplish. . . . He could grasp the bearings of a subject, hold his theme well in hand, and deploy his thoughts like troops in tactical movements. He was never "at sea." . . . All was orderly arrangement."[8]

Yet again, notes Douglas,

> Could any face more fully express geniality, friendliness, warmth of affection, and overflowing hospitality? We know of none in whom these traits so shone forth. His greeting was warm as sunshine. . . . It mattered not what might be the shadow on the spirit or the trouble of the heart—it all vanished away at the voice of his welcome. There was light on his countenance that instantly dispersed all gloom. I have never known one whose presence had such charm, or whose conversation was such a rich and varied feast.[9]

Second, although both faith and love are personal, they are hardly private and certainly never secret. They are visible and vocal in their expression. This was certainly the case with the Colossians, for Paul declares that he and others had "heard" (v. 4a) of their faith and love. Clearly, their faith in Jesus and love for one another had been sufficiently public and concrete that people had taken note of it and passed along the information to the apostle.

Yes, faith exists internally, in mind and heart and spirit, but it radically changes how one lives, talks, and relates to others. True faith energizes vocal proclamation and courageous witness concerning its glorious object: Jesus. Likewise, love is certainly a personal passion, a commitment of the heart. But Jesus declared that the *tangible expression* of affection for one another would be the hallmark by which the world would know that we are his disciples (John 13:35). True love is something seen and known by others.

One of the more stunning statements in Scripture concerning the nature of this love is found in Hebrews 6:10: "For God is not unjust so as to forget your work and the love which you have shown toward His name, in having ministered and in still ministering to the saints" (NASB). How does one demonstrate a love for God, a reverence for his name? Here we see that it is by ministering to and making sacrifice on behalf of his people. Loving God and loving people are not mutually exclusive. We are never forced to choose between the two. Calloused indifference toward the people of God is unmistakable evidence of a disregard for God himself. To love *them* is to love *him*.

Third, Paul is not impressed with faith. What moves him is faith "in Christ Jesus" (v. 4). The object of faith always determines its quality and worth. Mere sincerity, passionate devotion, clarity of conviction, and depth of insight are all ultimately useless unless they are rooted in and focused on the person and work of Jesus.

Fourth, the Colossians' love, which reached Paul's ears, was not selective. Had he discovered that they loved only some in the church, reserving their affection and sacrifice for those of a similar socio-economic achievement or an identical color of skin or a common ethnic or national heritage, I dare say he would not have experienced the sort of joy that is so obvious in his words. Their love was "for *all* the saints" (v. 4b), irrespective of those distinguishing features and public accomplishments that so often dictate whom and when and how much we will love.

May God so work in our hearts that our faith is affectionate and our passion is principled. May he energize us in ways that are both seen and heard and known by all, especially by those who as yet know nothing of Jesus. May his Spirit awaken and intensify faith, confidence, and satisfaction in Jesus. And may our love be as wide and all-encompassing as was and is his own.

## 7

# Hope: The Fountain of Faith and Love (1)

### Colossians 1:4–5a

We always thank God, the Father of our Lord Jesus Christ, when we pray for you, **since we heard of your faith in Christ Jesus and of the love that you have for all the saints, because of the hope laid up for you in heaven.**

Prepositions are wonderful things. No, I'm not crazy. Look with me at Colossians 1:4–5 and then draw your own conclusions.

Having heard of the faith and love among the Colossians, visibly and vocally displayed, Paul has declared his gratitude to God. But how did God produce these virtues in the hearts and lives of his people?

Some might suggest that he directed their thoughts away from heavenly reward to earthly responsibilities. If these people are going to be of any earthly good, so God supposedly said, they must get their minds off of heavenly glory. Well, not exactly.

In fact, precisely the opposite appears to be the case. We read in verse 5 that it was "because of the hope laid up for you in heaven" that faith in Christ and love for all the brethren flourished in Colossae. The preposition "because of" or "on account of" can only be taken as pointing to faith and love as in some sense a response to hope. *In some way, hope produces faith and love.* Hope, then, is the basis for faith and love.

That there is a distinctly future orientation to Paul's thought is confirmed by the description of hope as being "laid up for you in heaven" (v. 5a). By the way, this is *what* we hope for, the objective reality of our future inheritance, not the feeling of hope or expectation in our hearts. So what does Paul have in mind?

Since it is in the heavens, it could be Christ himself, the hope of glory (Col. 1:27). Or it could be our final salvation, our glorification, the blessedness of heaven itself. But these are appealing only because they give us Christ! In any case, thinking about and banking on and living in the expectation of the hope that awaits us in Christ in heaven is of immense practical, life-changing, faith-awakening, love-inspiring benefit.

In chapter 9 of my book *One Thing*,[10] I spoke in some detail of the practical benefits of being heavenly minded. For example, a contemplative focus on the beauty of heaven frees us from excessive dependence upon earthly wealth and comfort. If there awaits us an eternal inheritance of immeasurable glory, it is senseless to expend effort and energy here, sacrificing so much time and money, to obtain for so brief a time in corruptible form what we will enjoy forever in consummate perfection.

According to Philippians 3:20–21, knowing that "our citizenship is in heaven" enables the soul to escape the grip of "earthly things" (Phil. 3:19). Peter contends that the ultimate purpose of the new birth (1 Pet. 1:3–4) is our experience of a *heavenly* hope, an inheritance that is "imperishable," by which he means incorruptible, not subject to decay or rust or mold or dissolution or disintegration. This heavenly inheritance is "undefiled" or pure, unmixed, untainted by sin or evil. Best of all, it is "unfading." Not only will it never end, it will never diminish in its capacity to enthrall and fascinate and impart joy. It is "in heaven" for us, kept safe, under guard, protected, and insulated against all intrusion or violation. This hope is the grounds for the joy (v. 6) that sustains us in trial and suffering.

A few verses later he exhorts his readers to "set your hope fully on the grace that will be brought to you at the revelation of Jesus Christ" (1 Pet. 1:13). This is a commanded obsession. Fixate fully! Rivet your soul on the grace that you will receive when Christ returns. Tolerate no distractions. Entertain no diversions. Don't let your mind be swayed. Devote every ounce of mental and spiritual and emotional energy to concentrating and contemplating on the grace that is to come. What grace is that? It is the grace of the heavenly inheritance described in verses 3 to 6.

The expectation of a "city that has foundations" energized Abraham's heart to persevere in a foreign land. All the patriarchs are described as "seeking a [heavenly] homeland" (Heb. 11:14). Their determination in the face of trial was fueled by their desire for a "better country, that is, a heavenly one" (Heb. 11:16). As pleasant as it may be now, what we see and sense and savor in this life is an ephemeral shadow compared with the substance of God himself. Earthly joys are fragmented beams, but God is the sun. Earthly refreshment is at best a sipping from intermittent springs, but God is the ocean!

A contemplative focus on heaven enables us to respond appropriately to the injustices of this life. Essential to heavenly joy is witnessing the vindication of righteousness and the judgment of evil. Only from our anticipation of the new perspective of heaven, from which we, one day, will look back and evaluate what now seems senseless, can we be empowered to endure this world in all its ugliness and moral deformity.

A contemplative focus on heaven produces the fruit of endurance and perseverance now. The strength to endure *present suffering* is the fruit of meditating on *future satisfaction*. This is the clear message of several texts such as Matthew 5:11–12; Romans 8:17–18, 23, 25b; Hebrews 13:13–14; and 1 Peter 1:3–9.

Romans 8:18 is Paul's declaration that "the sufferings of this present time are not worth comparing with the glory that is to be revealed to us." We do not lose heart because we contemplate the unseen things of the future and nourish our souls with the truth that whatever we endure on this earth is producing a glory far beyond all comparison. Christians are not asked to treat pain as though it were pleasure, or grief as though it were joy, but to bring all earthly adversity into comparison with heavenly glory and thereby be strengthened to endure. The exhortation in Hebrews 13:13–14 to willingly bear the reproach of Christ is grounded in the expectation of a "city that is to come," namely, the heavenly New Jerusalem.

Nowhere is this principle better seen than in 2 Corinthians 4:16–18. Gazing at the grandeur of heavenly glory transforms our value system. In the light of what is "eternal," what we face now is only "momentary." Suffering appears "prolonged" only in the absence of an eternal perspective. The "affliction" of this life is regarded as "light" when compared with the "weight" of that "glory" yet to come. It is "burdensome" only when we lose sight of our heavenly future. The key to success in suffering, as odd as that sounds, is in taking the long view. Only when juxtaposed with the endless ages of eternal bliss does suffering in this life become tolerable.

There is yet another contrast to be noted. In 2 Corinthians 4:18 Paul juxtaposes transient things that are seen with eternal things that are unseen. Note especially the connection between verse 18 and verse 16. Our inner nature is being renewed *as we look* or *while we look* at the unseen, eternal things of the age to come. If you don't look you won't change! The process of renewal occurs only *as the believer looks to things as yet unseen*. As we fix the gaze of our hearts on the glorious hope of the age to come, God progressively renews our inner being, notwithstanding the simultaneous decay of our outer frame. Inner renewal does not happen automatically or mechanically. Transformation happens only *as* or *provided that* we "look not to the things that are seen but to the things that are unseen" (v. 18).

Nothing exerts such purifying power on the heart as does a contemplative focus on heaven. Meditation on the unseen glories of heaven energizes the heart to say no to fleshly desires. This is the clear witness of Colossians 3:1–4; 1 John 3:2–3; and 2 Peter 3:11–13. To be continued . . .

# 8
# Hope: The Fountain of Faith and Love (2)
## Colossians 1:4–5

We always thank God, the Father of our Lord Jesus Christ, when we pray for you, **since we heard of your faith in Christ Jesus and of the love that you have for all the saints, because of the hope laid up for you in heaven. Of this you have heard before in the word of the truth, the gospel,** which has come to you, as indeed in the whole world it is bearing fruit and growing—as it also does among you, since the day you heard it and understood the grace of God in truth, just as you learned it from Epaphras our beloved fellow servant.

*I* would be remiss if I didn't share with you the comments of John Piper on this passage in Colossians 1.

In a sermon titled "The Fruit of Hope: Love," preached on July 13, 1986, John addressed the objection that being heavenly minded is a threat to earthly productivity and fruitfulness and love toward those in need. Fixing our thoughts and hopes on heaven, so some contend, doesn't produce love, but escapism. And so we must ask, writes Piper,

> Is it true that when Christians set their hearts earnestly and intensely on the future prospect of sharing the glory of God, and seeing the risen Lord, and being freed from sin and sickness, and living in joy for all eternity—when Christians set their hearts with deep longing and strong

confidence on these things, do they become so heavenly-minded that they are of no earthly use? Do they become self-centered and fall prey to escapism?[11]

Piper's answer, like mine in the previous meditation in Colossians, is that the Bible teaches precisely the opposite:

It teaches and shows that a strong confidence in the promises of God and a passionate preference for the joy of heaven over the joy of the world frees a person from worldly self-centeredness, from paralyzing regret and self-pity, from fear and greed and bitterness and despair and laziness and impatience and envy. And in the place of all these sins hope bears the fruit of love.

The problem with the church today is not that there are too many people who are passionately in love with heaven. Name three! The problem is not that professing Christians are retreating from the world, spending half their days reading Scripture and the other half singing about their pleasures in God all the while indifferent to the needs of the world. The problem is that professing Christians are spending ten minutes reading Scripture and then half their day making money and the other half enjoying and repairing what they spend it on.

It is not heavenlimindedness that hinders love. It is worldlimindedness that hinders love, even when it is disguised by a religious routine on the weekend. Where is the person whose heart is so passionately in love with the promised glory of heaven that he feels like an exile and a sojourner on the earth? Where is the person who has so tasted the beauty of the age to come that the diamonds of the world look like baubles, and the entertainment of the world is empty, and the moral causes of the world are too small because they have no view to eternity? Where is this person?

He is not in bondage to TV-watching or eating or sleeping or drinking or partying or fishing or sailing. . . . He is a free man in a foreign land. And his one question is this: How can I maximize my enjoyment of God for all eternity while I am an exile on this earth? And his answer is always the same: by doing the labors of love.

Only one thing satisfies the heart whose treasure is in heaven: doing the works of heaven. And heaven is a world of love! It is not the cords of heaven that bind the hands of love. It is the love of money and leisure and comfort and praise—these are the cords that bind the hands of love. And the power to sever these cords is Christian hope.

I say it again with all the conviction that lies within me: it is not heavenlimindedness that hinders love on this earth. It is worldlimindedness.

And therefore the great fountain of love is the powerful, freeing confidence of Christian hope![12]

Well said, John! He then proceeds to cite several other texts in which the same truth is expressed. I'll take note of his comments on only one—Hebrews 10:34:

> The situation is that some of the church members had been imprisoned and the rest were faced with the moral dilemma of whether to go underground and save themselves, or whether to go visit the prisoners and risk losing life and possessions. Verse 34 describes what they did and why: "For you had compassion on the prisoners, and you joyfully accepted the plundering of your property, since you knew that you yourselves had a better possession and an abiding one."
>
> What was the power that drove them in love to the prison doors knowing their houses would be plundered? "Because you knew that you yourselves had a better possession and an abiding one." It was hope that drove them to love. Or to put it another way, it was heavenlimindedness that broke the power of worldly love for furniture and houses and security and freed the saints to risk their lives in love. Therefore, I say it again, it is not heavenlimindedness that hinders love. When religious people fail to love, it is not because they have fallen in love with heaven, but because they are still in love with the world.[13]

# 9

# The Word of Truth

## Colossians 1:5b–6

**Of this you have heard before in the word of the truth, the gospel, which has come to you, as indeed in the whole world it is bearing fruit and growing—as it also does among you, since the day you heard it and understood the grace of God in truth,** just as you learned it from Epaphras our beloved fellow servant.

Paul has focused on the hope we all have in Christ as the ground or fountain from which flow both faith and love. Of this hope, he now writes in Colossians 1:5–6, "You have heard before in the word of the truth, the gospel, which has come to you, as indeed in the whole world it is bearing fruit and growing—as it also does among you, since the day you heard it and understood the grace of God in truth."

Let me make four brief observations on this text.

First, the content of the gospel, at least in large part, is the "hope" that is "laid up" for us "in heaven." It was when the gospel was proclaimed that they "heard" of this hope. Many today argue that the gospel has little if anything to do with heaven in the future. Its primary focus is earth in the present. I understand their concern. We need to embrace a gospel that provides direction for life on earth, a gospel that transforms relationships and pursues social justice and labors for the expansion of the kingdom in this life. Yes, the gospel is about the lordship of Jesus over all of life *now*. It isn't merely a way to escape the corruption of this world and "go to heaven when you die."

But make no mistake: the gospel is most certainly (and perhaps primarily) concerned with life after death. It is most certainly concerned with the hope that is reserved for us in heaven and the glory of spending an eternity in God's presence (see 1 Pet.1:3–6). As Colossians 1:14 will make clear, the gospel is certainly about redemption, the forgiveness of sins.

Second, the gospel is something the Colossians *heard*. This is important, for we are being told that we no longer live in a world where oral communication is effective. Hearing the gospel, so they tell us, accomplishes little and must be replaced by presentations that focus on image and sight and color and taste and smell. The video clip has replaced the expository sermon. Theater has replaced teaching. Entertainment has replaced exegesis.

I suspect this may be offensive to some, but so be it. My opinion is that the alleged ineffectiveness or lack of appeal in the expository sermon is due less to the need of people for a more holistic sensory experience in church (as beneficial as that may be) and more to the laziness and lack of training on the part of pastors to expound and explain and apply the glorious truths in texts like Colossians 1:5–6.

The preparation and preaching of biblical texts that is true to the intent of the biblical authors and relevant to the lives of contemporary folk is hard work. It is demanding both of time and energy. Sadly, fewer and fewer pastors are willing to expend themselves in this way for the sake of their people. May I suggest you read my more extensive comments on this subject in a series of three articles that I wrote, titled "An Appeal to All Pastors: How and Why Should We Preach?"[14]

Third, the gospel that saves and heals and delivers us from the dominion of Satan (see Col. 1:13–14) is a word (*logos*), a proclamation, a propositional declaration, a message. Again, we are being told that we no longer live in a word-based culture. But we cannot so easily dismiss the logocentric or word-centered orientation of the biblical gospel. It comes to us as a multifaceted declaration or statement or assertion of truths regarding the work of God in Christ. Yes, the gospel is a story or narrative of what God has achieved for us in his Son. But the story must be stated, explained, unpacked, and applied in words. Such words are more than lifeless abstractions: they are life-giving, soul-saving, comprehensible truths that the Spirit awakens us to hear and understand and to trust and enjoy.

Fourth, this word of the gospel that we hear is *true*! Whether we translate this phrase "the word of the truth, the gospel" or "the true preaching of the gospel" or "the proclamation of the truth which is contained in the gospel," the result is the same: there is *truth* in the gospel of Jesus Christ that can be discerned, known, and cognitively embraced.

The very concept of *truth* has not fared well in the hands of postmodern critics. They typically say one of three things. Some, generally the more radical relativists, contend that absolute truth simply doesn't exist. Others say that if it does exist, we can't know it. Such truth, objective and real though it be, is inaccessible to the human mind. Then there are those who concede that truth exists but always in a variety of different and even contradictory forms, depending on the community in which one lives. Truth for one community of people, that is to say, what makes sense to them and enables them to function well in the world, may not be truth for another.

But the consistent testimony of Scripture, such as we find in Colossians 1, is that truth is absolute and accessible and universally relevant for all people in all times. Certainly we must be sensitive in how we communicate it. We must contextualize the gospel in a way that is both faithful to the revelation of Scripture and meaningful to the people to whom we minister. The truth of the gospel is not a hammer with which to oppress those who may disagree, but a key that unlocks the mind from slavery to idols, a light that dispels the darkness of errant thinking, a power that liberates and delivers us "from the domain of darkness" (Col. 1:13) and transfers us "to the kingdom of [God's] beloved Son" (Col. 1:13).

This truth is found in the gospel, in the good news that God has become human in Jesus Christ and has lived and died and risen from the grave for the redemption of his people. This truth is now embodied and expressed for us in the written Word of God, the Scriptures. Hear it. Study it. Ingest it. Relish it. And above all else, by God's grace, let it transform your heart and renew your mind and govern your steps each day.

# 10

# *In the Spirit*

## *Colossians 1:8*

He is a faithful minister of Christ on your behalf **and has made known to us your love in the Spirit**.

*I*n Colossians 1:4 Paul acknowledged the love these believers have toward one another. He praises and thanks God for having evoked this in their hearts. In verse 8 he mentions it yet again, but here explicitly describes it as being "in the Spirit."

Somewhat surprisingly, this is the only explicit reference to the Holy Spirit in the book of Colossians. Needless to say, there are countless activities and virtues and experiences mentioned in this book that are elsewhere in the New Testament attributed to the work of the Spirit, but in Colossians this is simply taken for granted rather than openly stated.

So, Paul has thus far said five things concerning Christian love: (1) it cannot exist independently of faith in Jesus (v. 4); (2) it is an affection for and commitment to "all the saints" (v. 4), not just those whom we find it easy to love and who in turn will love us back; (3) it is a public virtue, one that will make itself known in visible and vocal ways (v. 4); (4) it is the fruit of hope, which is to say that love flows from the fountain of confident expectation that what God has promised and laid up for us in heaven will indeed come to pass; and (5) it is ultimately the work of divine grace in our hearts, for it is God whom Paul thanks for its presence and expression in the lives of the Colossian believers (v. 3).

Colossians 1:8

To these five truths Paul now adds a sixth. In verse 8 he mentions the ministry of Epaphras (I'll return to him in the next meditation) who "has made known to us your love *in the Spirit.*" So, this love of the Colossians one for another is in some sense due to the work or operation of the Spirit in their lives.

This phrase "in the Spirit" could also be translated "by the Spirit" or "through the Spirit" in the sense that it is the Spirit who is responsible for the power and incentive and steadfast commitment to fulfill whatever is in view. For example, Paul exhorts us to pray at all times "in the Spirit" (Eph. 6:18), by which I think he means, among other things, (a) as the Spirit prompts us, (b) in the strength and power the Spirit supplies, (c) always asking the Spirit to bring to mind the truths of God's Word that are relevant to the person or subject of our intercession, and (d) always and ever dependent on the Spirit to cleanse our minds of sin and guard us against distraction and frustration. I should also mention that in view of Paul's description of tongues as praying "in the Spirit" (same Greek phrase; 1 Cor. 14:13–19) he may also have this in mind in Ephesians 6:18 (although, as noted, praying in the Spirit encompasses far more than merely praying in tongues).

Therefore, to experience and express "love in the Spirit" points us yet again to the divine origin of this affection. It is a God-given love, one that cannot be cranked up or willed into existence by human grit and determination. James Dunn put it best when he described this love as one that "can only be aroused and sustained by the Spirit of God. The phrase carries overtones of an inspiration that wells up from within, charismatically enabled (Rom. 2:29; 1 Cor. 12:3, 9, 13; 14:16; 1 Thes[s]. 1:5), and that depends on continued openness to the Spirit if its quality of unselfish service of others is to be maintained."[15]

Clearly, then, this love that the Colossians have for Paul and for all the saints is not a love that is natural to the human heart. We are by nature selfish and guarded and absorbed with our own concerns. If we are to love as the Colossians loved, it must happen "in the Spirit," which is to say, as the Spirit reminds us of Christ's love expressed in the cross, as the Spirit works to direct our thoughts from self to the saints, as the Spirit awakens in us a recognition of the presence of Christ in other believers, as the Spirit overcomes our inclination to harbor bitterness and unforgiveness toward those who have hurt us, as the Spirit energizes our hearts to believe that it is truly more blessed to give than to receive. This is why "love" is a fruit of the Spirit, as Paul states in Galatians 5:22.

There is yet a seventh, and final, observation Paul makes about this love. He has already said that love (and faith) flows from that hope laid up for us in heaven (v. 5a) and that this hope is an essential component in the gospel which the Colossians (and we) heard (vv. 5–6). Indeed, this gospel is bearing fruit and growing in the Colossians (and in us; v. 6). This fruit, in part, is love. So, the way this love will continue to be nurtured and nourished and sustained in our hearts through the activity of the Spirit is by listening to and reading about and trusting in the truth of the gospel.

If hearing the gospel produces hope and hope produces love, we must be diligent to immerse our minds in the gospel by reading of it in the inspired Word, by meditating on its promises, obeying its warnings, memorizing those texts that speak of its blessings, and trusting that it will do for our souls what nothing else can.

As we, by God's grace, focus our faith on the promises of the gospel and relish its beauty, the Spirit will work to evoke and stimulate and sustain a supernatural love one for another that will redound to the glory of Jesus, for "by this all people will know that" we are his disciples, if we have "love for one another" (John 13:35).

# 11

# A Remarkable Man

## Colossians 1:7–8; 4:12–13

Of this you have heard before in the word of the truth, the gospel, which has come to you, as indeed in the whole world it is bearing fruit and growing—as it also does among you, since the day you heard it and understood the grace of God in truth, **just as you learned it from Epaphras our beloved fellow servant. He is a faithful minister of Christ on your behalf and has made known to us your love in the Spirit.**

**Epaphras, who is one of you, a servant of Christ Jesus, greets you, always struggling on your behalf in his prayers, that you may stand mature and fully assured in all the will of God. For I bear him witness that he has worked hard for you and for those in Laodicea and in Hierapolis.**

You may recall that in Philippians 2:25–30 Paul described a certain Epaphroditus who risked his life for the work of Christ. "*Honor* such men" (v. 29b), said Paul. Tragically, today we honor people in whom we find none of the characteristics of an Epaphroditus. It is the pompous, arrogant athlete, or the self-indulgent Hollywood actress, or the unscrupulous Wall Street financial wizard who wins our praise and adoration.

Perhaps it's time to reevaluate the criteria by which we deem one "honorable." Consider Epaphras. Although the name is a shortened version of Epaphroditus, virtually all scholars agree Epaphras is different from the man of that name mentioned in Philippians. But he was of the same character and virtue.

It's important to recall the background that accounts for his being mentioned in Colossians (in 1:7–8; 4:12–13; see also Philem. 23). Paul most likely wrote Colossians while imprisoned in Rome (Caesarea is another strong possibility). Epaphras, a native of Colossae, probably heard Paul preach in Ephesus and was converted. He evidently volunteered to take the gospel to his home town and faithfully preached there and in the neighboring cities of Laodicea and Hierapolis (see Col. 4:13). He traveled to Rome to bring Paul news of events in Colossae and, for whatever reason, was imprisoned with him (Philem. 23). Paul now sends greetings from Epaphras (4:12) and commends him to the church that he had so faithfully served.

So what was it about Epaphras that accounts for such glowing praise? What is it that moved the heart of the great apostle to commend him so passionately? Let's note ten things.

First, he was an evangelist. The Colossians "heard" the gospel from him (v. 6b). Try to envision the sort of courage and boldness required for a man to return to his home town preaching the gospel of Jesus Christ for the very first time. The threat of ridicule and rejection carried no weight with Epaphras. Such was his love for Jesus and his fellow Colossians.

Second, he was a teacher. They not only heard the gospel from Epaphras but learned (v. 7a) it from him. This suggests that he labored among them not simply by preaching but by expounding the truths of God's work in Christ and building them up in their faith.

Third, he was Paul's "*beloved* fellow servant" (v. 7a). Paul loved him. So, too, no doubt, did the Colossians. He was joined in mission and ministry and heart affection with the apostle. He was more than a servant. He was a "fellow" servant.

Fourth, he was a "*faithful* minister of Christ" (v. 7c). He was trustworthy. Epaphras's word was his life. His devotion to Christ was unqualified, unconditional, and constant.

Fifth, he was devoted to the Colossians and to their spiritual welfare and growth, for Paul says his ministry was "on your behalf" (v. 7d). Some Greek manuscripts have "on *our* behalf," which would suggest that Epaphras was Paul's representative to the church there. But if the former is correct, as I believe it is, Paul's point is that Epaphras labored with the Colossians in mind, expending himself for their sakes, not his own.

Sixth, he was more than a minister; he was a "servant" of Christ Jesus (4:12a). Whereas being a "slave" in the first century was, in most cases, grounds for reproach, Epaphras considered it an honor and a blessing, for he was owned by Christ Jesus, a purchased possession, bought with his precious blood.

Seventh, he was a committed intercessor on their behalf (4:12b). He "always" prayed for them. I can envision Paul listening each day as Epaphras brought the Colossians, by name no doubt, to the throne of grace. His commitment to intercede on their behalf deeply impressed the apostle. What love!

Eighth, his prayers for them were characterized by a determination to fight through all resistance and a refusal to give up when it became demanding, painful, and inconvenient, for Paul says he was "always struggling" (4:12c) on their behalf in prayer. No perfunctory, casual requests here. He worked hard at prayer. He persevered through temptations to quit. He was tolerant of no distractions.

Ninth, he didn't pray for frivolous things or worldly fame or material prosperity. His focus was their spiritual maturity and discernment and satisfaction in Jesus. Paul describes it this way: he was always praying "that you may stand mature and fully assured in all the will of God" (v. 12c).

Tenth, he has "worked hard" (v. 13a) for the Colossians, counting no cost too high to pay so that his fellow-Christians might flourish spiritually (the word here carries the thought of pain and distress). He didn't use his imprisonment as an excuse for self-pity or to justify turning his attention to his own welfare or concerns. He seized this time of imprisonment as a great opportunity to intercede incessantly for others.

So let me close by asking two questions. Who have been "Epaphrases" in your life? Have you taken steps to honor them? Have you thanked God for them? Have you expressed your profound gratitude to them for having sacrificed so much for your spiritual well-being?

Lastly, in whose life have *you* been an "Epaphras"? If you have no answer for that question, you can start today. I doubt if you are imprisoned or are suffering in any way comparable to what Epaphras endured. So why not commit yourself right now to struggling on behalf of others whom God has brought to your attention or into your life? Will you work hard so that they, by God's grace, might "stand mature and fully assured in all the will of God?"

# 12

# Intercession: Why, for Whom, and How Often?

## Colossians 1:9a

**And so, from the day we heard, we have not ceased to pray for you**, asking that you may be filled with the knowledge of his will in all spiritual wisdom and understanding, so as to walk in a manner worthy of the Lord, fully pleasing to him, bearing fruit in every good work and increasing in the knowledge of God.

Let's be sure we understand the nature of intercessory prayer. I've heard any number of definitions, but none better than that of Lloyd John Ogilvie who said that intercession is not so much placing our burdens on God's heart but "God putting his burdens on our hearts."[16]

I can't prove it, but I suspect that God takes greater delight in blessing me in response to your prayers on my behalf than he does when I ask him myself. That isn't to say I shouldn't pray for myself or that you shouldn't petition God for the needs in your life. It's simply to say that with intercession, unlike other forms or expressions of prayer, there is a mutual love, fellowship, and spiritual bond that develops in a way that can't occur if we pray only for ourselves and not for others.

This reminds me of what Paul said in 2 Corinthians 1:11 in the wake of his deliverance from the life-threatening circumstances he encountered in Asia. If God, on whom "we have set our hope," will "deliver us again" (v. 10), "you [Corinthians] also must help us by prayer, so that many will give thanks on our behalf for the blessing granted us through the prayers of many."

Note two things here. First, the "blessing" of protection and perseverance is granted "through the prayers of many" (v. 11). No prayer, no protection. We can emphasize the sovereignty of God all day long (and we should!), but the fact remains that God chooses to suspend many of his blessings on the intercessory prayers of his people (see also Philem. 22; Phil. 1:19; and Rom. 15:30–32).

Second, not only would Paul benefit from their prayers on his behalf but, more important still, God would be glorified by the many expressions of gratitude that would be uttered for the blessings he bestowed on Paul through these prayers. It's a win-win! Paul gets the protection and God gets the praise.

Now, let's return to Colossians 1:9 and observe the answer to my three questions.

First, *why* does Paul intercede in prayer for the Colossians? Literally, verse 9 opens with the words "for this reason" or "on account of this." He is obviously referring back to the news concerning their faith, love, and hope described in verses 3 to 8. I can just imagine Paul's reaction when Epaphras informed him of events in Colossae. He probably called in Timothy, Aristarchus, Mark, Justus, and Luke (cf. Col. 4:10–14), eager to share with them the good news of what God was doing in the lives of these saints.

I wish this were always the case, but it isn't. Oftentimes when Christians hear of other Christians flourishing and prospering they begrudge them such benefits or find envy rising up in their souls or even wonder aloud whether such folk are deserving of so much good from God (as if any of us are). Not Paul. Although he languished in prison, he rejoiced over the success and spiritual prosperity of those in Colossae. Unable to restrain his exuberance, he lifts these saints before the throne of grace with gratitude and intercedes on their behalf for yet more and even greater spiritual benefits. We don't read so much as a word of: "Hey, God, what about me? If it weren't for me those Colossians wouldn't even be believers. How come you bless them so abundantly and leave me in this stinking Roman jail?"

Second, *for whom* does Paul intercede? It's not enough simply to say, "the Colossians." Never forget that Paul had never met these people! As best we can tell, Epaphras brought the gospel to Colossae. Paul wouldn't have known a single name or recognized a single face in that church. Yet he prays for them passionately and persistently, which brings us to our third and final question.

*How often* did he pray for them? Unceasingly, Paul says in verse 9. "We have not ceased to pray for you," he happily declares. This doesn't mean that Paul never did anything else but pray, as if every waking moment was spent in intercession. It simply means that every time Paul prayed, and it was probably quite often and intense and prolonged, he came to the throne of grace with the Colossian believers in his heart and on his lips. Although Paul's "prayer list" must have grown daily as news of the success of the gospel reached him (cf. v. 6), he never failed to include the Colossians.

So, let's ask ourselves again: why do we pray for others? Is it only because we think they are praying for us? Is it only if we have prior assurance that they will continue to love us and provide for our needs? Is it only because we think that by doing so God will surely bless us in the way he has blessed them?

For whom do we pray? Is it only those we know and can recall by name and with whom we have shared much in life? No. You can pray fervently and successfully for that distant congregation in Sri Lanka about which you only read in the newspaper. You can intercede passionately on behalf of the persecuted church in Iran, for their good and God's glory.

Finally, how often does prayer occur in the midst of your daily routines? You may not have prolonged seasons free from the distractions of life, but you can find a minute here, or perhaps ten there, to bring to heaven those whom God has placed on your heart. And remember, God only places them on your heart because they are first on his.

# 13

# Intercession: What Should We Ask For?

## Colossians 1:9b

And so, from the day we heard, we have not ceased to pray for you, **asking that you may be filled with the knowledge of his will in all spiritual wisdom and understanding,** so as to walk in a manner worthy of the Lord, fully pleasing to him, bearing fruit in every good work and increasing in the knowledge of God.

So what did Paul pray for? What did he want most for those in Colossae? I wonder what they might have said to him had he asked, "How may I pray for you?" We'll never know, but what we do know is that Paul asked, apparently repeatedly, that God would fill them "with the knowledge of his will in all spiritual wisdom and understanding."

Let's be clear about one thing. Simply because Paul prayed for them to know God's will does not mean we are forbidden to ask for other things. There are countless blessings, both spiritual and material, for which we ought to intercede. But there is significance in the fact that this weighed heavily in Paul's value system.

I doubt if knowing God's will is at the top of many of our "want" lists. New cars, better paying jobs, respect, notoriety, physical comfort, all the latest technological conveniences are probably of more pressing importance to us than knowing the will of God. It's tragic, but all too true.

This prayer is similar to what we find in Ephesians 1:17 where Paul prays that God would give them "a spirit of wisdom and of revelation in the knowledge of him." Likewise, in Philippians 1:9 his prayer is that their "love may abound more and more, with knowledge and all discernment" (see also Philem. 6).

Clearly, knowledge was important to Paul. But not any sort of knowledge will do. He asks for knowledge of "God's will." At minimum, this would involve the understanding of all that Paul teaches in the remainder of this epistle and all other inspired writings as well. In one sense, then, this prayer is for illumination, or to use the words of Ephesians 1:18, it is for the "enlightenment" of the "eyes of their heart."

More specifically, he asks God to fill them with the knowledge of his will "in all spiritual wisdom and understanding" (v. 9b). There are three possible ways of understanding the relationship between "spiritual wisdom and understanding" and the "knowledge of God's will."

The NIV renders this: "the knowledge of his will *through* all spiritual wisdom and understanding." That is to say, *by means of* Spirit-imparted wisdom and the understanding he provides, we come to discern God's will. Others say the idea is more that wisdom and understanding *accompany* the impartation of divine knowledge.

Perhaps the best rendering is that the knowledge for which he prays *consists of* all spiritual wisdom and understanding. In other words, to know God's will is not only a matter of understanding what is pleasing to him but also consists of experiential wisdom in knowing how to apply God's desires to the concrete realities and crises and decisions of every day life.

In any case, don't miss Paul's emphasis on the word "spiritual" (which applies to both the wisdom and understanding that we need). Part of the problem in Colossae was the temptation to listen to the worldly and fleshly wisdom (cf. 2:8, 18, 23) of the false teachers who were disrupting the life of the community.

Before leaving this part of Paul's prayer, I must draw our attention to Isaiah 11:2. There we read of a similar experience in almost identical language of what was to be true of the Messiah: "And the Spirit of the LORD shall rest upon him, the Spirit of wisdom and understanding, the Spirit of counsel and might, the Spirit of knowledge and the fear of the Lord."

This is good news indeed! The same Spirit who anointed the Lord Jesus Christ and empowered him with wisdom and understanding and knowledge has anointed us (see 2 Cor. 1:21–22; 1 John 2:20, 27). Thus the knowledge of God's will and the spiritual wisdom and understanding to apply it in every circumstance is available to us as well. Oh, God, may your Spirit fill us up to overflowing that we might live as Jesus did, to your glory and in conformity with your will in all things.

# 14

# Fruitless Knowledge?

## *Colossians 1:10*

> And so, from the day we heard, we have not ceased to pray for you, asking that you may be filled with the knowledge of his will in all spiritual wisdom and understanding, **so as to walk in a manner worthy of the Lord, fully pleasing to him, bearing fruit in every good work and increasing in the knowledge of God.**

There is a reason why I put a question mark after the title for this meditation. I'm asking whether knowledge of God—true, soul-saving knowledge of God—can be fruitless. Can a person "know" God in the way Paul describes in Colossians 1:9 and *not* bear the fruit of holiness?

George Barna recently described seventy-seven million church-going Americans as "born again." In my review of his book *Revolution*, I took issue with this.[17] I didn't do so because I regard myself as the infallible judge of human hearts! I did it because the Scriptures tell me in no uncertain terms that genuine, saving knowledge of the Lord Jesus is transforming and life-changing and sin-killing and Christ-exalting in its effects. I fear countless people are living a religious charade, having been assured by undoubtedly well-meaning ministers that their "decision" for Jesus was unto eternal life in spite of the fact that there is little if any spiritual fruit in their experience.

Consider Paul's words in Colossians 1:9–10. He has prayed that we might be filled with the knowledge of God's will, which consists of spiritual wisdom and understanding (v. 9). But why? To what end?

For what reason? The answer, according to verse 10, is so that we might "walk in a manner worthy of the Lord, fully pleasing to him, bearing fruit in every good work and increasing in the knowledge of God."

The language of verse 10 is clear and inescapable. We know God and his will for this reason: to equip, enable, and encourage us to walk in holiness of life. Knowledge for knowledge's sake is fatal. To learn simply for the sake of learning expands the mind but does not necessarily transform the heart. Elsewhere Paul declares that "the grace of God has appeared" in the person of Jesus Christ to *train* us to "renounce ungodliness and worldly passions, and to live self-controlled, upright, and godly lives in the present age" (Titus 2:11–12). Indeed, the very reason Jesus gave himself for us was "to redeem us from all lawlessness and to purify for himself a people for his own possession who are zealous for good works" (Titus 2:14).

All this to say that the knowledge of God and his will is eminently practical in nature and purpose. Paul's aim in praying for the Colossians to be filled with spiritual wisdom and insight is so that they might be energized in the daily mortification of sin and the cultivation of spiritual fruit and good works. Had Epaphras informed Paul that the Colossians were loudly proclaiming their love for God and knowledge of his ways all the while living unrepentantly in sin and disobedience, I suspect Paul would have replied: "I beg your pardon!" Well, he probably would have said a lot more than that, but I trust you get my point.

It's interesting to note that what Paul said in 1:6 about the gospel he now says in 1:10 about the Colossians themselves: "It [the gospel] is bearing fruit and growing" (v. 6), and you are "bearing fruit . . . and increasing" (v. 10); the Greek word translated "increasing" in verse 10 is the same as that translated "growing" in verse 6; the ESV translates them differently for stylistic reasons. The point seems to be that the way in which the gospel is bearing fruit and increasing (v. 6) is by producing Christlike and holy lives, through the Spirit, in those who have received it in faith (v. 10).

Paul's closing words in verse 10 ("increasing in the knowledge of God") deserve close scrutiny. Two views have emerged.

First, some argue that we should render this phrase in an instrumental fashion, hence, "by means of" or "through" the knowledge of

God. If this be true, Paul's point is to reinforce what he said in verse 9, namely, that knowledge of God (of his will, his grace, his character, etc.) forms the basis from which or the means by which the bearing of fruit and the growth in good works comes about. As James Dunn notes, "repetition of the same . . . form (*epignosis* [= knowledge]) as in 1:9 doubles the insistence that such conduct can only grow from such knowledge."[18]

If this view is correct, it reminds us again that all efforts at Christian behavior without a solid foundation of orthodox, theologically robust, and wide-ranging Christian belief will eventually prove to be a mere vapor.

Second, others contend that Paul's point is that genuine transformation always *includes* growth in understanding of God. Heat without light eventually degenerates into fanaticism, much in the same way that light without heat breeds arrogance. The saving presence of the Spirit in our souls yields the rich harvest of both good deeds and deep insights, both orthopraxy (right behavior) and orthodoxy (right belief).

We simply can't live a life that is "pleasing to him" (v. 10) if we fail to increase in the knowledge of what he is like and how he acts and why he does what he does. This, then, is what the Lord says: "Let not the wise man boast in his wisdom, let not the mighty man boast in his might, let not the rich man boast in his riches, but let him who boasts boast in this, that he understands and knows me, that I am the LORD who practices steadfast love, justice, and righteousness in the earth. For in these things I delight, declares the LORD" (Jer. 9:23–24; cf. Hos. 4:1–6).

# 15

# Worthy of the Lord / Pleasing to the Lord

## Colossians 1:10

And so, from the day we heard, we have not ceased to pray for you, asking that you may be filled with the knowledge of his will in all spiritual wisdom and understanding, **so as to walk in a manner worthy of the Lord, fully pleasing to him, bearing fruit in every good work and increasing in the knowledge of God.**

There are two phrases in verse 10 that call for our careful attention.

First, observe that Paul speaks of the need for us to walk *worthy* of the Lord. The apostle uses similar language in a number of texts. For example, in Philippians 1:27 he exhorts the believers in that city to let their "manner of life be *worthy* of the gospel of Christ." In Ephesians 4:1 he urges believers "to walk in a manner *worthy* of the calling to which you have been called." Again, in 1 Thessalonians 2:12 he declares that he earlier encouraged them "to walk in a manner *worthy* of God." This is almost identical to the language of John in 3 John 6b: "You will do well to send them on their journey in a manner *worthy* of God."

Someone might get the wrong idea from this, especially given the strong emphasis throughout Colossians 1 on the necessity of good works and bearing fruit and the like. Paul is most assuredly not saying that by our efforts and deeds and commitment we prove ourselves to be worth God or worth the salvation he offers, as if it were by our merits that we gain eternal life. In other words, neither Paul nor John is suggesting that we should strive to earn a place in God's favor or by our good deeds put him in our debt such that he is obligated to acknowledge our efforts and reward us accordingly. This is the opposite of the gospel of grace that we find throughout Scripture.

The focus in Ephesians 4:1 is on the worth of our calling, not on our personal worth. The focus in Philippians 1:27 is on the worth and value of the gospel of Christ, not on the people who believe in it. In both 1 Thessalonians 2:12 and 3 John 6, the point is that God is worthy of our complete and unqualified dedication and devotion. And here in Colossians 1:10, the idea isn't that we are worthy by virtue of how we walk but that we should walk in a way that reflects or displays how much he is worthy of such obedience on our part.

Our great triune God and the marvelous and undeserved kindness that is ours in the gospel are of such infinite value, so exalted and beautiful and full of glory, that we should always live in such a way that it be known. Our lives, by his grace, should reflect positively on God. People should walk away from having observed us, saying, "My goodness, what an incredible God he [she] believes in!" Our aim isn't to evoke from them praise and admiration of who we are, but praise and admiration of who *he* is! Jesus, the cross, and the gospel of salvation by grace alone through faith alone are worthy of lives that reflect on *their* value, not ours.

The second thing to note here is that a life worthy of the Lord is one that is "fully pleasing to him" in all things.

The more literal rendering of this phrase would be something like, "every type or sort of pleasing," or "to please him in all respects." Whereas it is God the Father who fills us with the knowledge of his (God the Father's) will (v. 9), the "Lord" (v. 10) whom we please is probably Jesus.

This is the only place in the New Testament where the word "pleasing" occurs, but the verb occurs in such texts as Romans 8:8 ("those who are in the flesh cannot please God"); 1 Corinthians 7:32 ("how to please the Lord"); and 1 Thessalonians 2:4 ("to please God who tests our hearts"). (See also Rom. 15:1–2; Gal. 1:10; 1 Thess. 2:15; 4:1.)

In secular Greek this particular word most often signified "the behavior by which one sought to gain a favor, and therefore was most often employed with a negative connotation meaning 'obsequiousness.'"[19] To put it in common, somewhat vulgar language, it meant something along the lines of "brown-nosing."

My reason for highlighting the word here in Colossians 1:10 is twofold. First, it reminds us again that good works are pleasing to God! They make God happy. They evoke his pleasure. They incite joy in his heart. God is not devoid of emotions. He feels great delight in good deeds (and displeasure in bad ones; see below).

Of course, we must never forget the incredible words of Hebrews 13:20–21 where the author of that epistle prays, "Now may the God of peace who brought again from the dead our Lord Jesus, the great shepherd of the sheep, by the blood of the eternal covenant, *equip you with everything good that you may do his will, working in us that which is pleasing in his sight*, through Jesus Christ, to whom be glory forever and ever. Amen" (cf. also Phil. 2:12–13).

Thus, when God takes pleasure in our good deeds he is rejoicing in the work of his own grace and power. He is the one who works in us what pleases him. Thus, in rewarding our works God is crowning his own grace.

Another thing to keep in mind is that if our good works please him, our bad ones displease him. On more than one occasion the book of Proverbs speaks of certain deeds as being an "abomination" to the Lord. I can't think of anything more horrendous than a life that God regards as an abomination.

The great difference, of course, is that all good works that please him are the result (ultimately) of his gracious energy in us, whereas all bad works that displease him are our responsibility, for which we shall give an account.

# 16

# Power and Perseverance

## Colossians 1:11

**May you be strengthened with all power, according to his glorious might, for all endurance and patience with joy,** giving thanks to the Father, who has qualified you to share in the inheritance of the saints in light.

Paul's prayer in Colossians 1 actually frightens some people. It is intimidating to them for one of two reasons (or both): some are afraid they won't have the power to live worthy of the Lord and to bear fruit in every good work, while others fear that once they start out in their efforts to do so, they'll end up quitting; they simply won't have the endurance to persevere in what they have begun. So either the sense of personal weakness and spiritual impotence, on the one hand, or the lack of steadfastness, on the other, often paralyzes people from even trying to live as they know the Lord wants them to.

Thank God for Colossians 1:11! Here Paul continues his prayer by asking God to strengthen them with power and to sustain them in their endeavors.

One of my spiritual mentors, a man named Russ McKnight (now with the Lord), was often heard to say: "Whatever God requires, he provides." Never were words more relevant than they are here. Walking worthy of the Lord and pleasing him is a tall order. Living lives laden with spiritual fruit does not come easily to men and women who are by nature selfish and jealous and ambitious and prideful and . . . well, you get the idea.

Paul knew this. It was his struggle, too. That's why he prayed for the Colossians (and undoubtedly for himself as well) the way he did in verse 11. Let's note seven things about this prayer.

First, Paul does not say "strengthen yourselves," as if the power were inherently ours, resident within us, and we only need to flip a switch to release it in our pursuit of holiness. You may recall similar words in Ephesians 6:10 where Paul says, "Finally, be strong in the Lord and in the strength of his might." Needless to say, the key words are "in the Lord" and "in the strength of his might." When he prays, "may you be strengthened," he obviously means "by God"! He could as easily have said it more directly, "Oh, God, I ask that you strengthen these otherwise weak and impotent people to do your will."

Second, there is something of a redundancy in Paul's saying, "be strengthened with all power." It's as if he says, "be empowered with power." Well, yes, but with what else might one be empowered if not with power? Surely, Paul chose his words carefully. He knew what he was saying. His point is simply to reinforce the magnitude of what is available to us from God when we ask him.

Third, as if that weren't enough, he prays that we be strengthened with "all" power. This could mean power "of every kind" or the "fullness" of power or perhaps power in the "highest degree." Nothing second-rate here! Paul prays (as we should, too) for the best and most potent and most effective and wide-ranging power possible. God, being omnipotent, is more than up to the task of saying yes.

Fourth, when God empowers us with maximum power to do his will, he does it "according to his glorious might" (literally, "according to the might of his glory"). Since the word *might* is effectively a synonym for *power*, it may even be rendered "according to his majestic power." In that case we would have something like, "May you be empowered with all power according to his majestic power." Wow! God doesn't do anything second-class.

Fifth, the goal of this empowerment is endurance and patience, the former a reference to persevering in the face of difficult circumstances, the latter a reference to steadfastness that does not retaliate against those who resist us. Events and trials and hardship tempt us to quit, but God grants endurance. People and criticism and injustice tempt us to seek revenge, but God grants patience.

Sixth, as O'Brien reminds us, "this kind of endurance . . . does not derive from personal bravery or stoical fortitude. Rather, as in the Old Testament and later Judaism . . . it is seen to spring from God who is its source."[20] Paul was even more explicit on this point in Romans 15:5 where he describes God as "the God of endurance," i.e., the God from whom endurance ultimately comes. By the way, in that text in Romans Paul makes clear that the means God typically employs when he imparts endurance is the Scriptures (see Rom. 15:4).

Seventh, I don't want to press this point, but we should take note of the present tense in Paul's prayer: "May you be strengthened." We might render it, "May you be continually strengthened" or "strengthened repeatedly." The point is that the strength and power we need is available as the many and varied circumstances and challenges of life are confronted, one after another, day after day.

In sum, there is no addiction God's power cannot break, no sin God's power cannot defeat, no task to which we are called that God's power cannot fulfill, no fruit we are called to bear that God's power cannot produce, no rebellious child God's power cannot restore, no broken marriage God's power cannot reconcile, no physical disease God's power cannot heal. That's why Paul calls it "majestic power."

Russ said, so I'll say it again: "Whatever God requires, he provides."

## 17

# *Glad-hearted Gratitude!*

### Colossians 1:12a

May you be strengthened with all power, according to his glorious might, for all endurance and patience with joy, **giving thanks to the Father**, who has qualified you to share in the inheritance of the saints in light.

*I*f you are reading the ESV, as I am, you'll see that the words "with joy" are placed at the close of verse 11, as if to qualify the endurance and patience that God's power will enable us to experience. In other words, this rendering suggests that perseverance and longsuffering are to be joyful, not morose and sullen as if we were to submit to injustice and hardship grudgingly and with a long face.

I certainly think the Bible teaches this, but I'm not sure Colossians 1:11 does. In a footnote to this passage, the ESV indicates that we might want to take "with joy" in connection with verse 12. In this case, we would render it something like, "strengthened with all power according to his glorious might, for all endurance and patience, with joy giving thanks to the Father."

My preference is for the second of these two options (both the NASB and the NIV also render "joy" as qualifying the way we give thanks). I won't bother you with the technical reasons for this, but I would like to focus on the importance for our gratitude to God to be a joyful, heartfelt, rapturous thanksgiving.

But does this even warrant comment? After all, what other kind of gratitude is there but that which is joyful? Isn't all thanksgiving, by definition, characterized by joy? No.

The fact is, we often receive things we don't want. Not every gift brings a smile to our faces. There are times when we silently wish the donors would just return it and get their money back!

On other occasions we find ourselves suspicious of the motive of the givers. What are they up to? Do they want something from me? Is this gift just a way of flattering me? Am I being manipulated? Perhaps they are doing this to get me to lower my defenses so they can ask of me a favor they know I otherwise wouldn't be inclined to perform.

In any case, gratitude can all too often be lifeless and perfunctory. We say "thanks" with virtually no energy or sincerity. It may be due to our thinking we actually deserve whatever they have given. If we view their action or "generosity" toward us as the payment of a debt, there may well be little joy or delight when we receive it. Relief, yes, but very little if any rejoicing.

Perhaps we struggle with this because we have lost sight of how important joy is to God. Consider, for example, these words from Deuteronomy 28:47–48a: "Because you did not serve the LORD your God with joyfulness and gladness of heart, because of the abundance of all things, therefore you shall serve your enemies whom the LORD will send against you." Merely serving the Lord wasn't enough. Joyfulness and gladness of heart were essential for their service to be pleasing to the Lord.

Or consider the following, which is a small sampling of a pervasive theme in Scripture:

> But let all who take refuge in you rejoice; let them ever sing for joy, and spread your protection over them, that those who love your name may exult in you. (Ps. 5:11)
>
> I will be glad and exult in you; I will sing praise to your name, O Most High. (Ps. 9:2)
>
> You make known to me the path of life; in your presence there is fullness of joy; at your right hand are pleasures forevermore. (Ps. 16:11)
>
> As for me, I shall behold your face in righteousness; when I awake, I shall be satisfied with your likeness. (Ps. 17:15)
>
> O LORD, in your strength the king rejoices, and in your salvation how greatly he exults! . . . For you make him most blessed forever; you make him glad with the joy of your presence. (Ps. 21:1, 6)

Be glad in the LORD and rejoice, O righteous, and shout for joy, all you upright in heart! (Ps. 32:11)

They feast on the abundance of your house, and you give them drink from the river of your delights. (Ps. 36:8)

Delight yourself in the LORD; and he will give you the desires of your heart. (Ps. 37:4)

Then I will go to the altar of God, to God my exceeding joy, and I will praise you with the lyre, O God, my God. (Ps. 43:4)

Restore to me the joy of your salvation. (Ps. 51:12a)

But the righteous shall be glad; they shall exult before God; they shall be jubilant with joy! (Ps. 68:3)

One final thought, which will prepare us for the next meditation: one reason we don't give thanks "with joy" is that we know so little of the profound spiritual blessings that God has provided for us in Jesus. In Colossians 1:12–14 Paul will cite three stunning gifts from God, all ours because of what Jesus has accomplished on our behalf. Meditate upon them, and rejoice with thanksgiving.

# 18

# Qualified in Christ

## *Colossians 1:12*

May you be strengthened with all power, according to his glorious might, for all endurance and patience with joy, **giving thanks to the Father, who has qualified you to share in the inheritance of the saints in light.**

There is a slight difference between being "unqualified" and being "disqualified." In the former case, I may simply lack a talent or attribute or sufficient education to fulfill a task. There's really no shame or fault in being unqualified. We can always work harder or go to school to cultivate the necessary characteristics for whatever it is we desire to achieve.

But to be "disqualified" means you are unfit for the task, you are excluded because of specific failures or vices or behaviors that prove you to be morally unworthy of some high office or responsibility.

Now, maybe I'm pressing too far the distinction between these two words, but I want to make a point. You and I, in our natural, sinful state, apart from divine grace, are not merely unqualified for the kingdom of God, but we are profoundly disqualified. It's not as if God says to us, "If only you could perform this task or solve that problem or answer some question, then I would grant you entrance into my kingdom." Rather, he says to us, "By nature and choice you are the kind of person who is prohibited from entering my kingdom. You think thoughts and commit deeds that warrant exclusion from my presence. It's not simply that you would be admitted if you could do this or that, but you are excluded because you are the moral and spiritual antithesis of what is required of any who would share my fellowship." Ouch!

But thanks (joyful thanks!) be to God who has "qualified us" or "fitted us" or "made us sufficient" to inherit the blessings. How did he do it? By redeeming us (v. 14a) and forgiving us our sins (v. 14b) and clothing us in the righteousness of his Son (1 Cor. 1:30; 2 Cor. 5:21). Whatever qualifications we formerly lacked, we now have. Whatever deeds may have disqualified us, they are forever forgiven.

Whatever feelings of inadequacy or sense of shame or depths of despair may have crippled you till now, God has qualified you to share in the inheritance of the saints in light! If you find yourself saying, "I'm not up to the task. I'm a miserable failure. I'm a hell-deserving wretch. I don't deserve to stand in God's presence. The only thing I should inherit is death," God now says to those who are in Christ: "Qualified! Forgiven! Adequate in Jesus! Righteous in my Son! Come and receive and enjoy your inheritance together with all the saints in the life-giving, soul-cleansing light of my kingdom!"

And what is this inheritance in which all believers share? Ruling angels (1 Cor. 6:3)? Inheriting the earth (Matt. 5:5)? A glorified body (Rom. 8:17–25)? The kingdom of God (1 Cor. 6:9–11)? Yes, and much, much more.

But none of that means anything if God is not there. Not the forgiveness of sins, nor a glorified body, nor the new heavens and new earth—nothing, if God isn't there. Our inheritance is God! He is our exceeding great reward. John Piper said it best when he wrote that "the highest, best, final, decisive good of the gospel, without which no other gifts would be good, is the glory of God in the face of Christ revealed for our everlasting enjoyment. The saving love of God is God's commitment to do everything necessary to enthrall us with what is most deeply and durably satisfying, namely himself."[21]

Or again, "If you could have heaven, with no sickness, and with all the friends you ever had on earth, and all the food you ever liked, and all the leisure activities you ever enjoyed, and all the natural beauties you ever saw, all the physical pleasures you ever tasted, and no human conflict or any natural disasters, could you be satisfied with heaven, if Christ was not there?"[22]

I hope the answer is no.

Oh, God, fill us with joyful and glad-hearted gratitude for having qualified us to inherit you—your presence, your beauty, your glory forever and ever.

# 19

# Delivered from Darkness

## Colossians 1:13

**He has delivered us from the domain of darkness and transferred us to the kingdom of his beloved Son,** in whom we have redemption, the forgiveness of sins.

When the apostle Paul stood before King Agrippa, he gave an account of what happened to him on the road to Damascus. Jesus, he said, was sending him to the Gentiles "to open their eyes, so that they may turn from darkness to light and from the power of Satan to God, that they may receive forgiveness of sins and a place among those who are sanctified by faith in me" (Acts 26:18).

When Paul wrote to the Colossians, he portrayed their salvation in almost identical terms: You have been given a "share in the inheritance of the saints" and have been delivered "from the domain of darkness and transferred" to "the kingdom" of Christ, in whom is found "the forgiveness of sins" (Col. 1:12–14). This, Paul says, is why our gratitude is to be fervent and joyful.

The Bible clearly indicates that there are two and only two spiritual realms, and all of mankind belongs in one or the other. There are not multiple religious options, each of equal saving value. Those who do not as yet know Jesus Christ are in the realm of darkness, subject to the authority and power of Satan. The apostle John said it in unmistakable terms when he declared that "the whole world lies in the power of the evil one" (1 John 5:19). By "the whole world" John means everyone and everything that is not in Christ by faith.

The irony, of course, is that few, if any, who are under the authority of Satan and walking in spiritual darkness feel as if they are. If anything, they are entirely persuaded they live in light and freedom and power. In fact, they are utterly blind, in bondage to the enemy, and powerless to extricate themselves by their own efforts.

The word Paul uses in verse 13, translated "domain," is the standard Greek word for "authority," which indicates an active power or energy that Satan exerts over those who are his. His dominion is characterized by darkness: intellectual, moral, and spiritual. No matter how high your IQ, no matter how expansive your financial portfolio, apart from Christ you are under the authority of Satan and subject to the power of darkness. No matter how musically gifted you may be, no matter how athletically endowed and honored, apart from Christ you lie in the power of the evil one.

If you ever felt you needed a good reason to share the gospel with an unsaved neighbor or a coworker in the office, this is it. Don't be misled by what appears to be worldly success. Burgeoning careers, civil behavior, the respect of peers, backyard barbeques, and children who score high on the ACT notwithstanding, they are in the power of the evil one, energized by the domain of darkness.

There is only one hope, for them or us. It is the forgiveness of sins that is found only in Jesus Christ. Give thanks joyfully to the Father, says Paul, for you were once as they are, thinking yourselves wise when in fact you were fools, reveling in a freedom that only deepened and intensified your bondage.

But God has "delivered" you from Satan's tyranny and has placed you under the loving and kind authority of his Son. To be "transferred" suggests the notion of being uprooted from one kingdom and transplanted into another.

This is the kingdom or rule or reign of God's own "beloved Son" (v. 13b). This is a stunning description of Jesus, if only because he is the one who became the object of the Father's eternal wrath.

But how can this be? If the Father truly loved the Son, surely he would not have exposed him to such horrific suffering. How can the Son be the "beloved" of the Father and yet also the object of his wrath and judgment? Such is the glorious, soul-saving, redemptive mystery of penal substitutionary atonement.

It is possible because the Son and the Father are united in their love for the elect and together entered into a covenant to redeem them from their sins. This could only be accomplished by the Son's willingly and freely offering himself as a substitute who would wholly absorb the wrath of the Father, which those for whom he died deserved.

Had Jesus not satisfied the wrath of the Father, we would still be under the dominion of darkness, held captive in our sins, and subject to the authority of one who hates us. But thanks be to God, joyful and whole-hearted thanks, because he has, at great and unimaginable cost to himself and his beloved Son, extricated us from the grip of Satan and now embraces us with an eternal and irrevocable love.

# 20

# Forever Forgiven

## Colossians 1:14

He has delivered us from the domain of darkness and transferred us to the kingdom of his beloved Son, **in whom we have redemption, the forgiveness of sins.**

Jesus Christ, the one into whose kingdom we have been transferred (Col. 1:13), is also the one, indeed the only one, "in whom we have redemption, the forgiveness of sins" (Col. 1:14).

It isn't in the keeping of New Year's resolutions that forgiveness is found, or in the therapy of a psychiatrist's counsel. Neither good works nor good intentions nor the cultivation of a healthy self-esteem can wipe clean the slate of our souls. Forgiveness is found only in Christ.

And when it is found, it is found now and forever. Note Paul's use of the present tense, "we have." The forgiveness of sins isn't just a future hope, something that will one day be ours. It is ours now. It is an existing, ever-present, liberating, and life-changing reality in the present moment.

But how does one describe the forgiveness of sins? In my book *The Singing God: Discover the Joy of Being Enjoyed by God*,[23] I gave it a try, and I honestly don't think I can improve on it. So I want to take the liberty of citing what I said there.

Have you ever fooled around with an Etch-a-Sketch? It's that toy with what looks like a television screen and two knobs that enable you to sketch whatever fits your fancy.

I never was much good at it. I'm not an artist by any stretch of the imagination. The Etch-a-Sketch was made for people like me. If you don't like what you've "drawn" and especially don't want to be embarrassed should anyone else see it, you simply tip the screen and your work of "art" vanishes!

It's a crude and simple illustration, but that is a lot like what God does with your sin when he grants forgiveness. Through the course of our earthly existence we sketch an ugly scenario of sin and rebellion and ingratitude and jealousy and lust. There it is, vividly imprinted on the screen of our souls.

But when we confess our sin, God's loving and gracious hand tips the toy and the slate is wiped clean. No matter how often we return to deface our lives with ugly pictures of hatred and anger and pride and envy, God is faithful to tip the screen. All it takes is confession. All it takes is the blood of Christ.

But don't take my word for it. Listen to what God himself says: "I, I am he who blots out your transgressions for my own sake, and I will not remember your sins" (Isa. 43:25). When we confess our sin and plead the blood of the Lord Jesus, God promises never again to bring it up, either to himself, to you, or to others. That's forgiveness!

God is not finished yet. He's got another illustration to make his point. Hezekiah put it this way: "Behold, it was for my welfare that I had great bitterness; but in love you have delivered my life from the pit of destruction, for you have cast all my sins behind your back" (Isa. 38:17).

God has taken your sin and placed it out of sight behind his back. All he sees now when he sees you is the blessed righteousness of his own dear Son, the Lord Jesus Christ. Such is the love of forgiveness.

Still not good enough? Still not convinced? Still afraid that your sins will do you in? Then pay close attention to the word of the prophet Micah. He has something important to say about the kind of God we have: "Who is a God like you, pardoning iniquity and passing over transgression for the remnant of his inheritance? He does not retain his anger forever, because he delights in steadfast love. He will again have compassion on us; he will tread our iniquities under foot. You will cast all our sins into the depths of the sea" (Mic. 7:18–19).

How much more graphic do you demand God to be before you enter into the joy of his forgiving love? All vestige of condemning guilt is gone. Again, "just as God said he *put* our sins behind his back, so here he says he will *hurl* them into the depths of the sea. They will not 'fall overboard'; God will hurl them into the depths. He wants them to be lost forever, because he has fully dealt with them in his Son, Jesus Christ."[24]

Like you, I watched with amazement as the latest underwater technology scoured for remains of the *Titanic*, recovering from the bottom of the sea what everyone thought lost forever. No! No! It won't happen with your sins! The submarine has not been made that can submerge that deep. The equipment has not been found, and never will be, that can retrieve the slightest vestige of your transgressions. God forbids it. Such is the quality of his forgiving love.

I don't know how all this affects you, but I agree with David when he says (shouts?), "Blessed is the one whose transgression is forgiven. . . . Blessed is the man against whom the Lord counts no iniquity" (Ps. 32:1–2).

All hope for happiness is contingent on the forgiveness of sins. The word "blessed" in Psalm 32, by the way, is plural. As Charles Spurgeon said, "Oh, the blessednesses! the double joys, the bundles of happiness, the mountains of delight"[25] that abound to the forgiven.

Having experienced for himself the joy of forgiving love, David encourages others to seek God's pardoning favor: "Therefore let everyone who is godly offer prayer to you at a time when you may be found; surely in the rush of great waters, they shall not reach him. You are a hiding place for me; you preserve me from trouble; you surround me with shouts of deliverance" (Ps. 32:6–7).

God is like a high rock on which we stand when the flood waters of adversity begin to rise.

God is a hiding place, a shelter in whom we find safety and protection from all that threatens the soul.

And remember, all this for men and women like David who have spurned his ways and transgressed his will.

What accounts for this willingness in God to forgive? To what do we attribute the peace and release and joy that flood the pardoned soul?

David puts his finger on it in Psalm 32:10: "Many are the sorrows of the wicked, but steadfast love surrounds the one who trusts in the Lord." God's love is the bulwark of our lives, the bodyguard of our souls, the atmosphere of immutable affection in which we move and live and breathe.

# 21

# Who Is This Man?

## Colossians 1:15–20

He is the image of the invisible God, the firstborn of all creation. For by him all things were created, in heaven and on earth, visible and invisible, whether thrones or dominions or rulers or authorities—all things were created through him and for him. And he is before all things, and in him all things hold together. And he is the head of the body, the church. He is the beginning, the firstborn from the dead, that in everything he might be preeminent. For in him all the fullness of God was pleased to dwell, and through him to reconcile to himself all things, whether on earth or in heaven, making peace by the blood of his cross.

The Sea of Galilee on this particular night was unusually disturbed. A raging storm had suddenly arisen, tossing the tiny boat around like a toothpick in a whirlpool. Fearing for their lives, the disciples awakened their sleeping companion who calmly rebuked the wind and the sea and reduced the fury of the storm to a peaceful hush. Awestruck, they murmured among themselves, asking the question, "Who then is this, that even wind and sea obey him?" (Mark 4:41).

When this same individual proceeded both to heal the body and forgive the sins of a paralytic who had been brought to him, the scribes and Pharisees huddled among themselves, asking the question, "Who is this who speaks blasphemies? Who can forgive sins but God alone?" (Luke 5:21).

As reports of what this man had done spread throughout the land, news of him finally reached the palace of King Herod. Puzzled,

Herod said: "John I beheaded, but who is this about whom I hear such things?" (Luke 9:9).

When the man rode meekly, yet majestically, into the city of Jerusalem on a donkey, on what we call Palm Sunday, the reaction of the multitude was typical of what had already occurred numerous times before. "And when he entered Jerusalem, the whole city was stirred up, saying, 'Who is this?'" (Matt. 21:10).

There is no question as profound or fundamental or eternally significant as the one so many have asked before: "Who is this man, Jesus of Nazareth?" On your answer to that question hang suspended all the issues of life and death, good and evil, truth and falsehood, heaven and hell. The author of "Amazing Grace," John Newton, once wrote:

> What think ye of Christ? is the test;
> to try both your state and your scheme;
> You cannot be right in the rest
> unless you think rightly of him.

Imagine for a moment that you are the host of a neighborhood dinner party. Tonight in your home are gathered several individuals from a variety of different religious backgrounds. Sitting at your table are a Mormon, a Muslim, a Jehovah's Witness, a Moonie (Unification Church of Rev. Sun Myung Moon), a theological liberal, your next door neighbor, and you. The after-dinner conversation soon turns from politics to religion. Before long, someone asks, concerning Jesus: "Who is this man?"

The Mormon is the first to speak up:

> Let me tell you who Jesus was. He was the first-born child of Elohim. He was the product of the physical union between the Father-God and the Virgin Mary. Don't look so shocked. For a time, God and Mary were actually husband and wife and they had sexual relations, as any married couple would, and conceived Jesus! And the good news is that if we work hard enough we too can become sons of God in the same sense that Jesus is. Please, no coffee for me.

The Muslim protests:

> "No, no, no! You've got it all wrong. Jesus is just like Abraham and Moses and Isaiah. He was a prophet of God. But he was not himself God. In fact,

he wasn't even the most important of the prophets. Muhammad, who lived five hundred years after Jesus, was God's greatest prophet. Besides, Jesus didn't really die on the cross as Christians believe. He was rescued by God and carried to a safe place in the heavens. Since there was no death, there was no atonement for sin. Since there was no death, there was no resurrection either. Don't you dare disagree with me!"

The Jehovah's Witness can no longer hold his peace:

You're both wrong! Prior to his coming to this earth Jesus was Michael, the archangel. He's only a creature, the first product of Jehovah God's creative work. When he was born of the Virgin Mary, he was divested of his spiritual, angelic nature and became wholly and exclusively a man. Jesus isn't God. Would anyone like a tract?

The Moonie is next:

You people are so deceived. On the one hand, I agree with those of you who say that Jesus was a mere man. But what you don't know is that he was actually the illegitimate child of an adulterous relationship between Mary and Zacharias, the husband of her cousin Elizabeth. Jesus failed to establish the perfect family on earth, so God has sent to us his second Messiah to carry on the work. His name is Rev. Sun Myung Moon. By the way, I've got some nice roses left over that I'll sell real cheap.

Disgusted by what he perceives to be religious mythology, the theological liberal takes control of the conversation:

You're all fools! This is the twenty-first century, for heaven's sake. All of you talk like you live in the Dark Ages. Common sense alone tells us that Jesus was the natural-born son of Mary and Joseph, no different at birth from anyone else. But don't get me wrong. I'm no atheist. In fact, because of his exceptional virtue and humility and spiritual sensitivity, God adopted him to be his Son. He endowed him with miraculous powers and through him proclaimed the wonderful message of the Universal Fatherhood of God and the Universal Brotherhood of Men! You all probably believe in Santa Claus and the Tooth Fairy, too.

Your next-door neighbor is a bit bewildered by now:

Golly, gee. I always thought Jesus was just a good-old-boy who told us to love everybody and be nice. It's too bad he ended up getting killed like that. But as long as we all believe in the existence of God, does it really matter all that much? Is it really worth starting a neighborhood feud?

And there you sit, nervously sipping your coffee, as every eye at the table turns its attention to you, awaiting your opinion on who is Jesus. "Uh, well, let me see, uh . . . would anyone care for dessert?"

Colossians 1:15–20 is undoubtedly one of the most theologically profound and mysterious portrayals of Jesus in the New Testament. So, as we prepare to examine it, word by word, phrase by phrase, I'll ask again: "Who, then, is this man?"

# 22

# Seeing the Father in the Son

## Colossians 1:15

**He is the image of the invisible God, the firstborn of all creation.** For by him all things were created, in heaven and on earth, visible and invisible, whether thrones or dominions or rulers or authorities—all things were created through him and for him. And he is before all things, and in him all things hold together. And he is the head of the body, the church. He is the beginning, the firstborn from the dead, that in everything he might be preeminent. For in him all the fullness of God was pleased to dwell, and through him to reconcile to himself all things, whether on earth or in heaven, making peace by the blood of his cross.

Seeing is believing, or so we are told. But if that's true, how can we ever be expected to believe in God? Several biblical texts make it clear that God is, by nature, invisible. It isn't just that he has not been seen: he *cannot* be seen (cf. John 1:18; Rom. 1:20; 1 Tim. 6:16; Heb. 11:27). Even here in Colossians 1:15 he is described as "the invisible God."

In Romans 1:20 Paul says that God's existence and eternal attributes can be seen in the things that are made. In other words, the visible creation reveals an invisible creator. All well and good, but looking at a tree or a sunset or the majesty of the Grand Canyon isn't the same as looking at God himself.

So what hope is there for knowing and believing in God? The answer is Jesus! Philip certainly felt the urgency to "see" God. "Lord, show us the Father, and it is enough for us" (John 14:8), to which Jesus replied: "Whoever has seen me has seen the Father" (John 14:9).

This is very much Paul's point here in Colossians 1:15 where he declares concerning Jesus: "He is the image of the invisible God, the firstborn of all creation" (cf. 2 Cor. 4:4).

The word translated "image" refers to a likeness or visible representation. How exact or precise the resemblance is between the original and the copy must be determined by the context. To say someone is "like" another person often conveys the idea of moderate similarity, but not necessarily exact representation. On the other hand, you've undoubtedly heard someone described as "the spitting image" of another. If one may be reverent in saying so, God the Son (Jesus) is the spitting image of God the Father.

Of course, Paul's point isn't that Jesus "looks like" the Father, as if to suggest the Father has a physical frame and visage, which the Son reflects. The Son "images" the Father in terms of moral character, will, and the attributes of deity. The Father and the Son, together with the Holy Spirit, share a common divine nature, glory, and purpose.

I've spoken with people who almost choke when they hear that God is their "Father." The latter term reminds them only of abuse or abandonment, often evoking a bitter taste in their mouths. How, then, does one rebuild in the hearts of Christian people the image of God as Father? It can come only by pointing to the Son. He is everything the Father is, except for being the Father. Every virtue, every power, all glory, and the fullness of deity reside in the Son as they do in the Father. He is the perfect and exact image of the Father (cf. Heb. 1:3).

But if being the "image" of the Father seems to confirm the deity of the Lord Jesus Christ, the second phrase in verse 15 appears to destroy it, for there we are told that he is also "the firstborn of all creation."

This phrase seems to say that Jesus was the first created being in a series of other created beings. Does this mean the Jehovah's Witnesses have been right all along? No. Part of the problem is related to translation. We have to determine the best way to render this phrase. Is it, "the firstborn of all creation," or "the firstborn over all creation"? Either is grammatically possible but there is a world of difference between them. Is Jesus "of" creation in the sense that he belongs to it as its initial or original member? Or is Jesus "over" creation in the sense that he is its source and sovereign Lord and maker? I believe it is the latter, and for several reasons.

First, observe how verse 16 begins: "For by him all things were created." The word "for" indicates that what follows in verse 16 supports or explains what has preceded in verse 15. In other words, Paul is saying, "Here is 'how' or 'the sense in which' Jesus is the firstborn of (over) all creation: it is by virtue of his having created all things." If Jesus were merely one of the many and varied parts of creation, belonging to them as if he were himself a creature, Paul would not have said that Jesus created all things.

Second, to say that Jesus is himself a creature is inconsistent with Colossians 1:17. There Paul declares that the Son of God is "before" all things, similar to our Lord's claim in John 8:58 that "before Abraham was, I am."

Third, to say that Jesus is a creature would be inconsistent with what Paul clearly said about him elsewhere, primarily in Philippians 2:6–11 (esp. v. 6).

Fourth, to say that Jesus is a creature would be inconsistent with what John clearly said of him in John 1:3: "All things were made through him, and without him was not any thing made that was made."

Fifth, the word *firstborn* itself does not necessarily mean "first in a sequence" or "first in time." It can also mean "first in rank" or "supreme in dignity." The point is that the Son, by virtue of being the image of God, has a preeminence and exercises a sovereignty over everything else that exists. The word is used this way of King David in the Old Testament. In Psalm 89:27, God says of David: "And I will make him the firstborn, the highest of the kings of the earth."

The point, then, is that Jesus Christ is utterly unique, distinguished from all of creation because he is both eternally prior to it and supreme over it in the sense, as verse 16 makes clear, that he is its creator.

Who, then, is this man? He is the Lord Jesus Christ, who "images" the Father, displaying in himself as the second person of the Godhead every perfection and attribute of the first person of the Godhead (see Col. 1:19 and 2:9). He is also creator and sovereign Lord over all. Praise be to the Son!

# 23

# Praising Christ with Prepositions

## Colossians 1:16

He is the image of the invisible God, the firstborn of all creation. **For by him all things were created, in heaven and on earth, visible and invisible, whether thrones or dominions or rulers or authorities—all things were created through him and for him.** And he is before all things, and in him all things hold together. And he is the head of the body, the church. He is the beginning, the firstborn from the dead, that in everything he might be preeminent. For in him all the fullness of God was pleased to dwell, and through him to reconcile to himself all things, whether on earth or in heaven, making peace by the blood of his cross.

I admit it sounds pretty weird at first, but there's something stunning about prepositions. That's right, *prepositions*. I'm really not nuts. Trust me. Yes, I'm talking about those words like *in* and *over* and *through* and *by* and *for*, just to mention a few.

There is immeasurable spiritual wealth in those little words. I'm fascinated to think that God would entrust the revelation of his glory to something as mundane as prepositions, words that few of us ever pause in the course of a day to notice. But the more I meditate on prepositions, the more I see the beauty and majesty of Jesus. Let me prove it to you.

When Christians gathered for worship in the early church, they sang hymns of praise as we do. Many scholars contend that the words of one such hymn are found in the passage we are studying in Colossians. Read the passage closely and take special note of the prepositions (italicized) that it contains:

> He is the image of the invisible God, the firstborn of all creation. For *by* [literally, "in"] him all things were created, in heaven and on earth, visible and invisible, whether thrones or dominions or rulers or authorities—all things were created *through* him and *for* him. And he is *before* all things, and *in* him all things hold together. (vv. 15–17)

Perhaps an analogy will help make my point. Consider the stages involved in building a home. The first thing you do is hire an architect who draws up the blueprints. He formulates the plan and lists the many specifications on how everything is to be constructed. You then contract a builder, the person who actually puts brick to mortar and nail to wood. The house is then put to the use for which it was built: you move in. You occupy it and enjoy the many special features it contains, whether a special den or a hot tub on the deck. Finally, as its inhabitant and owner, you maintain it. You are careful to make timely repairs and perhaps a bit of remodeling here and there.

Here's my point. Jesus Christ is all of these in relation to the whole of the universe. He is the architect. This is what Paul means in Colossians 1:16a when he says that all things were created "in" him. He is the artisan. He is the one in whose eternal mind the blueprints for every nook and cranny of the cosmos were conceived.

And Paul is pretty specific about the extent of Christ's creative input. It encompasses literally everything: "all things" (v. 16a), by which he means everything "in heaven and on earth," be they massive galaxies billions of light years away or the dust mites beneath your feet. The "all things" include what you can see and can't see, whether visible but intangible, like a mirage or beam of light; whether invisible but tangible, like a summer breeze or the heat of the sun; whether visible and tangible, like an oak tree or a book or a baseball; even things invisible and intangible like a proton or gravity or a feeling or a dream. He conceived them all!

But it doesn't stop there. He is the architect of every spiritual being, here described as "thrones" and "dominions" and "rulers" and "authorities," typical Pauline language for every conceivable variety of angel, both good and evil, both hellish and holy. They were all Christ's idea.

He is not only the architect who conceived their existence and their manifold properties and powers, he is the artisan who actually constructed their being. They were made *through* him, says Paul (v. 16b). John echoed this thought by saying that "all things were made through him, and without him was not any thing made that was made" (John 1:3).

Yes, he is both architect and artisan, as well as the aim for which they were created. As Paul put it, "all things were created . . . *for* him" (v. 16c; oh blessed preposition). Whatever is, is, that he might be glorified and praised and enjoyed forever. He is the reason, the goal, the aim, the intent, the point, the purpose, the end, the terminus, the consummation and culmination of every molecule that moves.

Does that please you? Do you find unparalleled joy in knowing that it's about him and not you? Do you find delight in knowing that God didn't create the world so he could have you, but so that you could have him?

# 24

# Shaken, but Safe in Him

## Colossians 1:17

He is the image of the invisible God, the firstborn of all creation. For by him all things were created, in heaven and on earth, visible and invisible, whether thrones or dominions or rulers or authorities—all things were created through him and for him. **And he is before all things, and in him all things hold together**. And he is the head of the body, the church. He is the beginning, the firstborn from the dead, that in everything he might be preeminent. For in him all the fullness of God was pleased to dwell, and through him to reconcile to himself all things, whether on earth or in heaven, making peace by the blood of his cross.

I've never been in an earthquake, and I hope I never am. I've seen quite a few tornadoes in my life. Having grown up in Oklahoma and Texas, I actually grew somewhat accustomed to hearing the warning sirens and seeking shelter in the appropriate place. But I have no idea what it is like to have the ground beneath your feet shake and split open. That is one sensation from which I've been spared.

But the Colossian Christians knew what it was like. Ancient Colossae was located in the Lycus Valley, about one hundred miles inland from Ephesus. This was an area that was the center of repeated earthquakes (it was not unlike living in California). We know that a major, devastating earthquake hit this area sometime in A.D. 60 or 61. Much of the city was destroyed and numerous lives were lost.

Most scholars believe Paul wrote this letter during his Roman imprisonment around A.D. 60. Therefore, either just before or very soon after they received this letter, the entire city of Colossae and its inhabitants were seriously shaken!

Knowing this makes Paul's statement in verse 17 all the more significant. Of Jesus Christ he writes, "He is before all things, and in him all things hold together" (v. 17). Some translations render this, "in him all things cohere" or "in him all things subsist," the point being, whatever coherence or unity the universe displays, it is due to the continual exertion of divine power from the Son of God. The risen Christ sustains and upholds all things.

Jesus Christ is the sustaining and supportive power by which all that he has conceived and constructed should stay in being. He didn't create, only to skip town. From the moment of inception until now and for as long as he so wills, Jesus sustains all things, guides all things, and is in the process of providentially bringing all things to their proper consummation in and for him.

Jesus is the cohesive power that keeps all things intact. If I may say it reverently, he's the "divine glue" that holds it all in place. This world is a cosmos rather than a chaos because of the continuous exertion of divine power from the risen Christ.

The things that *are* don't exist by virtue of some power intrinsic to themselves. Cars and chairs and baseballs and butter and quarks and quasars—yes, everything, exists and is sustained in its present form by virtue of the incessant energy emanating from Jesus. If at any moment, for any reason, he should loosen his providential and preserving grip on any thing, it would disintegrate. It would vaporize and vanish into a vacuum of nothingness.

Every heartbeat, every flutter of an eyelid, every rustle of every blade of grass, every breath you breathe is sustained by the Son of God. Truly did Paul say in Acts 17:28 that "in him we live and move and have our being."

We can wake up each day confident that we will not freeze to death because in the sun that we so easily take for granted hundreds of billion billion billion billion (that's 10 with 38 zeros) fusion reactions take place every second. More than four hundred million tons of hydrogen are being converted into helium every second in the heart of the sun. And this is only one sun among billions of trillions of others, all of which are a constant inferno of chemical and nuclear reactions, all of which are the product of the power and sustaining energy of Jesus who sits enthroned at the right hand of God.

If that earthquake hit Colossae soon after their reception of Paul's letter, I suspect they would have encouraged one another with the reminder that in Jesus, their Lord and Savior, all things still cohere, all things are upheld. If there is a shaking, it is because the Lord has willed it. No matter how widespread the destruction, no matter how disconcerting the loss, Jesus has not lost his grip on this world or their lives.

The "shaking" may also be spiritual or political or economic in nature, but "in him all things [still] hold together." The world may appear to be swept up and away in moral chaos, but in him all things still hold together. One crisis may crash in upon another, like the incessant waves of the ocean pummeling the shoreline, but in him all things still hold together.

One more thing: don't think of Jesus as merely bearing up the world as if he were Atlas, holding aloft the globe on somewhat sunken shoulders, laboring intensely lest he crater under its incredible weight. No! The Lord Jesus is bearing the universe toward a consummation; he is moving and managing and orchestrating all that he sustains so that on that final day his glory will be radiantly seen and his purpose will have been perfectly attained (cf. Heb. 1:3).

So, I pray that you and I will do what I trust the Colossians did as they labored to put their lives back together following that incredible shaking: confidently rest and trust in the One who holds all things together and continues, unabated and undeterred, in the pursuit of his purpose, for our spiritual good and his everlasting glory.

# 25
# Preeminent in All Things

## Colossians 1:18

He is the image of the invisible God, the firstborn of all creation. For by him all things were created, in heaven and on earth, visible and invisible, whether thrones or dominions or rulers or authorities—all things were created through him and for him. And he is before all things, and in him all things hold together. **And he is the head of the body, the church. He is the beginning, the firstborn from the dead, that in everything he might be preeminent**. For in him all the fullness of God was pleased to dwell, and through him to reconcile to himself all things, whether on earth or in heaven, making peace by the blood of his cross.

If it weren't for biblical texts like Colossians 1:18, it would be easy to get discouraged about the local church. There Paul continues his description of Jesus Christ with the statement, "And he is the head of the body, the church. He is the beginning, the firstborn from the dead, that in everything he might be preeminent."

I've ministered in a lot of churches from a vast array of denominations: Presbyterian, Vineyard, Anglican, Methodist, Baptist, Nazarene, Assemblies of God, and Lutheran, as well as numerous independent and nondenominational congregations. It isn't always a pretty sight to behold. Many are struggling to stay open. Others are on the verge of schism. Political ambition and behind-the-scenes shenanigans prevail. In some, the proverbial "worship wars" are raging intensely, while others are laboring to overcome the devastation of moral failure in their leadership.

I don't want to sound unduly pessimistic. I'm thankful that some churches are flourishing and vibrant and maintain a faithful testimony to Jesus and a commitment to his Word. But far too many have compromised with the surrounding culture or have embraced worldly values that have largely muted their proclamation of the gospel.

As I said, it would be easy to get discouraged if it weren't for the fact that Jesus is the head of the church. The "church" here is probably a reference to the universal body of Christ, that spiritual organism comprised of all believers in all of history. But if Jesus is the head of the universal church in general, he is also the head of every local church in particular. These many and varied local expressions of his body belong to him. If a local church dissolves or strays off course, the church, the universal body, perseveres. When Jesus first promised to "build" his church (Matt. 16:18), he assured us that the gates of hell would not prevail against it. I have to keep reminding myself of this, as I suspect you do as well.

When Paul says that Jesus Christ is the "head of the body, the church," he means to tell us that Christ is the sovereign, ruling authority over his people, as well as the source from which we, his body, derive all spiritual sustenance and power. As such, we can rest assured that our Lord will not permit his body to drift into utter moral and theological chaos or to die of spiritual starvation and thirst.

Some professing Christians behave and "minister" as if Jesus is the head of the church only in name or title, much in the way Elizabeth is the Queen of England. When it comes down to the daily operations and administration of that country, she has very little if any role. The title "Queen" is merely honorary and traditional.

But such is not the case with our Lord Jesus Christ. He exerts a functional authority over his body. He can be trusted to govern and direct and provide instruction and power for the life of his church if we will but look to him and draw from the resources he so generously supplies. The relationship between Jesus as head and the church as body is organic and living and vital. He exercises sovereign control over us and we are ever and always dependent on his abiding influence and presence. As J. B. Lightfoot once wrote, Jesus "is the inspiring, ruling, guiding, combining, sustaining power [of the church], the mainspring of its activity, the centre of its unity and the seat of its life."[26]

Paul continues by describing him as "the beginning, the firstborn from the dead." That is to say, he was the beginning and founder of a new humanity, a new people, by virtue of his having been the first to rise, never to die again. When God the Father raised him from the dead and glorified and exalted him to the right hand of the majesty on high, he became the firstfruits of that resurrection guaranteed for all who are united to him (cf. 1 Cor. 15:20–23; Rev. 1:12–18).

There is a reason for this. There was a goal in view. It was so that Jesus might be seen and known and glorified as preeminent in everything. God raised Jesus from the dead and placed him in authority over the church so that he, and only he, might be seen and savored, recognized and relished, exalted and enjoyed as the sovereign Lord, the one for whom all things were made and to whom all praise should be given.

To what extent does your life reflect the preeminence of Christ? Are the affairs of your daily existence so ordered that Jesus is seen to be preeminent? Is there any doubt in the way you use your time, your money, and your talents that Jesus is the source and center of it all? Is he your treasure, or is it found in the documents and deeds lying in a bank vault? Does he govern your life in such a way that all may know he is Lord? How visible is the supremacy of Christ in the way you talk and relate to others and fulfill your responsibilities at work and in the home?

Resist the temptation to restrict the preeminence of Christ to one day a week, as if he were Lord and worthy of praise for only one hour on a Sunday morning. He is to be honored as preeminent not only over all things but at all times, in every context, in every circumstance.

Resist the temptation to isolate the preeminence of Christ or to confine it to "religious" matters. He has been given preeminence "in all things." Everything in all of life, both inside and outside the church, exists to make him look good. Not to make him good, for he is eternally and self-sufficiently good, but to reveal and disclose and enable all to see that he is, in fact, good and glorious and worthy of our wholehearted and exclusive devotion.

# 26

# *Wholly God (1)*

## Colossians 1:19; 2:9

He is the image of the invisible God, the firstborn of all creation. For by him all things were created, in heaven and on earth, visible and invisible, whether thrones or dominions or rulers or authorities—all things were created through him and for him. And he is before all things, and in him all things hold together. And he is the head of the body, the church. He is the beginning, the firstborn from the dead, that in everything he might be preeminent. **For in him all the fullness of God was pleased to dwell**, and through him to reconcile to himself all things, whether on earth or in heaven, making peace by the blood of his cross. . . . **For in him the whole fullness of deity dwells bodily,** and you have been filled in him, who is the head of all rule and authority.

In my travels I've had the opportunity to visit a wide variety of churches. Not long ago I was in a mainline Protestant denominational church where I couldn't help but notice a variety of Sunday school classes that were being promoted in the foyer. On the table were a number of books to be studied in the respective classes. To say I was shocked to see a volume by the Episcopalian bishop John Shelby Spong is an understatement.

Spong has become (in)famous in recent years for his blatant and boastful denial of virtually every foundational Christian doctrine. Spong mocks belief in the incarnation of Christ, his deity, his virgin conception, his atoning death, and his bodily resurrection, just to mention a few. That any of his wretched books should be used as the basis for a Sunday school class is a sad commentary on the state of spirituality in too many churches today.

I suppose I was especially energized by the presence of this book because I happened to be preparing this meditation in Colossians at the time. Contrary to Spong and other likeminded heretics, there is hardly a more explicit affirmation of the deity of our Lord Jesus Christ than what we find in Colossians 1:19 (and again in 2:9). Here is how this verse is rendered in three different translations:

> For in him all the fullness of God was pleased to dwell.

> For it was the *Father's* good pleasure for all the fullness to dwell in Him. (NASB)

> For God was pleased to have all his fullness dwell in him. (NIV)

Paul literally says that "all the fullness" was "pleased" to dwell in Christ. But "fullness" is not a person and only a person has conscious and willful intent; only a person can be "pleased" to do something. So both the NASB and the NIV translate the verse to indicate that God the Father is the subject of the verb: it was his good pleasure that the fullness of the divine nature dwell in Christ. In this and subsequent meditations we are going to think deeply about this truth.

Let me begin by urging you not to be misled by the word "dwell." Paul is not suggesting that there was a man named Jesus in whom deity or divinity resided. In other words, the fullness of deity didn't dwell in Jesus the way the Holy Spirit dwells in you and me. When God the Son became a human, the fullness of the divine nature "became flesh" (John 1:14), yet without ceasing to be divine. The divine and the human united in the one person of Jesus Christ.

The early church wrestled with how best to articulate this marvelous and mind-bending mystery and reached its conclusions at the Council of Chalcedon in A.D. 451. Here is that portion of the statement that attempts to explain what Paul is saying in Colossians and elsewhere in the New Testament. Jesus Christ is "to be acknowledged in two natures [one divine, one human], without confusion, without change, without division, without separation; the distinction of natures being by no means taken away by the union, but rather the property of each nature being preserved, and concurring in one Person and one Subsistence, not parted or divided into two persons, but one and the same Son, and only begotten, God the Word, the Lord Jesus Christ."

The authors of this statement had three primary goals in mind. First, their point in saying the two natures were not confused or changed is to prevent us from concluding that the divine and human were so united that an altogether different third thing, neither truly divine nor truly human, was created. For example, if you have a glass of water and a glass of wine and mix them together in a pitcher, you end up with something different from what you started out with. The water is now somewhat alcoholic and the wine is now somewhat diluted, but the substance in the pitcher is different from what was in either of the two glasses.

Contrary to what some in the early church suggested, the divine nature did not "swallow up" the human (as the ocean would a drop of ink), nor did the human dilute the divine into something less than truly God.

Second, their point in saying there was neither separation nor distinction is to prevent us from concluding that the divine and human natures in Christ were artificially bonded, almost as one would glue together two separate pieces of wood. There was more than an external "connection" between the divine and human: there was and is a true union of the two.

Third and finally, they wanted to be certain that the union of the divine and the human not be construed in such a way that we think of the incarnate Christ as if he were two separate persons. He is one person, wholly divine and wholly human, neither less divine because he has a human nature nor less human because he has a divine nature.

Yes, I know it's mind boggling! But if our Lord Jesus Christ were anything less or other than the God-man, one person who is truly divine and truly human, we would still be in our sin.

# 27

# *Wholly God (2)*

## Colossians 1:19; 2:9

He is the image of the invisible God, the firstborn of all creation. For by him all things were created, in heaven and on earth, visible and invisible, whether thrones or dominions or rulers or authorities—all things were created through him and for him. And he is before all things, and in him all things hold together. And he is the head of the body, the church. He is the beginning, the firstborn from the dead, that in everything he might be preeminent. **For in him all the fullness of God was pleased to dwell**, and through him to reconcile to himself all things, whether on earth or in heaven, making peace by the blood of his cross. . . . **For in him the whole fullness of deity dwells bodily,** and you have been filled in him, who is the head of all rule and authority.

*I* generally loathe tautologies. Needless redundancies drive me nuts. Saying the same thing twice when once will do generally ruins my day. Well, I hope you get my point!

But there are biblical tautologies that need to be noted. They are often theologically profound and deserving of careful attention. One such tautology is found in Colossians 1:19 where Paul says that in Christ "all the fullness" of God was pleased to dwell. But what other kind of "fullness" is there: "partial" fullness or "half" fullness? If any part or aspect of the divine "fullness" were absent from Christ it would be absurd to say that "fullness" was in any sense present in him. Clearly, Paul is going out of his way to make a point. But what point?

As I noted in the previous meditation, this passage is an explicit and unashamed declaration of the deity of Jesus Christ. This appears in several ways.

First, the word "fullness" has provoked a lot of discussion (which I will mercifully spare you). I agree with Peter O'Brien, who argues that the word points to the fact that "all the attributes and activities of God—his spirit, word, wisdom and glory—are perfectly displayed in Christ."[27] In Colossians 2:9 Paul makes it clear: it is all the fullness of "deity" that dwells in Christ, which is to say the divine nature, the essence and attributes and infinite qualities that make God, God.

What glorious redundancy! What marvelous tautology! It means that deity dwells in him extensively: he is not partially God, he is wholly God. Everything you wanted to know about God but were afraid to ask is found and embodied and expressed in Jesus.

Not only is deity found extensively in Jesus, it is found exclusively in Jesus. He alone is God, which means that no one else is. Not Buddha, nor Muhammad, nor any other religious leader or philosopher or sage. In his comments on Colossians 2:9, James Dunn argues that "the importance of the language is to indicate that the completeness of God's self-revelation was focused in Christ, that the wholeness of God's interaction with the universe is summed up in Christ."[28]

Second, someone may well ask, "When was God pleased for the divine fullness to dwell in Christ?" This question comes from the verb tense Paul employs. This is what Greek scholars call an *ingressive aorist*, which suggests that the fullness of God "took up residence" in the person of Christ. Did this happen at his baptism in the River Jordan? No, for that would imply an adoptionist Christology according to which Jesus, a mere man, was adopted or selected by God to act in the role of Son or to perform the duties of Messiah. In other words, it would mean that before his baptism Jesus wasn't God and that after it he was only "god" by virtue of his having been chosen by the Father.

Given Paul's unequivocal affirmation of the eternal deity of God the Son (see Phil. 2:6, for example), he surely has in mind the moment of his conception in the womb of Mary, his mother. As we will see when we come to Colossians 2:9, this "fullness" not only "indwelt" (in the past) but now (in the present) and evermore (in the future) "indwells" Jesus Christ.

Third, don't miss the little word "for" with which verse 19 begins. It is "for" or "because" Jesus Christ is fully and wholly and exclusively God (in bodily form, 2:9) that he is Lord over creation and head of the church (Col. 1:18). If he were not truly and wholly God he would not be either of the two.

Don't think for a moment that the blasphemous arguments of Dan Brown's *The DaVinci Code* are unimportant. If Brown is right and Paul is wrong, we lose our Savior and our Lord and our living head. The Fathers of the early church fought and sacrificed their lives for the truth of Christ's deity not because it served political or personal agendas but because of statements like this in Colossians 1:19 and 2:9.

Fourth, and finally, in light of what we have seen in Colossians 1:19, consider Paul's words in Ephesians 3:19. There he prays that we would come to know the love of Christ so that *we* "may be filled with all the fullness of God."

It's important to note that the NASB is a bit more literal than the ESV at this point. It renders Paul's prayer this way: "to know the love of Christ which surpasses knowledge, that you may be filled up to all the fullness of God." Similarly, the NIV has "that you may be filled to the measure of all the fullness of God." In other words, the "fullness of God" is "the standard or level to which they [and we] are to be filled."[29]

But *with what* are we to be filled? Is it the "power" of God or the "Spirit," as Ephesians 3:16 might suggest, or "Christ" who in verse 17 is said to indwell us already, or perhaps his "love" (as suggested by v. 19)?

Since we are to be filled *by God*, up to the fullness *of God*, it would seem the ESV is correct after all that it is *with God* himself that we are to be filled, not in the sense that we become God but that we are energized and empowered as his radiant presence permeates our being. Whereas the church as Christ's body "already" shares in, embodies, and expresses his fullness (Eph. 1:23), we have "not yet" experienced the plenitude of God in the way that is available for us. That is why Paul now prays as he does.

If that doesn't raise your expectations of what is available and possible for us in this life, nothing will.

So, how do you pray? Do you long for and labor by means of intercession that the "fullness" of God himself, as was and is and ever will be present in Christ, may fill you now so that by his grace and empowering presence you may accomplish what mere human flesh never could? I hope so.

# 28

# *Wholly God (3)*

## Colossians 1:19; 2:9

He is the image of the invisible God, the firstborn of all creation. For by him all things were created, in heaven and on earth, visible and invisible, whether thrones or dominions or rulers or authorities—all things were created through him and for him. And he is before all things, and in him all things hold together. And he is the head of the body, the church. He is the beginning, the firstborn from the dead, that in everything he might be preeminent. **For in him all the fullness of God was pleased to dwell,** and through him to reconcile to himself all things, whether on earth or in heaven, making peace by the blood of his cross. . . . **For in him the whole fullness of deity dwells bodily,** and you have been filled in him, who is the head of all rule and authority.

After speaking at a recent conference, I was approached by an inquisitive man who asked for clarification concerning something I had said about the incarnation of Christ. "Yes, you heard me correctly," I responded. "The incarnation of Christ never ends."

He was understandably befuddled. "I always just assumed," he replied, "that once we were all in heaven, Jesus would somehow divest himself of his human nature and revert to his former mode of existence, as he was with the Father and Holy Spirit in eternity past."

I have to admit that the Bible isn't as explicit on this point as we might wish. But two things are to be noted. First, there is no text of Scripture that says, or even implies, that the Incarnation was temporary. Nowhere are we led to believe that John's amazing utterance in chapter 1, verse 14, of his gospel will ever be reversed or cease to be true. In other words, when "the Word became flesh," I believe he became flesh forever. If it were otherwise, given the momentous nature of this truth, one would expect some hint of it somewhere in Scripture.

You might say, "But, Sam, that's an argument from silence. Isn't that a flimsy basis on which to build your case?" I suppose so, which brings me to my second point. There are a few texts that actually speak to this issue. One of them is our text in Colossians 2:9 (an obviously parallel passage to 1:19). There Paul declares of Jesus Christ, "In him the whole fullness of deity dwells bodily." The NIV renders it, "For in Christ all the fullness of the Deity lives in bodily form." Several things are worthy of note.

First, we see here yet again the incredible importance of affirming the revelation of God in Christ as "bodily." That is to say, God made himself known to us as and in the form of a human being. Jesus was not a ghost or a phantom or a make-believe human.

One of the fundamental errors of Gnosticism was its denial that God the Son assumed a true human nature: body, soul, spirit, flesh, blood, bones, skin, hair, etc. The Gnostics were Docetists. The latter term comes from the Greek word *dokeo* which means "to seem" or "to appear." Jesus, they argued, only "seemed" to be human. When his contemporaries looked at him, he "appeared" to be like them, but was not literally, substantially, and essentially human.

Just how important is our affirmation that the incarnation entailed the literal assumption by God the Son of a truly physical body? How important is it that we affirm that he possessed (and possesses, as I'll note shortly) human nature in its totality? Let me be brief and to the point and simply quote the apostle John: "Every spirit that confesses that Jesus Christ has come in the flesh is from God, and every spirit that does not confess Jesus is not from God. This [i.e., the denial that Jesus Christ has come in the flesh] is the spirit of the antichrist" (1 John 4:2–3). Enough said.

Second, Paul wrote this statement in Colossians 2:9 *after* the resurrection, glorification, and exaltation of Christ to the right hand of the Father. Furthermore, we know that when Christ returns at the end of the age he will come in the same body in which he departed. So the incarnation most definitely lasts at least until the new heavens and new earth. As I said before, nothing in Scripture suggests it ends at any time thereafter.

Third, there are two things to note about Paul's use of the verb translated "dwells." In the first place, it is in the present tense (unlike the aorist tense used in Col. 1:19). The fullness of deity did not merely dwell in Christ in bodily form in the past, or for a momentary season in human history. The fullness of deity even now continues to dwell in him bodily, says Paul. And second, some render this word "resides," because the verb Paul uses (*katoikeo*) suggests a permanent, timeless presence rather than a mere sojourning or temporary abode (which would, more likely, have called for the use of the verb *paroikeo*; see also 2 John 7 and its use of the present tense, as well as 1 Cor. 15:28).

Thus, the plenitude, or to use Paul's language, the "fullness," of the divine nature dwells in Christ bodily now and for eternity. Even now, and forever, Christ is not merely God. He is also man. He is God in bodily form. As I said: the incarnation never ends! Before the incarnation Christ was certainly the "fullness" of God, but not in bodily form. He has always been God (see Phil. 2:6), but he has not always been God—or the fullness of God—in bodily form.

We might, then, envision Jesus saying: "I am now what I always was: God (or Word). I am now what I once was not: man (or flesh, or fullness of God in bodily form). I am now and forever will be both: the God-man."

# 29

# Will Everyone Be Saved? (1)

## Colossians 1:20

He is the image of the invisible God, the firstborn of all creation. For by him all things were created, in heaven and on earth, visible and invisible, whether thrones or dominions or rulers or authorities—all things were created through him and for him. And he is before all things, and in him all things hold together. And he is the head of the body, the church. He is the beginning, the firstborn from the dead, that in everything he might be preeminent. For in him all the fullness of God was pleased to dwell, **and through him to reconcile to himself all things, whether on earth or in heaven, making peace by the blood of his cross.**

Yes, insists Carlton Pearson, pastor of Higher Dimensions Family Church of Tulsa, Oklahoma. But not everyone agrees. Pearson's church, whose membership swelled to five thousand before he announced his theological convictions, has dwindled to about five hundred. Pearson was ordained by the Church of God in Christ, the largest black Pentecostal denomination in the U.S. According to Pearson, everyone will end up in heaven whether or not they exercise conscious faith in Jesus Christ. The door even remains open to Satan himself, if he'd only repent (one immediately wonders why Satan need repent to enter the kingdom but all other non-Christians need not).

There are some who agree with Pearson. Reverend Bill Wiseman, a minister at Trinity Episcopal Church of Tulsa, is quoted as saying: "We like him and we agree with what he's saying."[30] Following foreclosure on Higher Dimensions's building, Trinity has allowed Pearson's congregation to meet in its facilities.

I haven't heard how Pearson defends his belief, but I suspect he may well appeal to Paul's statement in Colossians 1:20. There the apostle writes that God was pleased, through Christ, "to reconcile to himself all things, whether on earth or in heaven, making peace by the blood of his cross."

Although at first glance it might appear that Pearson has a case, there are two possible ways of interpreting Paul's words that avoid the heresy of universalism (in fact, there are others, but I don't find them persuasive).

The first view begins by noting that Paul has clearly asserted in verse 16 that Jesus Christ is the creator of "all things," whether angelic or human, visible or invisible. The "all things" in that verse unmistakably refer to the "original creation" and are inescapably universal in scope.

But observe that in verse 18 and the following verses Paul turns to a description of the new creation, the church, of which Christ is the head and the beginning and the first among those who will be raised from the dead.

Could it then be that the "all things" in verse 20 which are said to be reconciled by the blood of the cross, are those that belong to this new creation, the church? If so, the "all things" of the original creation in verses 16 and 17 and the "all things" of the new creation in verses 18 to 20 are not coextensive. The former is quite universal and all-inclusive in scope (humans, both good and evil, as well as angels, both good and evil). The latter is restricted to those who are the beneficiaries of the blood of the cross and who have thereby experienced "peace" with God.

With this view we would then take the phrase, "whether on earth or in heaven" to refer respectively to both elect humans and elect or holy angels.

But how can holy, elect angels experience "reconciliation"? The fact is, the ministry of angels brings them into constant contact with sin and its evil and corrupting effects (cf. Heb. 1:14). It is from the disheartening and disturbing necessity of ministering within such a fallen world that the holy angels will one day be released. It isn't so much that they are personally reconciled. They are, after all, "holy."

Furthermore, Jesus didn't die for angelic beings, whether good or evil. Their release into the unqualified purity and beauty of heaven, rather, is the fruit of a reconciliation that Christ effected by means of his cross.

The strength of this view is that it pays close heed to the context in which verse 20 appears and the progression in Paul's thought from the first creation to the second, from the universality of all things made to the particularity of all things redeemed.

But is there another possibility? Yes . . .

# 30

# Will Everyone Be Saved? (2)

## Colossians 1:20

He is the image of the invisible God, the firstborn of all creation. For by him all things were created, in heaven and on earth, visible and invisible, whether thrones or dominions or rulers or authorities—all things were created through him and for him. And he is before all things, and in him all things hold together. And he is the head of the body, the church. He is the beginning, the firstborn from the dead, that in everything he might be preeminent. For in him all the fullness of God was pleased to dwell, **and through him to reconcile to himself all things, whether on earth or in heaven, making peace by the blood of his cross.**

We considered in the previous meditation the suggestion that when Paul says "all things, whether on earth or in heaven," have been reconciled to God through the blood of the cross, that he had in mind the redeemed citizens of the new creation, those who are now and will be members of the church of which Christ is the living head and beginning (thereby maintaining a close connection between v. 20 and vv. 18–19).

But there is another possibility that we need to consider. According to this view, the "all things" in verse 20 refer back to the "all things" in verse 16. They are indeed coextensive. How, then, does one avoid universalism?

We first need to understand the need for reconciliation. As we noted in verse 16, all things were created in, by, and for Christ. What Paul does not mention here is what happened to this creation after it came into existence. Because of the fall of Adam, the unity, harmony, and consonance of the original creation have suffered a devastating rupture. That pristine beauty of Eden has been horribly marred. Disharmony was brought to bear on God's handiwork. Alienation (between God and man, between man and man, and between man and nature) now characterizes the cosmos. In a word, the totality of creation is mired in disruption and suffers from what one can only describe as moral, spiritual, and physical discombobulation.

This is clearly Paul's point in Romans 8:18–23, where he speaks of the creation being subjected to futility, yet one day to be delivered from the bondage of corruption into the liberty of the children of God (v. 21; see also 2 Pet. 3:13). In other words, Adam's sin had cosmic repercussions that require reconciliation. This much we can all understand. But how can it be that "all things" are embraced by this reconciliation?

How can Paul say that wicked and unbelieving humans as well as wicked and rebellious demons (including Satan, no doubt) are in any sense "reconciled"? After all, when Paul later relates the cross of Christ to the demonic hosts, he describes its effect as one of despoiling and conquering, not redeeming (see Col. 2:15). Fallen angels are consistently portrayed as irrevocably hostile to the kingdom of God with no hope of "salvation" in any sense of that term (see 1 Cor. 15:24–25; Matt. 25:41; Jude 6; Rev. 20:10).

What this suggests is that the "reconciliation" Paul has in mind includes the notion of subjugation and the bringing to nought of God's enemies. God's reconciliation of all things includes the triumph and victory over those who are and ever will be his enemies. Some have wondered how this constitutes a "victory" for God. Does not the perpetual presence in hell of unbelievers signify his failure, perhaps even his defeat? No. It would be failure only if they were to escape the punishment their sin merits. Divine justice prevails and holy wrath is revealed, all to the glory of God.

As John Murray explains, the consummated order of the new heavens and new earth, "however we may describe it in the various designations Scripture provides, is one from which all conflict, enmity, disharmony, warfare will be excluded; it will mean the final triumph of righteousness and peace, in a word, of reconciliation. The powers of darkness will be cast out and by the judgment executed made to 'confess that Jesus Christ is Lord to the glory of God the Father' (Phil. 2:11). Bowing the knee in compulsive submission, this will be the reconciliation as it bears upon them; it will constitute the ultimate unconditional surrender, the confessed defeat of age-long assault upon the kingdom of God. We can and must see in this grand climax of victory the fruit of the blood of Christ's cross."[31]

Thus the demonic hosts and unbelieving humanity may be spoken of as encompassed by and participating in the "reconciliation," not in the sense that they are ultimately saved, but insofar as they will be subjugated, pacified, and rendered incapable of any longer disrupting the harmony and beauty of God's creative handiwork. According to Scripture, all evil will be excluded from heaven, all wickedness banished from its boundaries, all unbelief confined in hell (see Rev. 21:8, 27; 22:15).

The point is that "peace" can be achieved in one of two ways: either by the removal of hostility through grace or by the pacification and subjugation of enemies through power and judgment. At the close of World War II, hostilities ceased. Battles came to an end. The threat of Nazi domination was terminated. The Axis Powers were defeated, subjugated, and compelled to submit to the oversight and authority of their conquerors. There was undoubtedly lingering hatred and disdain toward the Allies, but the latter were still victorious. Harmony and order and peace, as much as is possible this side of heaven, were restored. There was, in a word, reconciliation.

Likewise, although all creation will ultimately bow the knee and confess that Jesus Christ is Lord, to the glory of God the Father (Phil. 2:10–11), the elect will do it voluntarily, by grace, whereas the nonelect will do it by compulsion, as one element in their judgment. Reconciliation can occur, therefore, without entailing the restoration of all to fellowship with God.

There will be no conflict in the age to come. There will be no warfare to threaten the security of God's people. There will be no corruption of nature or demonic temptation or opposition to the kingdom of God.

Paul used similar language in Ephesians 1:10 when he described God's eternal purpose as the "summing up" or the "uniting" of "all things" in Christ, "things in heaven and things on earth." His final purpose will have been achieved: (1) his grace and mercy will have been glorified by the salvation of his people, (2) his holiness and justice will have been glorified by the condemnation of his enemies, and (3) heaven and earth will have been restored under their divinely created and determined order, the universe placed once again under its head.

I'm not certain which of these two views is the correct one (perhaps there is yet another alternative). But I am certain of this: there is no hope for reconciliation and peace with God apart from the blood of the cross of Christ.

# 31

# *Before*

## Colossians 1:21

**And you, who once were alienated and hostile in mind**, doing evil deeds, he has now reconciled in his body of flesh by his death, in order to present you holy and blameless and above reproach before him, if indeed you continue in the faith, stable and steadfast, not shifting from the hope of the gospel that you heard, which has been proclaimed in all creation under heaven, and of which I, Paul, became a minister.

I don't know who it was that first conceived the idea, but one of the more durable and effective advertising schemes is the "before-and-after." I can remember as a young boy turning to the back page of my Superman comic book only to find myself looking at the less-than-flattering, black-and-white picture of a pathetically scrawny, virtually emaciated man, under which was written one word: "Before." On the other side of the page was the impressive, color portrait of a smiling, robust, muscular individual (allegedly the same guy), under which was written: "After."

To what miracle drug or exercise program they attributed this miraculous and altogether unbelievable transformation, I can't recall. But the point was well made.

The authors of the New Testament, in their own unique and far more dignified way, also portray for us a "before" and an "after." But in their case the transformation they describe isn't physical. It isn't from weakness to strength, or from obesity to a lean, taut frame, or from ugliness to beauty. Far less is it a change that occurs instantaneously, or even one that can be achieved over the course of a few months.

The transformation they repeatedly describe is spiritual and moral in nature, from unrighteousness and enmity with God to holiness and peace. It is the "before" and "after" of the Christian who formerly was immersed in immorality and religious apathy but now is devoted to the Lord Jesus Christ and conforming to his likeness. This is a transformation attributed to sovereign, saving, sanctifying grace.

To use a different analogy to make the same point, Christians are portrayed as if they were a book with two chapters. Chapter 1 is their "before Christ," or as people often say, "My B.C. days." This story is characterized by darkness, enmity, rebellion, and unbelief.

Chapter 2 is a different story. The "after" is a description of progressive, incremental growth in grace and love and knowledge. It is a chapter not of enmity but peace, not of unbelief but trust, not of darkness but the light of the knowledge of the glory of God revealed in the face of Jesus Christ (2 Cor. 4:6).

We read of the "before" and "after" of the Christian, of the two chapters in our book of life, here in Colossians 1:21–22: "And you, who once were alienated and hostile in mind, doing evil deeds, he has now reconciled in his body of flesh by his death, in order to present you holy and blameless and above reproach before him." Colossians 1:21 is the "before," the B.C. side of life, and to that I want to devote our brief attention.

Perhaps you're wondering why Paul even bothers to describe that season of our earthly sojourn that most of us would just as soon forever forget. I assure you that it isn't out of some morbid fascination with lust and greed and pride, but rather to highlight and magnify the wonder and majesty of God's grace and kindness in Jesus. It isn't in our sinful past that Paul's emphasis lies, but in the mighty mercy of God in reconciling us to himself through Jesus.

Note how he describes the "before" of the Colossians (and us). He mentions three things.

First, we were "alienated." Alienation is an ugly word. All of us know what it means in human relationships. The hurt, the misunderstanding, and the bitterness toward another feel like insuperable barriers. In terms of our relationship with God, or lack thereof, our sin has alienated or divorced or separated us from him, while his holy wrath poses what appears to be an insurmountable obstacle to any form of reconciliation.

Second, we were "hostile in mind." Whereas in other texts God is portrayed as being at enmity with us, here it is we who were at enmity with God. Contrary to how most non-Christians want to portray themselves, they are not neutral about religious matters. They are not indifferent about God or apathetic when it comes to the claims of Christ. They may speak publicly of a "supreme being" in whose existence they believe, but when it comes to the one true God of holiness and justice and absolute supremacy, rage, rebellion, and hostility dominate the heart.

Paul said it with even greater force in Ephesians 4:18: "They are darkened in their understanding [notwithstanding their claim to intellectual brilliance and scientific enlightenment], alienated from the life of God because of the ignorance that is in them [notwithstanding their claim to be 'in touch' with the divine and 'at one' with his will and ways], due to their hardness of heart [notwithstanding their professed spiritual sensitivity and openness to all things good]."

And let's not miss Paul's point that the problem is in the "mind," in how unbelievers think about God and envision his character and reflect on the claims of Christ. Their ideas (and our ideas "before" we were graciously converted) are perverted, distorted, prejudiced, and vile.

Third, we were given over to "evil deeds." Bad beliefs inevitably yield the rotten fruit of bad behavior. The willful, conscious, intellectual antagonism of being "hostile in mind" ultimately poisons daily conduct. The social climate of our day strains to acknowledge that there is actually something someone can do that merits the adjective *evil*. In our live-and-let-live, personal-and-postmodern, politically correct, don't-you-dare-judge-me-or-my-lifestyle world, it's dangerous to call certain behaviors "evil." But such is surely what they are.

"But now . . ." Oh, blessed contrast! Estranged, hardened, perverted people can be reconciled, softened, and set straight. Praise God! There is indeed a glorious and Christ-exalting "after" to the "before" of our experience.

# 32

# But Now

## Colossians 1:22

And you, who once were alienated and hostile in mind, doing evil deeds, **he has now reconciled in his body of flesh by his death, in order to present you holy and blameless and above reproach before him**, if indeed you continue in the faith, stable and steadfast, not shifting from the hope of the gospel that you heard, which has been proclaimed in all creation under heaven, and of which I, Paul, became a minister.

Thank God that there is something "after" the "before"! Before Jesus there was only alienation, hostility, and evil deeds (v. 21). Not a very flattering picture! But now . . . (v. 22a). Oh, my. But now—were ever more glorious words spoken to otherwise hopeless and helpless sinners? But now!

Were it not for the divine and gracious "but now," we would be forever mired and entrenched in the "always" of sin and death and darkness. There would be no purpose in speaking of a "before," because there would be no hope of an "after."

The contrast evoked by the transitional words "but now" with which verse 22 begins is lost in most English translations. There are several places in the New Testament where we encounter these or similar words. The words "but God" (cf. Eph. 2:4) often follow the dire description of humanity in sin. In Ephesians 2:11–12 Paul paints a rather ugly and disheartening portrait of the plight of Gentiles before the coming of Jesus. "But now" (v. 13a), "in Christ Jesus," he happily shouts, we have been drawn near and our former alienation has given way to friendship and intimacy and forgiveness.

The apostle uses the same terminology in Colossians 1:22 to tell us yet again that "now," because of God's gracious activity in removing the hostility that alienated us from his presence, we can stand confident in his presence.

> Lord, I was blind; I could not see,
> In Thy marred visage any grace;
> *But now* the beauty of Thy face,
> In radiant vision dawns on me.
>
> Lord, I was deaf; I could not hear,
> The thrilling music of Thy voice;
> *But now* I hear Thee and rejoice,
> And all Thine uttered words are dear.
>
> Lord, I was dumb; I could not speak,
> The grace and glory of Thy name;
> *But now*, as touched with living flame,
> My lips Thine eager praises wake.
>
> Lord, I was dead; I could not stir,
> My lifeless soul to come to Thee;
> *But now*, since Thou hast quickened me,
> I rise from sin's dark sepulcher.
>
> Lord, Thou hast made the blind to see,
> The deaf to hear, the dumb to speak,
> The dead to live; and lo, I break,
> The chains of my captivity. (Matson; emphasis added)

Dead! Blind! Dumb! Alienated! Hostile! *But now*! Well did John Newton say it in that famous hymn:

> "Amazing grace, how sweet the sound,
> that saved a wretch like me;
> I once was lost *but now* I'm found,
> was blind, *but now* I see!" (emphasis added)

These are words that embody and express an indescribably encouraging and hopeful truth.

When your conscience is pricked by the memory of failure and sin, a simple cry of *but now* will bring healing and hope.

When the enemy assaults your soul with reminders of how unworthy you were, a simple cry of "Yes, *but now* I've been made worthy in Christ" will suffice.

When he insinuates that no one with a history so filled with failure, ingratitude, and selfishness could possibly be a Christian, rebuff him with a hearty and defiant, "*But now* I have a clean slate and new life and joy and the promise of God's abiding presence."

Fight the paralyzing power of past transgressions and the crippling fear of what may lie ahead by strengthening your soul with the inspired promise that *now*, because of Christ and in Christ, you are reconciled and redeemed.

# 33

# After

## Colossians 1:22

And you, who once were alienated and hostile in mind, doing evil deeds, **he has now reconciled in his body of flesh by his death, in order to present you holy and blameless and above reproach before him**, if indeed you continue in the faith, stable and steadfast, not shifting from the hope of the gospel that you heard, which has been proclaimed in all creation under heaven, and of which I, Paul, became a minister.

If "before," we were alienated, then "after," we are reconciled. What a wonderful word, *reconciliation*. But what does it mean? Perhaps more than any other word in the language of the New Testament, reconciliation highlights the personal and relational nature of our salvation. Justification points to the forensic (or legal) declaration that we are righteous in Christ. Redemption emphasizes our being ransomed from bondage to sin. Sacrifice has in view the Old Testament ritual order. But it is reconciliation that speaks of the restoration of a relationship formerly characterized by animosity and rancor and lack of trust.

There are several senses in which we use this term. For example, there is the situation where you persuade your friends Mike and Tom to give up their anger against each other. You, in this instance, are the one who "reconciles" the other two.

Then there is the case where you persuade Mike to forsake his anger against you. This is what Jesus has in mind in Matthew 5:23–24.

*The Hope of Glory*

A final form of reconciliation is when you choose to give up your anger against Mike.

But none of these scenarios describes what God did for us in Jesus. Paul clearly envisions another category in which God removes from us that which is the cause of his anger against us. Of course, that would be our sin! In this case, the initiative clearly lies with God. In order to restore peace and fellowship between us and God something must be done about the cause of the alienation. In our unregenerate state, we neither can nor want to do anything about it. But God both can and will. He removes the cause of alienation by redirecting his wrath against us to a willing and sufficient substitute: Jesus Christ (see especially Rom. 5:10 and 2 Cor. 5:18–21).

Paul makes it clear in Colossians 1:22 that the means by which reconciliation has occurred is the death of Jesus on our behalf: we have been "reconciled in his body of flesh by his death" (v. 22a). In that death is the wrath of God against our sin satisfied, and thereby are we reconciled or put right with God.

But to what end? What is the purpose for this act of reconciliation? It was "in order to present you holy and blameless and above reproach before him" (v. 22b).

Almost identical language appears in Ephesians 1:4 where Paul describes the purpose for our election. God chose us "that we should be holy and blameless before him." Some think the words "holy and blameless" refer to the daily experience of each believer, what we call progressive sanctification. If that is true, the goal of both election and reconciliation is to secure for Jesus Christ a people whose lives are characterized by purity and obedience to his will (an idea that is certainly substantiated by other passages in the New Testament: see Titus 2:14; 1 Thess. 4:7; 1 Pet. 1:14–15).

No one doubts that the word *holy* is frequently used to describe the character of Christian living, but what about the word *blameless*? It sounds like "sinless perfection," although in Philippians 2:15 Paul urges believers "to be blameless and innocent, children of God without blemish in the midst of a crooked and twisted generation, among whom you shine as lights in the world" (cf. Rev. 14:5). Therefore, it is surely possible that in Colossians 1:22 and Ephesians 1:4 Paul is referring to the holiness and blamelessness of the Christian in the here and now of daily life.

On the other hand, the word translated "blameless" is used in Ephesians 5:27 of the church in its final state of perfection and glory. This is also the case in Jude 24. The only other occurrences of this word in the New Testament are in Hebrews 9:14 and 1 Peter 1:19, both of which refer to the blamelessness of Jesus Christ. We should also note that in our text, as well as in Ephesians 1:4; 5:27 and Jude 24, we find the notion of being presented blameless and without reproach "before him," that is, before God.

All this persuades me that Paul is referring to that absolutely sinless, holy, and blameless condition in which we shall be presented to God at the second coming of our Savior. Of course, this by no means excludes the notion of progressive sanctification. Indeed, experiential purity and holiness in this life are but a prelude to our ultimate glorification in the next. The latter is but the consummation of the former.

Before I close, note again the words "before him" (v. 22b). This is incredibly encouraging to struggling Christians. To think that we will stand in God's presence, regarded by him as "above reproach," that is to say, as people against whom no legitimate charge can be brought, is breathtaking. Note well: it is "before him," face-to-face with infinite righteousness, that this verdict will be rendered. As John Eadie put it, "The phrase denotes the reality or genuineness of the holy and blameless state. God accounts it so. The elect are not esteemed righteous 'merely before men.' . . . Their piety is not a brilliant hypocrisy. It is regarded as genuine, 'before Him' whose glance at once detects and frowns upon the spurious, however plausible the disguise in which it may wrap itself."[32]

# 34

# No Continuation, No Presentation

## Colossians 1:23

**And you, who once were alienated and hostile in mind, doing evil deeds, he has now reconciled in his body of flesh by his death, in order to present you holy and blameless and above reproach before him, if indeed you continue in the faith, stable and steadfast, not shifting from the hope of the gospel that you heard, which has been proclaimed in all creation under heaven, and of which I, Paul, became a minister.**

If you're among Christians, talking about politics will rarely lead to an angry debate. Disagreement, yes, but usually a civil and constructive one. Sports? Even Christians have their favorite players and teams and will defend them vigorously, but not at the expense of unity. There is a way of creating a furor, if you're so inclined. Just bring up the question of whether or not a believer can lose his or her salvation. State your position, and then duck!

I've been in a few of those theological donnybrooks myself. They are rarely resolved peacefully. On more than one occasion the dispute focused on Colossians 1:23. Paul has just made the glorious declaration that by virtue of the death of Christ we have been reconciled to God, all with a view to his presenting us holy and blameless and without reproach before him. Then he drops this bombshell: "*If* indeed you continue in the faith, stable and steadfast, not shifting from the hope of the gospel that you heard, which has been proclaimed in all creation under heaven, and of which I, Paul, became a minister."

This is no place to engage in a full-orbed discussion of this issue.[33] So let me make just a few brief comments that I hope prove helpful in our understanding of this passage.

Paul seems rather clearly to say that if you don't persevere by continuing in "the faith," you will not be presented before God holy and blameless and without reproach. Whether "the faith" is a reference to one's personal trust in Jesus or the objective body of truths we call "the Christian faith," the fact remains: if you don't continue in it you will not experience the inestimable joy of standing forever in the presence of God.

So, yes, there is truly a conditional element involved—"if indeed." The condition for final presentation is faithful perseverance. The notion espoused by some that one "act of faith" in Jesus Christ eternally secures final salvation irrespective of how one lives is unbiblical. But that's for another day.

Having said this, there appear to be three options worthy of our consideration. There are probably others, but I want to focus on three.

First, the Arminian view says it is possible for the truly regenerated (born again) soul to fail to meet the condition and thereby fail to be presented holy and blameless and without reproach before God. The salvation once gained by faith alone may be forfeited and lost by the disappearance and death of said faith. My aim here is not to challenge this view.[34]

Second, some Calvinists read Colossians 1:23 as saying that perseverance is the proof that one's "act of faith" in Jesus Christ was genuine. Perseverance or continuing stable and steadfast in the faith, not shifting from the hope of the gospel, is evidence of the authenticity of one's initial conversion and commitment to Christ. Likewise, the failure to persevere, or the decision to shift from the hope of the gospel and abandon one's "commitment" to it, is proof that one's profession of faith in Jesus was spurious and false, an act of self-delusion.

This concept is undoubtedly true, in my opinion, and other biblical texts affirm it. The passage in 1 John 2:19 clearly speaks to this scenario. There John writes, "They [i.e., the false teachers] went out from us, but they were not of us; for if they had been of us, they would have continued with us. But they went out, that it might become plain that they all are not of us."

The phrase "they went out from us" most likely points to their willful and voluntary separation. In spite of their external membership or alliance with us, says John, they did not share the inner life or spiritual bond of the body of Christ. "For if they had been of us they would have continued with us." If they had truly and authentically shared our unity and life in Christ, it would have displayed itself in fruitful perseverance. "But they went out, that it might become plain that they all are not of us." This is to say that there was a divine purpose in their secession, namely, exposure of those who were merely professors, not genuine possessors, of spiritual life. Their departure was their unmasking (cf. 1 Cor. 11:18–19).

So again, abiding or continuance or endurance is the sign of the saved, just as apostasy reveals the counterfeit character of one's initial profession of faith. Note the emphasis of the phrase: "for if they had been of us, they would have continued with us" (cf. Heb. 3:6, 14). The presence of saving faith ("of us") implies (necessitates) perseverance.

Third, the other Calvinist option interprets Paul's purpose in Colossians 1:23 somewhat differently. All Calvinists believe that the elect will fully and finally persevere and thus be eternally saved. (In fact, some "Arminians" believe this too.) They will not fail to fulfill the condition of Colossians 1:23. Yet according to this third option, God preserves us in faith and holiness of life by stirring our hearts to avail ourselves of his sustaining grace. One way he does this is *by means of the warning implicit in the condition*. What is the warning? Simply this: no continuation, no presentation. In other words, God preserves and keeps us safe, and thus we persevere, by heeding the warning that, if we don't, we will not be presented blameless and without reproach before God.

On both Calvinist options, the elect will persevere. According to the first, Colossians 1:23 is backwards looking. As we consider whether or not a person continues in the faith, we are directed to draw one of two conclusions concerning the authenticity of their initial profession of trust in Jesus.

According to the second, Colossians 1:23 is forward-looking. Christian, take heed to this undeniable fact: if you don't persevere by continuing in the faith, you won't be presented before God. Christian, take heart in knowing that God will work in you "that which is pleasing in his sight" (Heb. 13:21). Be encouraged with the assurance that "he who began a good work in you *will* bring it to completion at the day of Jesus Christ" (Phil. 1:6), so that you will persevere and not shift from the hope of the gospel which you believed.

Some people insist that the idea that God will preserve us undermines and vitiates the urgency to make certain that we continue in our faith. I would argue precisely the opposite. The reason I commit myself fervently to the pursuit of holiness of life is that God has assured me that he will be ever present to energize my heart "to will and to work for his good pleasure" (Phil. 2:12–13). Praise God for his preserving presence and power!

If you are inclined to indulge in unrepentant sin and then justify your licentiousness on the grounds that God has promised to preserve you, there is a strong likelihood that your alleged "faith" in Christ is not saving. Given what Paul says in Colossians 1:23, it would be irresponsible of me to assure you that following such a life you will, nevertheless, be presented before him holy and blameless and without reproach. Remember: no continuation, no presentation.

# 35

# Joy in Suffering?

## Colossians 1:24

> **Now I rejoice in my sufferings for your sake, and in my flesh I am filling up what is lacking in Christ's afflictions for the sake of his body, that is, the church**, of which I became a minister according to the stewardship from God that was given to me for you, to make the word of God fully known, the mystery hidden for ages and generations but now revealed to his saints.

"Now I rejoice in my sufferings for your sake" (Col. 1:24a). Does that strike you the way it does me? Who in their right mind would ever "rejoice" in their "sufferings"?

I suppose people who take a perverse pleasure in pain for its own sake might conceivably utter such words (minus the "for your sake," of course). But why would a Christian, like Paul, say it?

The New Testament perspective on suffering is truly unique. In Matthew 5:10–12, Jesus pronounced a blessing on those "who are persecuted for righteousness' sake" (v. 10a) as well as those who are reviled or slandered "falsely" on his account (v. 11). "Rejoice and be glad," said Jesus, "for your reward is great in heaven" (v. 12a). Jesus saw no benefit or profit in suffering for suffering's sake, far less in suffering that is the consequence or penalty of some wrong or crime or sin you may have committed. But suffering for his name's sake was altogether something else.

After being beaten, the apostles left their persecutors, "rejoicing" (Acts 5:41). The beating hurt. It was undoubtedly quite painful, perhaps permanently debilitating. But they rejoiced that they had been "counted worthy to suffer dishonor for the name [of Jesus]."

In Romans 5:3–4, Paul again declares, "we rejoice in our sufferings." Why? Because we know "that suffering produces endurance, and endurance produces character, and character produces hope," and this hope is not the sort that disappoints or puts us to shame. In and of itself, suffering is senseless. But Paul saw it as a means to a higher and spiritually superior end: the development of Christlike character and despair-defeating hope.

Paul goes so far as to describe suffering "for his sake" as something we should acknowledge as a divine gift (Phil. 1:29). Peter gently rebuked his readers for being surprised that they suffered, describing it as a blessing and an indication that "the Spirit of glory and of God rests" on them (1 Pet. 4:12–16).

Suffering for sin (1 Pet. 4:15) is a reproach. Suffering for suffering's sake is perverted. Suffering for the sake of Christ and his people is grounds for joy (1 Pet. 4:13, 16).

The only way to account for this perspective is on the assumption that there is something spiritually and morally superior, both here and in the age to come, that can only be attained by means of willing and joyful submission to suffering. This was certainly Paul's point in 2 Corinthians 1:8–9 where he acknowledged the providential design in his having been "so utterly burdened beyond" his "strength" that he "despaired of life itself." It was orchestrated, so he says, "to make us rely not on ourselves but on God who raises the dead" (v. 9).

To suffer "for Christ's sake" is to endure hardship because of one's loyalty to him, or with a view to the advancement of his kingdom, or to demonstrate his incomparable worth. We rejoice in suffering because we believe that something is more important and more precious and more valuable than physical comfort and convenience. It may be the spiritual welfare of other Christians (hence Paul's "for your [the Colossians'] sake"). It may be the proclamation of the gospel. It may be the declaration that the treasures of the age to come infinitely exceed those of the age that now is (cf. Rom. 8:18; Heb. 10:34; see especially Heb. 11:25–26).

In any case, if we do not look beyond suffering to the greater spiritual goal that it achieves, it will breed bitterness and resentment rather than joy. If we regard suffering as an end in itself, that is to say, if we fail to take "the long view"—to see it in the light of its eternal consequences (cf. 2 Cor. 4:14–16), God will appear cruel and life meaningless.

But this is by no means all that Paul says about suffering in Colossians 1. We must reckon with the stunning statement in the second half of verse 24: "Now I rejoice in my sufferings for your sake, and in my flesh I am filling up what is lacking in Christ's afflictions for the sake of his body, that is, the church."

What is meant by "Christ's afflictions"? How can it be said that something is "lacking" in them? And in what way can Paul or any Christian be described as "filling up" this alleged deficiency? These questions will be our focus in the next lesson.

# 36

# Filling Up the Afflictions of Christ

## Colossians 1:24

**Now I rejoice in my sufferings for your sake, and in my flesh I am filling up what is lacking in Christ's afflictions for the sake of his body, that is, the church**, of which I became a minister according to the stewardship from God that was given to me for you, to make the word of God fully known, the mystery hidden for ages and generations but now revealed to his saints.

Colossians 1:24 has consistently baffled and bothered Christians for centuries. Understandably so! Look at it again: "Now I rejoice in my sufferings for your sake, and in my flesh I am filling up what is lacking in Christ's afflictions for the sake of his body, that is, the church." Here are a few of the interpretive possibilities, concluding with the two I find most convincing.

First, let's be clear about what this text does not mean. Paul is not saying that the redemptive sufferings of Jesus on the cross are deficient or incomplete or need to be supplemented by something that Paul or any of us might supply. I say this for several reasons: (a) everywhere in his epistles, Paul says the opposite: Christ's death has once for all secured eternal redemption and is perfect and altogether sufficient (cf. Col. 1:12–14, 19–20; 2:13–14); (b) Jesus himself said, "It is finished" (John 19:30); (c) every other New Testament author says the same (see Heb. 1:3; 9:12–14, 24–28; 10:11–14); (d) he word translated "afflictions" is never used in the New Testament of Christ's redemptive work at Calvary. Whereas the persecution and abuse he experienced on the earth were part of his messianic calling and qualified him to serve as our savior (see esp. Heb. 2:10, 17–18), it was his suffering and death on a cross that satisfied the wrath of the Father and secured our forgiveness.

Second, some have said that Paul is referring to the afflictions he endures "for the sake of Christ" in order to glorify him and advance the cause of the kingdom. This is true enough, but does not explain the phrase, "what is lacking in Christ's afflictions," nor does it account for how Paul can fill them up or complete them.

Third, others appeal to a typological meaning. Paul, they argue, thought of his sufferings as being like those of Christ. The sufferings of Jesus were a type or prefigurement of what all Christians would encounter. Paul's sufferings, then, correspond to those of Jesus. Again, this is true enough, but it fails to explain the "lack" in what Christ suffered or how Paul filled them up.

Fourth, there is the eschatological view. Here, the afflictions of Christ refer not to what Jesus suffered but to those trials and tribulations that immediately precede the end of the age, what some have called the "Messianic woes." The idea is that there is a prescribed amount or definite measure of afflictions that Christians must endure before the end of the age. That limit, that quota, as it were, of messianic woes has not yet been reached or filled up. There is, therefore, a lack or deficiency that Paul by his suffering hopes to fill. The sufferings of the apostle, together with the sufferings of all believers, contribute to the sum total of these afflictions.

The final two views are more likely than any of the first four. I often find myself vacillating between them. The next one, the fifth option, has been defended by John Piper:

> Paul's sufferings complete Christ's afflictions *not* by adding anything to their worth, but by extending them to the people they were meant to save. What is lacking in the afflictions of Christ is not that they are deficient in worth, as though they could not sufficiently cover the sins of all who believe. What is lacking is that the infinite value of Christ's afflictions is not known and trusted in the world.... So the afflictions of Christ are "lacking" in the sense that they are not seen and known and loved among the nations. They must be carried by the ministers of the

Word. And those ministers of the Word "complete" [or "fill up"] what is lacking in the afflictions of Christ by extending them to others.[35]

What is lacking, then, in Christ's afflictions is not *propitiation* but *presentation*. In other words, the sufferings of Jesus fully satisfied the wrath of God, but there is lacking "a personal presentation by Christ himself to the nations of the world. God's answer to this lack is to call the people of Christ (people like Paul) to make a personal presentation of the afflictions of Christ to the world. In doing this, we 'fill up what is lacking in Christ's afflictions.' We finish what they were designed for, a personal presentation to the people who do not know about their infinite worth."[36]

The amazing thing about this text is how Paul envisions himself (and others) filling up this lack. It is in his "flesh." In other words, "God intends for the afflictions of Christ to be presented to the world through the afflictions of His people. . . . Our calling is to make the afflictions of Christ real for people by the afflictions we experience in bringing them the message of salvation. Since Christ is no longer on the earth, He wants His body, the church, to reveal *His* suffering in *its* suffering."[37]

Sixth, and finally, it may be that in some sense Paul is experiencing afflictions in the place of Jesus, afflictions that Jesus otherwise would have endured were he on earth. By doing so Paul is convinced that he is providing an example of endurance and faith that will encourage and be of benefit to the Colossians.

The key to this final option is the concept of a spiritual union that exists between Christ and his people. We read of something similar in Paul's encounter with Jesus on the Damascus Road: "And falling to the ground he [Saul/Paul] heard a voice saying to him, 'Saul, Saul, why are you persecuting me?' And he said, 'Who are you, Lord?' And he said, 'I am Jesus, whom you are persecuting'" (Acts 9:4–5; cf. Gal. 2:20; Phil. 3:10). Everything done to the body of Christ, the church, is done to Christ himself, and vice versa.

The afflictions of Paul were the afflictions of Christ: the latter suffered in and with the former because of their spiritual union. In a sense, the sufferings of Paul (and of all Christians) are simply the continuation of the world's quarrel with our Lord. Jesus, because of the brevity of his earthly life, did not bear the full brunt of the world's hatred and animosity. Thus, we are the objects of it in his place.

The world hated and afflicted Jesus without ceasing. But since he is not here, their arrows of persecution, meant especially for him, strike his followers. By virtue of our spiritual union and identity with him, as well as our commitment to him, we endure the persecution and affliction that he otherwise would experience. What the world believes is lacking in his suffering, we fill up. We bear the afflictions which are still intended for him (see especially John 15:18–21; 2 Cor. 1:5; 4:10; Gal. 6:17). As Mark 13:13 states, "You will be hated by all for my name's sake."

Whichever of these last two options proves to be correct (or perhaps a combination of them, or even another view we have not considered), the point is the same: the calling of Christians is to willingly and joyfully endure suffering for the sake of Christ and his kingdom, for the sake of Christ and his body, the church. In this way we are seen to be his own. In this way others see him, through us, in his love for sinners. In this way we "share his sufferings, becoming like him in his death" (Phil. 3:10).

# 37

# The Hope of Glory

## Colossians 1:25–27

Now I rejoice in my sufferings for your sake, and in my flesh I am filling up what is lacking in Christ's afflictions for the sake of his body, that is, the church, **of which I became a minister according to the stewardship from God that was given to me for you, to make the word of God fully known, the mystery hidden for ages and generations but now revealed to his saints. To them God chose to make known how great among the Gentiles are the riches of the glory of this mystery, which is Christ in you, the hope of glory.**

If I thought, for a moment, that this life is all there is or ever will be, I would fall immediately and irretrievably into utter despair. If "this," as the beer commercial suggests, "is as good as it gets," I think I'd pop a pill or pull the trigger or find some way to escape as quickly and painlessly as possible the futility and meaningless of this life.

But I have hope. I am confident that "this slight momentary affliction is preparing for us an eternal weight of glory beyond all comparison" (2 Cor. 4:17). I have hope. I am confident that "the sufferings of this present time are not worth comparing with the glory that is to be revealed to us" (Rom. 8:18). I have hope. I am confident that when Christ who is my life appears, I "also will appear with him in glory" (Col. 3:4).

As you can see, my hope is in the experience of a future glory. In some sense, in some way, this life and its pain and deprivation and disappointment and ugliness will yield to an unyielding and eternal glory. That is my hope.

But on what grounds do I have such hope? What makes my hope any different from the religious fantasies and pipe dreams of so many others? The answer is found in something Paul said in Colossians 1:27. But to get there, indeed to see how Paul got there, we need to back up to verse 25 and follow his thought. Trust me, it will yield rich rewards!

At the close of verse 24 Paul mentions the church, Christ's body, "of which," says the apostle, "I became a minister according to the stewardship from God that was given to me for you, to make the word of God fully known" (v. 25).

Feel free to insert your name or that of your church in the place of "you," a reference to the Colossians in its original context. God enlightened, empowered, and entrusted Paul with a message for them and for us. This is the meaning of the stewardship given him. His task was "to make the word of God fully known." We might translate this a bit more literally as "to complete the Word of God" or "to fulfill (or finish) the Word of God."

But what specifically is the "word" that Paul is determined to make fully known? He answers the question in verse 26. It is that mystery concerning the salvation of the Gentiles which until the time of Christ was hidden, but has now been revealed to the saints. But it's more than merely that Gentiles would be saved. That in itself was no mystery. The Old Testament spoke often of Gentile salvation. No, it is that they would be saved as "fellow citizens" (Eph. 2:19) and "fellow heirs, members of the same body" (Eph. 3:6) with Jewish believers. The mystery, long hidden but now revealed, is that Gentiles and Jews are no longer two but rather one new man (Eph. 2:15), equal in every way in Christ.

Don't take this lightly or think it unimportant, for Paul refers to "the *riches* of the *glory* of this mystery" (Col. 1:27). There is a glory or divine splendor or radiant majesty in this truth that is indescribably rich and unfathomably deep. Why, you ask? What could possibly be deserving of such lavish language?

Here is Paul's answer. The mystery is that the Lord Jesus Christ, the Lord of Glory, is now in you (v. 27), that is, Gentiles who believe in him. He lives and abides in you, not merely with you or beside you or above and below you, but *in* you!

This, says Paul, is the hope of glory (v. 27). Christ living in you is the ground and foundation and cause of your hope that you will enter into the fullness of divine glory. Christ living in you is the assurance, trumping all evidence to the contrary, that you and I will share in the glory that is to come.

That glory I earlier mentioned, as promised in 2 Corinthians 4:16–18, Romans 8:18, and Colossians 3:4 (among others), will be ours because the Christ who died and rose again to secure it on our behalf lives in us now and forever.

But remember this: Christ is not simply the reason we can hope for glory, but *Christ is himself that glory.* The glory for which we long, the glory for which we have been predestined, the glory that makes all suffering and pain and disappointment in this life unworthy of comparison is the person and presence of Jesus Christ himself. He is our glory. Being with him, to know him, to see him, to relish and rejoice in his beauty, is the glory for which we hope.

Forgiveness of sins and justification and adoption and all the other blessings of the gospel are good and glorious, but only so far as they make it possible for us to experience the permanent presence and vision and splendor of Jesus himself. Our hope is Christ. Period. He is our exceeding great reward. And he lives in us now. Not figuratively or symbolically or merely "as it were." He lives and abides in us now. And this is the ground and assurance we have for the glory of being with him and enjoying him forever.

# 38

# Everyone for Everyone

## Colossians 1:28

> Him we proclaim, warning everyone and teaching everyone with all wisdom, that we may present everyone mature in Christ.

What is your responsibility to other believers with whom God brings you into contact and relationship? Have you yielded to the temptation to give them over to someone else to warn and admonish and instruct concerning Jesus? Do you read about the life and ministry of the apostle Paul and say to yourself: "Well, that's Paul. It certainly isn't me. I'm no apostle, that's for sure. I can't possibly read how he related to others and think that I should do the same."

If that's how you think, look more closely in Colossians 1:28 at Paul's description of his ministry among the saints: "Him we proclaim, warning everyone and teaching everyone with all wisdom, that we may present everyone mature in Christ."

Allow me a brief aside. If one were to look closely at many churches today and assess the shape and form of ministry, verse 28 would likely need to be rewritten as follows: "Him we mention only in passing, lest we offend seekers or sound excessively religious. [Rather than warning and teaching . . .] we seek to please and entertain everyone so that they might feel good about themselves and be reassured that all is well in the world."

As cynical as that might sound, it is all too tragically true. We have abandoned admonishment and warning, for it would require that we speak of "sin," a forbidden word in many congregations. To instruct or teach would require both that pastors study and prepare and that Christians listen and learn. But we live in an age where people refuse to "endure sound teaching" but with "itching ears" they "accumulate for themselves teachers to suit their own passions" and they "turn away from listening to the truth and wander off into myths" (2 Tim. 4:3–4). Well, enough of that. Now back to Paul.

In verse 28 he describes ministry as consisting of two tasks: warning or admonishing other believers (concerning the dangers of sin and the need to repent) and instructing or teaching them, all in a wise and discerning way. Some say the admonishment is directed to unbelievers and consists of a warning concerning divine wrath for those who do not embrace the gospel. Teaching or instruction, on the other hand, focuses on believers. But there are numerous passages where Paul uses this Greek word translated "warning" that describe ministry to believers (see Acts 20:31; Rom. 15:14; Eph. 6:4; Col. 3:16; 1 Thess. 5:12, 14; 2 Thess. 3:15).

Note Paul's emphatic reference to "everyone" (three times in this one verse; literally, "all men"). As Murray Harris has said, "There is no special gospel or teaching for a spiritual or intellectual elite."[38] All the truth of God is for all the people of God, no exceptions allowed.

And to what end does Paul labor this way? So that he might "present" all men mature or complete or fully equipped in Christ on that final day of judgment.

"That's great for Paul," you might be inclined to say, "but I'm certainly not up to the task, nor am I remotely gifted to do this myself." Oh really.

Look at what Paul says later in Colossians 3:16 about the responsibility of *every* Christian: "Let the word of Christ dwell in you richly, teaching and admonishing one another in all wisdom." In case you missed it, the very words that Paul uses in Colossians 1:28 to describe *his* apostolic ministry on behalf of all men is used in Colossians 3:16 to describe *your* responsibility in ministry on behalf of others in the body of Christ. The words translated "teaching" and "admonishing" and "in all wisdom" in 3:16 are the same Greek terms found in 1:28.

The growth and maturity in Christ of every believer is, in a certain sense, the responsibility of every other believer in Christ. We must look not only to ourselves but to one another, passionately admonishing and wisely teaching so that we all might stand complete in Christ on that day.

# 39

# His Power Divine (1)

## Colossians 1:29

> For this I toil, struggling with all his energy that he powerfully works within me.

There's simply no restrained or measured way of saying it: Colossians 1:29 is a stunning passage of Scripture! The NASB renders it this way: "For this purpose also I labor, striving according to His power, which mightily works within me."

There are several reasons why I'm excited about this text. Let me begin with Paul's description of his ministry. But don't disengage. Don't think this passage is irrelevant to you simply because you are neither an apostle nor in vocational ministry. Remember what we saw in the previous lesson: the very words Paul uses in Colossians 1:28 to describe his apostolic ministry on behalf of all men ("teach," "admonish," "in all wisdom") are used in Colossians 3:16 to describe your responsibility in ministry on behalf of others in the body of Christ.

So how does Paul envision ministry? Put simply, it's really hard work! Look at his words: "For this I toil, struggling . . ." By "this" Paul probably has in mind the full scope of ministry described in verse 28: proclamation of the gospel of Christ, admonition concerning sin and repentance, instruction in the truths of the faith, all with a view to presenting every person complete in Christ.

The reason it requires toil (the focus of this word is not on mere labor but on the exhaustion and weariness that it induces) and struggling is not hard to understand. On the one hand, there are our own fleshly desires and bodily weaknesses to contend with. The physical demands of ministry are obvious. For people like Paul, one must also include persecution and pain and imprisonment (cf. 2 Cor. 11:22–29).

There is also the instinctive tendency toward laziness and self-indulgence. We are prone to quit when times get tough. It's so much easier to just give up. The frustration and discouragement and disillusionment of dealing with human sin on a daily basis make it all too easy to rationalize abandoning the hard work of ministry.

We shouldn't forget the obstacles to ministry posed by those to whom we minister. Notwithstanding our best and most compassionate efforts to be of help, they often want nothing more than to argue and to dispute our doctrine. When you expend yourself in service of another and all you receive in return is either ingratitude or the misinterpretation of your motives and the slander it so often brings, it's hard to stay the course. To use Paul's words, it's a struggle!

As if that weren't enough, we also have to do battle with the devil. The daily barrage of accusation, temptation, and multiple efforts to undermine what we have accomplished weighs heavily on the human soul.

These and countless other expressions of resistance and opposition are undoubtedly what Paul had in mind. So, yes, there is toil and struggle and strain and effort in ministry that can so easily discourage and dishearten those who are not reliant on the power that God supplies.

"You're laying a pretty heavy burden on us, Sam. Consistently proclaiming Christ, especially in the face of ridicule, resistance, and worldly opposition, not to mention demonic assault, is a tall order. Then telling us we are responsible, as Paul was, to admonish and instruct one another—I can barely find strength and incentive to get through the day. What makes you think I can pull this off?"

Needless to say, some don't. We hear all too often of "burn out," of those who run dry, whose disillusionment is greater than their determination. The prospect of facing another day of pouring out oneself for the sake of those who couldn't care less can take its toll on the human soul. I can't tell you how many times I've heard pastors say, "I'm fed up, beat up, worn out, done in. Enough's enough. I'm out'a here."

So how did Paul pull it off? Far from being exempt from the trials we face, he endured more than any of us ever will. So what accounts for his endurance? What was the secret to his perseverance?

The answer is twofold. In the first place, *he retained an eternal perspective.* "We do not lose heart," said Paul, "as we look not to the things that are seen but to the things that are unseen. For the things that are seen are transient, but the things that are unseen are eternal" (2 Cor. 4:16, 18).

But second, as stated in our passage in Colossians 1, *he relied on an eternal power.* Look again at verse 29. Paul toils and struggles "with all his [God's] energy that he powerfully works within me." The ultimate antidote to the burning out of the human spirit is the burning in of the divine. That is our focus in the next lesson.

# 40

# His Power Divine (2)

## Colossians 1:29

*For this I toil, struggling with all his energy that he powerfully works within me.*

The secret of Paul's success was not his education, his cultural heritage, his homiletical techniques, nor the appeal of his personality, but God's power working in him. To make this point he piles up, one upon another, words that focus our attention on the energy and activity of God: "For this I toil, struggling with all his *energy* that he *powerfully works* within me." Or again, "For this purpose also I labor, striving according to His *power*, which *mightily works* within me" (NASB).

Note that the NASB says Paul strives "according to" God's power. This doesn't so much mean "in proportion to" God's power but "with" or "by means of" or "in reliance upon" God's power. The word translated "energy" by the ESV and "power" by the NASB always in the New Testament refers to supernatural power, divine energy. The energy for the work here below comes from above.

But let's be specific. The power Paul has in mind is the power that raised Jesus from the dead. In Ephesians 1:19–20, a passage parallel in emphasis with Colossians 1:29, Paul points us to "the immeasurable greatness of his [God's] power toward us who believe, according to the working of his great might that he worked in Christ when he raised him from the dead and seated him at his right hand in the heavenly places."

Apart from conscious, consistent, concentrated reliance on the power of God that raised Jesus from the dead, burnout is a sure thing. Paul toiled without losing heart and struggled successfully because he drew deeply from the well of the infinite and unending energy of God.

"By the grace of God I am what I am," wrote Paul in 1 Corinthians 15:10, "and his grace toward me was not in vain. On the contrary, I worked harder than any of them, though it was not I, but the grace of God that is with me." Here again we see the emphasis on his own efforts, his own hard work, empowered by the infinite energy of God himself.

I suspect many are tempted to ask: "Why bother, Paul? If God's power is so great and so effective and so readily available, why do you feel it necessary to exert yourself so passionately and no doubt painfully? Why toil? Why struggle? Shouldn't you just 'let go and let God'?"

Absolutely not! The presence of God's power does not preclude Paul's personal struggle or energetic striving or laboring. Rather, it makes it possible. God's power is not designed to eliminate our responsibility to work hard but to enable us to fulfill it. Paul is able to work hard because God is working hard. The latter doesn't destroy or undermine the former.

I can't repeat this often enough: the operation of divine energy does not eliminate the physical and emotional exhaustion that Paul feels. God's working in and through us is not the sort that enables us to put our efforts on cruise control.

What we see here in Colossians 1:29, with reference to ministry in particular, is similar to what Paul wrote in Philippians 2:12–13, with reference to the Christian life in general: "Therefore, my beloved, as you have always obeyed, so now, not only as in my presence but much more in my absence, work out your own salvation with fear and trembling, for it is God who works in you, both to will and to work for his good pleasure."

Virtually every theological and ethical problem can be traced either to an elevation of divine power in a way that minimizes human toil, or the exaltation of human effort in a way that marginalizes the sovereignty of God. But Paul will have neither. He toils because of God's power. And divine power is released in and through human struggling to enable us to accomplish in our labor what we otherwise never would.

Again, God's sovereignty doesn't undermine human activity but inspires it. Any attempt to justify sloth or irresponsibility by appealing to divine power will meet with a harsh biblical denunciation.

J. I. Packer perhaps put it best when he said, "The Holy Spirit's ordinary way of working in us is through the working of our own minds and wills. He moves us to act by causing us to see reasons for moving ourselves to act. Thus our conscious, rational selfhood, so far from being annihilated, is strengthened, and in reverent, resolute obedience we work out our salvation, knowing that God is at work in us to make us '. . . both . . . will and . . . work for his good pleasure.'"[39]

Thus we see that God has chosen to operate not independently of but only through and by means of human effort and labor. God's energy doesn't fall from heaven haphazardly and amorphously, but comes to us through human ministers and ministry, via human toil and struggle.

We know from other biblical texts that the infinite energy of the Godhead upholds and sustains and directs the world. In Christ, says Paul, "all things hold together" (Col. 1:17). Again, "in him we live and move and have our being" (Acts 17:28). But here in Colossians 1:29 we see a unique manifestation of divine energy. Although in one sense divine energy sustained Paul in existence and was alone responsible for his life and breath, in another sense divine energy is focused and laser-like, to empower him in daily ministry.

So, how might we know when God is energetically and powerfully working in us? If, when you are slandered, you respond by entreating (1 Cor. 4:13), you can rest assured that divine energy is working mightily in you. If, when you are reviled, you bless instead of curse (1 Cor. 4:12), you can rest assured that divine energy is working mightily in you. If, when you are persecuted, you endure (1 Cor. 4:12), you can rest assured that divine energy is working mightily in you. If, when you are afflicted but not crushed, are perplexed but do not yield to despair, are struck down but not destroyed, you may rest assured that divine energy is working mightily in you (2 Cor. 4:8–9). If, when you are sorrowful and still rejoice, possess nothing yet are rich, you may rest assured that divine energy is working mightily in you (2 Cor. 6:10). If, when you are in poverty and give generously and joyfully (2 Cor. 8:1ff.), you may rest assured that divine energy is working mightily in you.

You probably won't feel anything. There's no guarantee that your body will vibrate or your appearance will change. But if you find yourself responding and thinking as Jesus would, if you find yourself acting and choosing contrary to every fleshly and sinful impulse, you may rest assured that divine energy is mightily at work in you. Only in this way can we, like Paul, continue to serve and love and minister and not lose heart.

Part 2

# Colossians 2:1–23

# 41

# A Most Fervent Wrestle with the Lord

## Colossians 2:1–3

For I want you to know how great a struggle I have for you and for those at Laodicea and for all who have not seen me face to face, that their hearts may be encouraged, being knit together in love, to reach all the riches of full assurance of understanding and the knowledge of God's mystery, which is Christ, in whom are hidden all the treasures of wisdom and knowledge.

Paul opens chapter 2 of his epistle to the Colossians with this description of his prayers on their behalf: "For I want you to know how great a struggle I have for you and for those at Laodicea and for all who have not seen me face to face, that their hearts may be encouraged, being knit together in love, to reach all the riches of full assurance of understanding and the knowledge of God's mystery, which is Christ, in whom are hidden all the treasures of wisdom and knowledge."

Paul's "struggle" is surely a reference to his prayer life. On this, virtually all students of Colossians agree. Intercession, says Paul, is a battle, an agonizing war that demands concentration, effort, and sustained devotion.

Paul exhorted the Christians in Rome to join him in his "struggle" by praying to God on his behalf (Rom. 15:30; cf. Col. 4:12). But with what or whom does one "struggle" and "wrestle" in prayer? Is it the distractions of the world against which we fight? Is it the temptations of the enemy? Is our struggle with the fear that perhaps prayer is a waste of time? Or perhaps we wrestle with the weakness and lethargy of our own flesh, struggling to overcome the natural tendency to give in too quickly. Could it possibly be God himself with whom we strive and struggle? More on this below.

What makes Paul's statement even more stunning is that he had never even met the people for whom he prayed with such agonizing effort. "They 'have not seen me face to face,'" says Paul, "yet I intercede on their behalf unceasingly.'" Never forget that it was Epaphras, not Paul, who brought the gospel to Colossae. But no amount of geographical distance or relational anonymity could hinder Paul's prayers for these saints. This ought forever to put to rest the excuse some use for not praying for others: "But I don't know them. They don't know me. I can't even mention them by name. Does God really hear such prayers?" Yes, he does!

I'm often encouraged in my own intercessory "struggle" by the example of others. Consider David Brainerd (1718–1747), missionary to the American Indians, who for a season lived in the home of Jonathan Edwards. Brainerd frequently wrote in his *Diary* of "wrestling" with God in prayer. The entry for Monday, April 19, 1742, reads in part, "God enabled me so to agonize in prayer, that I was quite wet with sweat, though in the shade, and the wind cool. My soul was drawn out very much for the world; I grasped for multitudes of souls."[1]

On the next day, Brainerd wrote: "I think my soul was never so drawn out in intercession for others as it has been this night. Had a most fervent wrestle with the Lord tonight for my enemies."[2] Again, "[I] was enabled to cry to God with a child-like spirit, and to continue instant in prayer for some time. Was much enlarged in the sweet duty of intercession. Was enabled to remember great numbers of dear friends and precious souls, as well as Christ's ministers. Continued in this frame, afraid of every idle thought, till I dropped asleep."[3]

Joseph Alleine's (1634–1668) wife once wrote of him: "At the time of his health he did rise constantly at or before four of the clock, and would be much troubled if he heard smiths or other craftsmen at their trades before he was at communion with God; saying to me after, 'How this noise shames me. Does not my Master deserve more than theirs?'"[4]

Martin Luther certainly knew how to "struggle" in prayer on behalf of other believers. Of his intercession on behalf of his friend and colleague Philip Melanchthon he wrote, "This time I besought the Almighty with great vigor. I attacked him with his own weapons, quoting from Scripture all the promises I could remember, that prayers should be granted, and said that he must grant my prayer, if I was henceforth to put my faith in his promises."[5]

On this point James H. Thornwell once wrote: "We pray; but what is there of agony in our prayers? Who wrestles with God? Whose soul is burdened with the weight of a perishing world? Or who takes an hour from his sleep or foregoes a single meal in order that he may plead the cause of millions upon millions that know not God? And are such prayers sacrifices? Are they more than breath? And can there be any wonder that mere breath should not move the Lord of hosts?"[6]

This sort of striving and struggling with God in prayer is proper so long as it does not degenerate into a conflict of wills. The function of prayer is not to bend God's will to ours or to wrench from him what he is reluctant to give. We must never believe ourselves capable of overpowering the Creator or forcing his hand. C. E. B. Cranfield reminded his readers that "to entertain any notion of trying to exert pressure upon God to compel him to do that which he himself does not will to do or of mobilizing one's fellow-Christians with a view to constraining him by a combination of forces is to lapse into paganism."[7]

That being said, when was the last time you had "a most fervent wrestle with the Lord" on behalf of those you know and love, not to mention those whom you have not seen face-to-face? Would that God might energize us in the struggle, empower us to agonize in our intercession, and stir us to strive without ceasing in prayer for one another.

# 42

# The Anatomy of a Prayer

## Colossians 2:1–3

For I want you to know how great a struggle I have for you and for those at Laodicea and for all who have not seen me face to face, that their hearts may be encouraged, being knit together in love, to reach all the riches of full assurance of understanding and the knowledge of God's mystery, which is Christ, in whom are hidden all the treasures of wisdom and knowledge.

That Paul agonized and struggled in prayer for the Colossians is obvious. That we should do the same for other believers, whether we know them or not (cf. Col. 2:1), is also beyond dispute. But what did he pray for? What should *we* pray for?

To answer this question we need to look closely at verse 2. There are two different ways of interpreting this passage. According to one view, Paul is informing them of his struggle on their behalf so that their knowledge of his labor and suffering will encourage their hearts and facilitate a bonding in love between them and him. This is certainly a possible way of reading the text, but let me suggest another.

The principal way in which he struggled on their behalf was through intercessory prayer, as we noted in the previous lesson. In verse 2 Paul turns to inform them of precisely what it is that he is asking God to do. The aim of my struggle, says the apostle, is that your hearts would be encouraged. This comes about primarily as you are knit together, one with another, in love and mutual support. The intended result of this ever-increasing unity and affection is that you might experience a deeper assurance that comes from increased understanding as well as a more profound and life-changing knowledge of Jesus Christ himself.

Let's begin with the first two elements in this "intercessory chain." Paul's purpose is (1) to encourage them and (2) to entwine them. The word translated "encourage" means more than simply to comfort: it means to strengthen or to fortify, and has in view not so much the physical maltreatment they might face but the heretical teaching and philosophical deception that could lead them away from the truth of Christ (v. 4 makes this clear; see also 2:8ff.).

This strengthening of the heart to stand firm and resolute when tempted by false teaching comes about only to the degree that they are "knit together" or "entwined" by their love for one another (for the use of this word "knit together," see Col. 3:19 and Eph. 4:16). Love is the glue, so to speak, that binds and bonds their hearts one to another, prevents them from being ripped apart by schism and conflict, and equips them to not lose heart in the face of opposition.

"Yeah, yeah, Storms. We've heard it all before. Our hearts need encouragement. We're supposed to love one another. Boring!" I understand your response. And if that were all Paul said, I might join the choir and sing the same song as you. But look at the second half of verse 2.

The result of encouraged and entwined hearts is full assurance and the knowledge of God's mystery, namely, Jesus. Implicit in Paul's language is the assumption that you can't grow up in God in isolation from other believers. Gaining the assurance of our faith and expanding our knowledge of Jesus are communal endeavors.

In other words, the result of affection and unity in the body is not merely a more passionate feeling but a more profound insight. Yes, thinking brings knowledge. But so too does love! Paul resists every temptation to cease praying; he strives and agonizes to overcome the listlessness of his physical frame and the alluring temptations of the devil. Why? Because he wants the hearts of these folk to be strengthened for battle and bonded in love *so that* they can be ever more assured of the truths of the faith and ever more entranced with the beauty and all-sufficiency of Jesus Christ.

Yes, I suppose it's possible for a believer, in isolation from others, to grow in knowledge and assurance. But that's not the way God intends for it to happen. There is a strange and elusive spiritual dynamic at work when Christian men and women corporately and in loving, covenant relationship one with another commit themselves to the pursuit of the knowledge of God. The insights we gain from one another, the mutual accountability, the collective wisdom that is generated in the context of the local church, all serve to enhance our growth in godliness and understanding in a way that can never be fully attained when we venture out on our own.

It has never been nor will it ever be God's design for you to pursue your relationship with him independently of other believers in the body of Christ. It is not only unbiblical to think otherwise; it is arrogant. A finger is effective only if it is united to a hand. An eye can see only if embedded in a head. A foot is good for movement only if attached to a leg. "For the body does not consist of one member but of many.... [Therefore] you are the body of Christ and individually members of it" (1 Cor. 12:14, 27).

I'll have more to say about assurance and knowledge and the mystery, which is Christ, in the next lesson. But let's not lose sight of Paul's primary point: "I'm praying for you," he writes, "that God would encourage you and entwine you in that most powerful of all affections, love, so that your minds might rest, without wavering, fully convinced of all that God has promised, and that you would be ever more enriched by the knowledge of that great mystery, which is his Son, our Lord Jesus Christ."

# 43

# Defeating Doubt

## Colossians 2:1–3

For I want you to know how great a struggle I have for you and for those at Laodicea and for all who have not seen me face to face, that their hearts may be encouraged, being knit together in love, to reach all the riches of full assurance of understanding and the knowledge of God's mystery, which is Christ, in whom are hidden all the treasures of wisdom and knowledge.

Doubt or uncertainty isn't always bad. It can often be productive, by driving us into deeper study and investigation. If we are absolutely convinced about everything, beyond the shadow of a doubt, we face the even bigger problem of arrogance and pride. Doubt humbles. It reminds us that we are finite and that our knowledge is always subject to improvement and increase.

But doubt can also be crippling in a way that undermines our relationship with God. If we are constantly doubting his word or wondering if he will fulfill his promises or are cynical of his stated intentions, it's hard to grow spiritually.

I've known many who are tormented by fears that God can't be as good as he portrays himself in Scripture. Or they are paralyzed by uncertainty concerning the forgiveness of their sins. Some experience a gnawing anxiety about whether Jesus was really God and whether he can be trusted with their lives. This sort of incessant second-guessing of God's revealed purposes is ultimately counterproductive to a healthy relationship with him and others.

This is why Paul's statement in Colossians 2:2 is so important for us. One of his goals in praying for the Colossians was that they might "reach all the riches of full assurance of understanding."

Let me note three important things in this statement. First, full assurance is a very real possibility for us. That doesn't mean we will never again scratch our heads in bewilderment or wonder if a biblical statement can really mean what it seems to mean. But it does mean there is a degree of certainty concerning the most basic and foundational truths in Scripture that is attainable in this life. Our knowledge will never be infallible or exhaustive, but it can be sufficiently accurate and adequate to sustain our hope and energize our hearts to persevere in what God has called us to do.

I don't think it's possible, at least not this side of heaven, for us to banish every wayward thought that might run counter to what God says in his Word. Until Christ comes, Satan will continue to sow the seeds of doubt in our minds. Adverse circumstances, what appears to be unanswered prayer, an affliction that isn't healed, a friend who abandons us in a moment of profound crisis, among other things, all have the potential to undermine, in varying degrees, our confidence in who God is. But that doesn't mean we can't experience what Paul refers to as "full assurance" (v. 2).

Second, this assurance or conviction concerning the truth of the gospel is characterized by riches or wealth. There is great treasure in knowing that the gospel of Christ is true. There is indescribable spiritual value in resting confidently in the veracity of God's Word. I think this is Paul's way of saying that indescribable blessing and unfathomable joy and ineffable peace fill the human heart when it attains "full assurance" of all that God has made known of himself.

But third, and perhaps most important of all, look closely again at Paul's words: "full assurance *of understanding.*" We could as easily render this, "full assurance that comes from understanding" or "unshakable confidence that is produced by knowledge" or something similar.

The point is that assurance is a function of knowledge. Our confidence in God's promises is subject to varying degrees, depending on the depth of understanding that we have attained in the things of God. Not everyone is equally confident about what God has revealed to us in Christ, because not everyone is equally informed.

When knowledge is made an end in itself, or is prized for its own sake, it breeds arrogance and pride, and it "puffs up" (cf. 1 Cor. 8:1). But when a person humbly applies himself to the pursuit of knowledge and looks to the power of the Spirit to bring illumination and insight, the wealth of our assurance increases and the riches of confident hope expand.

Although we can have full assurance of eternal life the moment we trust in Christ (John 3:16), our confidence grows and intensifies in direct proportion to our cognitive grasp of the broad expanse of what God has revealed. Knowledge is the soil in which the seeds of peace and certainty germinate.

For some, ignorance is bliss. But not when it comes to the assurance of faith. Ignorance of God and his revealed Word is the breeding ground for heresy and skepticism. As our understanding deepens, so too does the peace and tranquility of "knowing that we know" that God is true and that he will do what he has said he will do.

Simply put: defeat doubt by immersing your mind in the Word of God. This is the ordained means by which the Spirit will indelibly imprint on your heart the joyful and undeniable assurance that what God has said, God will do.

Paul said much the same thing when he prayed that the Romans might "abound in hope" (Rom. 15:13b). But abundant hope or full assurance only comes "in believing" (Rom. 15:13a) or in connection with and as a result of our faith in what God has made known. Sin-killing, Satan-silencing confidence doesn't fall from heaven like manna, nor do we serendipitously bump into it as we skip blissfully and ignorantly down the yellow brick road to a heavenly Oz. The Spirit imparts hope and confidence and assurance by means of and only in connection with our growth in the knowledge and understanding of God in his Word.

# 44

# Treasuring Christ

## *Colossians 2:1–3*

> For I want you to know how great a struggle I have for you and for those at Laodicea and for all who have not seen me face to face, that their hearts may be encouraged, being knit together in love, to reach all the riches of full assurance of understanding and the knowledge of God's mystery, which is Christ, in whom are hidden all the treasures of wisdom and knowledge.

We've come to the conclusion of Paul's intercessory prayer in Colossians 2:1–3. But it's not simply a conclusion; it's more of the climax, the pinnacle, the ultimate aim, if you will, of all that Paul has prayed. Read these verses one more time:

> For I want you to know how great a struggle I have for you and for those at Laodicea and for all who have not seen me face to face, that their hearts may be encouraged, being knit together in love, to reach all the riches of full assurance of understanding and the knowledge of God's mystery, which is Christ, in whom are hidden all the treasures of wisdom and knowledge. (Col. 2:1–3)

Paul prays for their hearts to be encouraged and entwined in love so that they might experience the riches of assurance that flow from their understanding of all God has revealed. But that understanding, that knowledge, has a unique and particular focus: Jesus Christ.

Perhaps the most pernicious and threatening myth among "religious" people is that there is knowledge of God apart from a personal relationship with Jesus Christ. Many claim to be "spiritual" who have no taste or relish for Jesus. "I want the divine," they are often heard to say. "I want to touch the transcendent. I want an encounter with that supernatural dimension of reality that exceeds the limitations of my own humanity. But I don't want Jesus. I refuse to acknowledge his deity or submit to his lordship." (Contrast this with 1 John 2:23.)

This Christless spirituality, which permeates our world, must be identified and repudiated with unyielding fervor. There is no existential value apart from Christ. There is no ultimate meaning in life apart from Christ. Good and evil, true and false, are little more than personal preferences with no objective reality apart from the revelation of God in the incarnation, life, death, and resurrection of Jesus Christ.

Paul prays that we might attain to the knowledge of this mystery, which is Christ, because assurance that is grounded in anything or anyone else is, at best, wishful thinking. Confidence in who God is and what he has purposed to achieve comes only by knowing and receiving, relishing and rejoicing in the person of Jesus of Nazareth. Whatever else we learn in our study of Scripture, it serves us well and for eternity only to the degree that it points to and consummates in the person of Jesus. Not just "in him" but "in him *alone*" are hidden all the treasures of wisdom and knowledge. (I feel justified in adding and emphasizing the word "alone," given Paul's emphasis on the exclusivity of Christ in Colossians 1:14, 15–20, 27–28; 2:8–9, 17; 3:1–4, 11, 17.)

Don't be misled by Paul's language. When he speaks of Christ as God's mystery in whom all the treasures of wisdom and knowledge are hidden, he does not mean to suggest that who Jesus is and what he has accomplished are concealed from us. A "mystery" in Paul's language was simply a truth that remained inaccessible until such time as God took the initiative to reveal it and make it clear. Paul is not saying that Christ is mysterious in the sense that we can't figure him out. He is a mystery in the sense that it wasn't until the revelation of God in the historical person of Christ that we gained total access to the truth of God's redemptive purposes through him. And knowledge and wisdom are hidden in him, not in the sense of being impenetrable or beyond understanding but rather in the sense of being deposited or stored up in him. In other words, he is the only person and place where authentic, accurate knowledge of God and his ways with mankind can be found.

*The Hope of Glory*

When Paul says that "all" the treasures of wisdom and knowledge are in Christ, he isn't saying that a person can't know anything at all if he isn't a Christian. The world is filled with brilliant atheists. Our universities and think tanks are populated with highly intellectual and well-educated scholars who know nothing of Jesus beyond their concession that a man by that name lived two millennia ago.

Rather, his point is that true knowledge of the ultimate meaning of human existence is found only in light of the identity and redemptive accomplishment of Jesus Christ. Insight into the character of God and his relationship with his creation is found only by looking to the person and work of Jesus. The nature and eternal destiny of the human soul, the grounds on which we differentiate between good and evil, the wisdom of God's ways in the world, as well as the pathway to reconciliation with him, are all tethered to Christ. If we know him, we know them.

Paul's language is both extensive and intensive. He declares that all (not merely some) of the treasures (not the trivialities) of wisdom and knowledge are in Christ. His point here is twofold.

First, there is a vast reservoir of riches in knowing Jesus. That is to say, "all the treasures" points to the lavish, inexhaustible, far-reaching, mind-blowing, breathtaking realities that we discover and enjoy when we grow in our knowledge of him.

Second, and of equal importance, Paul's language reminds us that knowledge of Christ is to be honored and valued above all else. Is that not how we would treat any treasure that we discovered? The knowledge and wisdom that we find in Christ, and in Christ alone, are not to be treated casually or flippantly or presumptuously. The light of the knowledge of the glory of God as revealed in the face of Jesus Christ (2 Cor. 4:4–6) is a treasure of infinite worth and value. Ponder it deeply. Pray for it daily. Plunder its riches. Protect it from defilement. Penetrate its mysteries. Prize it above all earthly wealth, all human wisdom, all fleshly gain.

In simple summary: There's nothing you could ever hope to know about God, his will and his ways, that you won't find in Jesus. And you'll find it only in Jesus. He alone is the treasury of divine wealth and wisdom.

This is what Paul prayed that the Colossians would experience. Is that how you and I pray for each other and for ourselves? Ought it to be?

# 45

# How's Your Faith?

## Colossians 2:4–5

I say this in order that no one may delude you with plausible arguments. For though I am absent in body, yet I am with you in spirit, rejoicing to see your good order and the firmness of your faith in Christ.

How would you describe your faith? What characteristics would you attribute to it?

Would you use adjectives like *passionate, orthodox, vibrant, creative*, or something similar? Or would you employ a theological or denominational tag to identify the nature of your relationship with Jesus? Perhaps you would describe yourself as being of the Reformed faith or as having traditional faith or maybe even "Word of Faith."

Some, in a more vulnerable and honest moment, might describe their faith as half-hearted or hesitant or even faltering.

I ask this question because of something Paul wrote in Colossians 2:4–5. After describing the way he prays for them, he writes: "I say this in order that no one may delude you with plausible arguments. For though I am absent in body, yet I am with you in spirit, rejoicing to see your good order and the firmness of your faith in Christ."

The phrase, "I say this," is retrospective and looks back to what he has just written in verses 1 to 3 (and perhaps even to what he wrote in the closing verses of chapter 1). The point is that Paul willingly suffers and preaches and teaches and agonizes in prayer so that these believers will not be led astray or deluded by "plausible arguments," by which he means clever and impressive speech that gives the appearance of being sophisticated and substantive but ultimately proves false and destructive. If you want an example of this sort of thing in our day, turn on religious TV and wait. You are sure to run across several frightening examples in the course of a few hours.

In what sense was Paul present with them? You may recall that he used similar language in writing to the Corinthians concerning the discipline of a wayward church member: "For though absent in body, I am present in spirit; and as if present, I have already pronounced judgment on the one who did such a thing. When you are assembled in the name of the Lord Jesus and my spirit is present . . ." (1 Cor. 5:3–4). In both instances, Paul was truly present, although not physically so. I don't think he means "I am present in your thoughts and prayers," but rather that he was present by virtue of his union with them in Christ. He was in Christ and they were in Christ and thus, wherever Christ was, they were together in him.

But my primary concern is the way Paul describes their faith or the depth and quality of their commitment to Jesus. He uses two words in verse 5 that I suspect few would employ today. Such words just aren't exciting enough for twenty-first-century Christians. There's not enough glitz and bling to them. People like the Colossians could never raise enough money to subsidize a national television program. And if you're into building a mega-church, I suspect you'll need something more than good order and firmness in your faith. But such are the words of praise from the apostle.

The word translated "good order" points to the well-ordered behavior of the Colossians. He has in mind lives that are aligned with biblical revelation, daily habits of life that reflect the values of Jesus, unwavering obedience to the will of God, no matter how unpopular or "unsuccessful" that may prove to be.

The word rendered "firmness," used here to describe their faith, means steadfast, stable, resolute, solid, not given to flights of fancy or open to the influence of flashy, fleshly preachers whose "ministries" are built on novelty, bizarre and sensational experiences, or some new revelatory "word" that is strangely absent from Scripture and, upon closer examination, in direct conflict with it.

There wasn't much to set apart these believers except for their commitment to good order in godly living and resolute solidarity in their commitment to Jesus Christ. But isn't that enough? Where did the church ever get the notion that God is more impressed with new and unprecedented insights, or scintillating discernment on the signs of the times, or perhaps the latest sure-fire strategy for financial prosperity?

Here is what brings a smile of approval to the face of our heavenly Father: faithful Christians who set their personal and corporate spiritual experience in that "order" set forth in Scripture. Here is what evokes a heartfelt "Well done!" from our great and glorious God: people whose lives are fixed and riveted on Christ alone, whose faith does not bend with every blast of new doctrinal wind, whose commitment is not compromised by threat or fear of persecution or loss of personal convenience and comfort.

No, it's not very exciting, at least not as the world measures excitement. It may not draw huge crowds or bring in massive offerings or lead to lucrative book contracts. But whose favor are we seeking, anyway—God's or man's? If the latter, good order and firmness of faith in Christ won't get you very far. But if it's the favor and pleasure and joy of your heavenly Father that you most desire, commit yourself in the power of his Spirit to put all things in good order and stand firm and resolute and unwavering in your single-minded, wholehearted, world-denying, devotion to Jesus.

# 46

# Thanks, I Needed That!

## Colossians 2:6–7

> Therefore, as you received Christ Jesus the Lord, so walk in him, rooted and built up in him and established in the faith, just as you were taught, abounding in thanksgiving.

*I* desperately need the encouragement of this passage. My guess is that a lot of you do, too. I need it because of what it tells me about my past and my present. Earlier in Colossians we noted how Paul emphasized our future, the hope we have in Christ of inheriting and experiencing eternal and unchanging glory (see Col. 1:5, 21–23, 27). But here in Colossians 2:6–7 it is the past and present that concerns us.

In order to see this, we need to take note of how this passage is translated in both the ESV and the NASB. Although I prefer and use the former, the latter provides us here with a more accurate and literal rendering of Paul's words. Here is the ESV translation of verses 6 and 7: "Therefore, as you received Christ Jesus the Lord, so walk in him, rooted and built up in him and established in the faith, just as you were taught, abounding in thanksgiving."

Compare that with the NASB: "Therefore as you have received Christ Jesus the Lord, *so* walk in Him, having been firmly rooted *and now* being built up in Him and established in your faith, just as you were instructed, *and* overflowing with gratitude."

Did you see the difference? According to the NASB, we *have been* firmly rooted in Christ and are *now being* built up in him. I won't go into the technical distinction between the perfect passive participle and the present passive participle in the original Greek text, but I think you can see it for yourself from this English translation.

*I have been* rooted in Christ. So, too, have you if you believe in him for life and salvation. *I am being* built up in Christ. So, too, are you if you believe in him for life and salvation. And that's why I'm so profoundly encouraged by this text. Let me explain.

This world can be pretty brutal at times; in fact, most of the time. People disappoint us. We disappoint them. The flesh gets the upper hand. Satan is relentless in his assault, whether by accusation or temptation or taunting. Circumstances get out of hand and dreams are shattered. Society as a whole just seems to unravel before our eyes. And worst of all, we begin to wonder if our lives are going anywhere or producing anything of value.

That's why I'm so wonderfully encouraged by Paul's choice of words (and verb tenses) in Colossians 2:6–7. No matter how tenuous and free-floating life sometimes seems, I "have been rooted" in Jesus Christ. God has graciously seeded my soul into the soil of Christ's unchanging and unconquerable grace. My life is rooted in him. My hope is grounded in his goodness. This is my identity. This is my security. This is my strength when I feel like I'm wandering aimlessly and hopelessly through one disappointment after another. Whatever I may encounter, whether good or bad, of this I may be certain: I have been rooted in Christ!

But what about those times when so little spiritual progress is being made? Again, it feels like I'm stuck in concrete, immobile, immovable, unchangeable. That's when I remind myself once more of Paul's words: Not only have I been rooted in Christ in the past; I am being built up in Christ even now, in the present. I may not always see it or feel it or be aware of major developments. In fact, there are times when I feel like I'm regressing rather than progressing. If I'm moving at all, it must be backwards.

No! Paul assures us that however imperceptible it may be, we are being built up in Christ. We are ever and always under ongoing construction. A brick here, a board there, but always and persistently being built up by divine grace. Yes, every so often we dismantle what God has done, tearing down his handiwork and experiencing momentary, though painful, disintegration. But God will not give up on us. What he began by grace, he'll finish by grace. The building will be completed. Our souls will grow in conformity to Christ and one day we will be like him for we shall see him as he is (1 John 3:1–3).

I don't know about you, but it helps me to know that. I desperately need to be reassured that my life, body, soul, and spirit are rooted in Christ and what he has done for me. Being rooted and grounded in my own good intentions or the promises of other people or whatever worldly and financial success I might attain doesn't do much when life stinks and my soul sinks. I need to know that I'm rooted in him.

I desperately need to know that he's still at work in me, slowly but surely building up what I've torn down, conforming and shaping my soul to look like his. Oftentimes our spiritual and moral failures look massive and seem to dwarf our achievements. But I'm assured of this: nothing will lead him to forsake his work in me.

In fact, Paul goes on to say that we are also "being established" in the faith. The word here was often used to describe the practice of guaranteeing legal contracts. God has bound himself to me. He has formally pledged himself to my growth in grace in his Son. He has sealed the document of ownership. I am his and he is mine and he will continue to confirm and solidify me in the experience and knowledge of all that he has made known of himself and his purposes for me in Christ.

There's only one appropriate response to such breathtaking realities: thanksgiving. No wonder Paul's final phrase in verse 7 reminds us of the importance of "abounding in thanksgiving" or "overflowing with gratitude" (NASB).

Okay. Thanks, God (and Paul). I needed that!

# 47

# Fullness for Life

## Colossians 2:8–10

> See to it that no one takes you captive by philosophy and empty deceit, according to human tradition, according to the elemental spirits of the world, and not according to Christ. For in him the whole fullness of deity dwells bodily, and you have been filled in him, who is the head of all rule and authority.

So far in our study of Colossians I've avoided saying anything in depth about the problem that led Paul to write this letter in the first place. There is good reason for that. I long ago lost count of the number of theories concerning the essence of the so-called Colossian heresy (it probably consisted of an odd mix of Gnosticism, asceticism, and an inordinate emphasis on the importance of angels; some have contended there was also a Judaizing element in it).

But we can no longer afford to ignore this issue, and the reason is obvious. Here in Colossians 2:8–10 Paul explicitly warns his readers: "See to it that no one takes you captive by philosophy and empty deceit, according to human tradition, according to the elemental spirits of the world, and not according to Christ. For in him the whole fullness of deity dwells bodily, and you have been filled in him, who is the head of all rule and authority."

There are four observations that need to be made. First, contrary to what some have said, Paul is not condemning all philosophy, as if the discipline is itself inherently dangerous. I've actually run into a few individuals who, upon entering college, believed that this passage prohibited them from majoring in philosophy. "The idea of a 'Christian philosopher,'" said one, "is a contradiction in terms." Now, there may well be reasons why one should opt for another major, but this verse isn't one of them!

Paul is clearly referring to one specific expression of philosophical thought that was a threat to the faith of the Colossians in the first century (note the presence of the definite article, although left out by most English translations, hence more literally, "*the* philosophy"). This is a philosophical perspective characterized by empty deceit. It is *deceitful*, as over against the word of *truth* (Col. 1:5). It is *empty*, as over against the glorious *riches* (Col. 1:27) and *treasures* (Col. 2:3) that are in Christ.

Philosophy, more generally considered, is an extremely helpful discipline designed to help us think through ultimate issues such as the existence of God, the meaning of life, the nature of good and evil, how we use language, and a variety of other tough topics. Philosophical reasoning, therefore, that is subject to the final authority of Scripture can shed great light on our search for and understanding of truth.

Second, on the other hand, Christians do need to be cautious about any form of philosophy that is "not according to Christ" (v. 8), That is to say, if it is in any way contrary to the revelation of God in Christ or diminishes from his supremacy and glory, it is to be shunned.

That Paul has in mind a particular philosophy that detracts from the centrality of Christ and undermines our confidence in his sufficiency to be and do for us all that we need is evident from verses 9 and 10. Note the word "for" with which verse 9 begins. Paul's point is that *because* (for) all the fullness of the divine nature dwells in Christ and *because* we have been made complete in him and in no other, we have no need for human reasoning that purports to give us something that Christ didn't provide. Any philosophy (or theology) that says, "Christ was necessary, but not sufficient; we have more, we have the 'fullness' of divine wisdom and power that isn't available merely in a relationship with Jesus Christ," is demonic and must be rejected.

Third, the philosophy that Paul condemns is according to human tradition (v. 8). In other words, it is earthly in origin. This is a philosophy that was conceived in the mind of man and did not come by means of divine revelation. It may well be compatible with and confirm human traditions, and make sense when looked at from a this-worldly perspective, but it has nothing in it of God.

Fourth, and perhaps worst of all, this philosophy is "according to the elemental spirits of the world." Since the Greek word *stoicheia*, translated "elemental" (the word "spirits" is not in the original text), was employed in the ancient world to refer to the letters of an alphabet, it may be used here as a reference to first principles or the fundamental elements of something, hence the rudimentary concepts of human thought or the basic ideas of human reasoning.

But it is more likely that by this word (*stoicheia*) Paul is referring to spiritual beings, i.e., demons, that were thought to be active within and exercising influence over the physical universe. In other words, this would be another way of referring to those spiritual beings which Christ created and over whom he exercises sovereign rule, as well as those demonic spirits that Paul will soon declare (Col. 2:15) were defeated by means of the cross.

If this is the case, no wonder Paul warned them so strongly lest they be taken captive. There is demonic energy behind any philosophy, says the apostle, that undermines or detracts from or tries to supplement the work of our Lord Jesus Christ. He, and he alone, is truly enough! He is all we will ever need.

The NASB makes this clear by translating the first half of verse 10 as, "in Him you have been made complete." There is fullness in only one: Jesus. In him, and therefore in no one else, you will find every resource, every truth, and all power. Look again at Colossians 2:3 where Paul declared that it is in him we find all the treasures of wisdom and knowledge.

Besides the translation "made complete," this word has also been translated "you have been filled" or even "fulfilled." The same verb is used to describe Christians as being filled with the fruit of righteousness (Phil. 1:11), joy and peace (Rom. 15:13), as well as goodness and knowledge (Rom. 15:14), not to mention the Spirit himself (Eph. 5:18). The false teachers tried to convince the Colossians that the fullness they desired was unattainable in Christ alone. Paul responded by reminding them that everything they need to be complete, full, and fulfilled is in Jesus, and Jesus alone.

The "Colossian heresy" no longer exists in precisely the form it did in Paul's day. But there is still great relevance in his words of warning. We must be diligent, constantly on guard, and ever alert to those deceitful and ultimately destructive philosophies and theologies that to the slightest degree draw us away from reliance on Christ and his all-sufficient grace.

Any idea or system of thought that would suggest he is not supreme and sovereign or that he is not infinitely and exclusively worthy of our absolute devotion and adoration is demonic at its core. Beware, says the apostle, of any such philosophy. Identify it. Denounce it. Deliver others from its destructive clutches.

# 48

# Glorious Truths in Gruesome Terms

## Colossians 2:11

**In him also you were circumcised with a circumcision made without hands, by putting off the body of the flesh, by the circumcision of Christ,** having been buried with him in baptism, in which you were also raised with him through faith in the powerful working of God, who raised him from the dead.

The apostle Paul was many things, but "politically correct" wasn't one of them. He rarely shied away from using graphic and often gruesome language if he thought it effective in making a point. If he thought he could help people, he wasn't averse to offending them to do it.

How else does one account for the language of Colossians 2:11? There Paul declares that in Christ "you were circumcised with a circumcision made without hands, by putting off the body of the flesh, by the circumcision of Christ."

It's not altogether clear why Paul abruptly introduces the subject of circumcision at this point in his argument. Perhaps the heretics at Colossae were insisting on physical circumcision as a condition for full acceptance with God (although there's little evidence for that; indeed, were it true, one would expect him to explicitly denounce the practice somewhere in Colossians, but he doesn't). Whatever the case, Paul's point is unmistakable: the only circumcision that has any religious significance is a spiritual one. Let me try to explain this by taking each phrase separately.

First, physical circumcision was the token or seal of the covenant God made with Abraham and his seed. It was the distinctive sign, the ethnic badge, so to speak, of an Israelite in covenant relationship with Yahweh. But it was always intended to symbolize an inward, altogether spiritual cleansing and purification from sin.

When Paul declares that we "were circumcised" (v. 11a), I'm inclined to believe he is referencing our conversion. In other words, we experienced a spiritual circumcision of the heart at the time of our regeneration. This is what Paul had in view in Romans 2:28–29 where he said that true circumcision is not "outward and physical" (v. 28) but is "a matter of the heart, by the Spirit" (v. 29). See also 2 Corinthians 3:3 and Philippians 3:3.

It's possible, however, that Paul is referring to our identification with Christ in his death on the cross. With this view, to say "you were circumcised" would be another way of declaring, in obviously metaphorical language, "you died." When Christ died, when he experienced "circumcision" by the stripping away of his physical body in death, we died. But I still think the first view is more likely.

Second, Paul describes this circumcision as one that is "made without hands" (*acheiropoietos*). This word was typically used in the New Testament to contrast what is made by humans with what is made by God. It also points to the contrast between the external material aspects of the old order of Judaism under the Mosaic covenant and the internal spiritual efficacy of the new order under the new covenant (Mark 14:58; Acts 7:48; 17:24; Heb. 9:11, 24).

Thus, to speak of something not made by human hands or made without hands is to assert that God himself has created it (as in the case of the temple that Jesus would build in three days, in Mark 14:58, as well as the heavenly house [i.e., body] which believers receive at death, in 2 Cor. 5:1). Paul's point is that the circumcision performed in the flesh with human hands is no longer the real or spiritually meaningful circumcision (note especially Galatians 5:6, "for in Christ Jesus neither circumcision nor uncircumcision counts for anything, but only faith working through love").

Third, Paul says it was achieved by a "putting off the body of the flesh" (v. 11). This is most likely a reference to the physical body and death of Christ himself. The only other place this phrase appears in the New Testament is in Colossians 1:22 where it refers to the physical body of Christ, and the three earlier uses of "flesh" in Colossians all denote physical flesh (see Col. 1:24; 2:1, 5).

Thus, the "putting off the body of flesh" does not refer to the believer's experience but to the violent stripping away of Christ's physical body in his death on the cross.

When we combine this phrase with the one that follows ("by the circumcision of Christ") we see that "the body of flesh was stripped off when Christ was circumcised, that is, when he died; the whole statement is 'a gruesome figure for death.' . . . Here is a circumcision which entailed not the stripping off of a small portion of flesh but the violent removal of the whole body in death."[8]

Fourth, as just noted, when Paul then refers to "the circumcision of Christ" at the conclusion of verse 11, he does not mean his circumcision as a Jewish infant of eight days (cf. Luke 2:21), but he has in view the literal death of Christ. In other words, Paul envisions the crucifixion itself as a circumcision.

[I would be remiss not to mention an alternative interpretation of the phrase "the body of the flesh." According to this view, by "flesh" Paul means not the physical body of Christ (as above, in an ethically neutral sense) but our sinful, fallen, unregenerate nature, or everything we were in Adam before we came to be in Christ. In this view, "the body of the flesh" would be similar to what Paul had in mind in Romans 6:6 when he spoke of "our old self" that was "crucified with him in order that the body of sin might be brought to nothing, so that we would no longer be enslaved to sin."]

It's not a pleasant image and these are not easy words, but it sure gets the point across! It is not by "human hands" (whether our effort, good intentions, or a reformed life) but by the Spirit of God that our hearts have been circumcised and renewed and regenerated unto life eternal.

# 49

# Why I Am a Baptist

## Colossians 2:12

In him also you were circumcised with a circumcision made without hands, by putting off the body of the flesh, by the circumcision of Christ, **having been buried with him in baptism, in which you were also raised with him through faith in the powerful working of God, who raised him from the dead.**

Why do I believe that only believers should be baptized in water? Why am I a credo-baptist rather than a paedo-baptist (the term *credo* comes from the Latin that means "I believe," hence baptism for believers only; the term *paedo* comes from the Greek word for infant).

Before I answer that question, it may be helpful to explain briefly why some Christians baptize their infants. The primary reason comes from their understanding of the relationship between Old Testament circumcision and New Testament baptism.

In the Old Testament, male infants were circumcised as the outward sign of entrance into the covenant community of Israel. This did not guarantee their salvation, but marked them out as recipients of the external blessings of a national covenant into which they were introduced by physical birth.

Christian baptism, so goes the paedo-baptist argument, is the New Testament counterpart to Old Testament circumcision. It does not guarantee the salvation of infants but sets them apart as children of covenant parents who are thus included in the external blessings and responsibilities of the people of God. Baptized infants are thus "under the umbrella," so to speak, of God's new covenant blessings. Parents of the infant pray that he or she will personally receive the blessings of salvation in Christ, which baptism signifies. They hope and trust that baptism is the foreshadowing of what will take place when their child personally embraces Jesus as savior. This is closely related to the idea that God deals not merely with individuals based on personal faith but with corporate entities based on covenant promise.

Paedo-baptists also appeal to what they call "household" baptisms in the New Testament (see Acts 16:15, 33; and 1 Cor. 1:16). Surely, they contend, there must have been infants in these households. Infants of Christian parents, therefore, were made recipients of water baptism.

Why am I not convinced by this? Very briefly, for these reasons. First, the narrative examples in the New Testament portray baptism as being administered only to believers. (See Acts 2:41; 8:12; 10:44–48.)

Second, baptism is portrayed in the New Testament as a symbol of the beginning of spiritual life (Gal. 3:27; Rom. 6:3–4; Col. 2:12), as well as "an appeal to God for a good conscience" (1 Pet. 3:21). Unless one is prepared to predicate salvation and spiritual life of unbelieving infants, or suggest that they are capable of making a conscious appeal to God for a good conscience, it would appear that baptism is restricted to those who consciously trust Christ.

Third, baptism is consistently portrayed as inextricably tied up with (conscious) faith and repentance (e.g., Acts 2:38, 41; 8:12–13, 36; 10:47–48). This is especially the case with Colossians 2:12, which I'll deal with below.

Fourth, in all examples of so-called household baptisms the broader contexts make clear that only believers were baptized. As for Acts 16:15 and 16:33, members of the household were old enough to hear and understand the word of the Lord spoken to them (Acts 16:32, thereby excluding infants) and old enough to understand what it meant for a person to believe in God and thus have reason to rejoice because of it (Acts 16:34, thereby again excluding infants; see also John 4:53).

As for 1 Corinthians 1:16, we see in 1 Corinthians 16:15 that the household of Stephanas, whom Paul baptized, were the first converts in Achaia who devoted themselves to the service of the saints. As for the children in Acts 2:39, they are at least old enough to be called by the Lord (v. 39). And then, as if to confirm it, Luke records that "those who received his word were baptized" (Acts 2:41). There is no indication that those who were too young to respond to the call of God and too young to receive God's word were baptized.

Fifth, and finally, I can't help but notice the absence in the New Testament of any explicit portrayal of an infant ever being baptized.

But let's look more closely at Colossians 2:11–12, where Paul writes, "In him also you were circumcised with a circumcision made without hands, by putting off the body of the flesh, by the circumcision of Christ, having been buried with him in baptism, in which you were also raised with him through faith in the powerful working of God, who raised him from the dead."

Contrary to the paedo-baptist argument, the New Testament counterpart to Old Testament circumcision isn't baptism; it's regeneration or the new birth. Or again, it is spiritual circumcision of the heart, not water baptism, that corresponds in the new covenant to old covenant physical circumcision of the flesh. (By the way, even if one were to concede that water baptism is the new covenant counterpart to old covenant circumcision, the former is consistently predicated on the faith of the individual, unlike the latter. Indeed, this is the very point of Colossians 2:12, as I'll note below.)

Water baptism is a sign of the circumcision of the heart and the new life and cleansing from sin that it brings. The sign of the new covenant isn't baptism, but spiritual circumcision or regeneration or the "cutting away" of the heart of flesh, of which water baptism is an outward, symbolic expression.

But more important still is Paul's reference to faith in verse 12. John Piper has summarized this better than anyone I've read, so let me close by quoting his words:

> If baptism were merely a parallel of the Old Testament rite of circumcision it would not have to happen 'through faith' since infants did not take on circumcision "through faith." The reason the New Testament ordinance of baptism must be "through faith" is that it represents not the

Old Testament external ritual, but the New Testament, internal, spiritual experience of circumcision "without hands."

Those two words, "through faith," in verse 12 are the decisive, defining explanation of how we were buried with Christ in baptism and how we were raised with him in baptism: it was "through faith." And this is not something infants experience. Faith is a conscious experience of the heart yielding to the work of God. Infants are not capable of this, and therefore infants are not fit subjects of baptism, which is "through faith."[9]

I love my paedo-baptist friends and rejoice in their love for God. But I remain unconvinced by their arguments. Needless to say, this is a subject deserving of book-length treatment, but I hope my brief comments here are of help as you seek to obey Scripture with regard to this precious ordinance of God.

# 50

# Faith in What?

## Colossians 2:12

In him also you were circumcised with a circumcision made without hands, by putting off the body of the flesh, by the circumcision of Christ, **having been buried with him in baptism, in which you were also raised with him through faith in the powerful working of God, who raised him from the dead.**

There is a fascinating phrase in Colossians 2:12 that few commentators mention. It concerns the focus of our faith. Here again is verse 12: "having been buried with him in baptism, in which you were also raised with him through faith in the powerful working of God, who raised him from the dead."

I find it interesting that Paul says our faith is in the powerful "working of" God and not simply in God or even in Jesus Christ. Of course, this isn't to deny for a moment that we are to trust and put our faith in the person of Jesus Christ who is the incarnation of God himself. But there is something significant in the fact that Paul here declares our faith is in God's "power." [It is grammatically possible, although noticeably awkward, to translate this, "through faith of the power of God," which is to say, "through faith that comes from God" or is "produced by" God. Whereas it is true that faith is a gift of God that is evoked in us by the Holy Spirit, it is highly unlikely that Paul is saying that here.]

The word translated "powerful working" is the same Greek word (*energeia*) used earlier by Paul in Colossians 1:29 where he described himself as struggling with all God's "energy" (*energeia*) to accomplish the ministry he had been given.

But why would he say that our faith (indeed, our saving faith) is in God's energy or power? Someone might answer by saying that we shouldn't differentiate between God and his power. In other words, our faith is in the God whose power is responsible for raising us to newness of life in Christ. I certainly agree with that. It isn't just any power at all, as if raw, independent power has saved us. It is specifically *God's* power. Indeed, it is the very power that was manifested and expressed when God the Father raised God the Son from the dead (v. 12b; see especially Eph. 1:19–20).

But we are still left with the fact that Paul thought it important, for whatever reason(s), to highlight the power of God as the focus of faith. In what sense do we trust in or believe or exercise faith in God's power?

Surely part of the answer is in the verses that follow. In Colossians 2:13 Paul says we were dead in our trespasses. To bring to spiritual life what was formerly dead is no small feat! Nothing could accomplish this other than the power of God regenerating and renewing our lifeless hearts.

As if that were not enough, God also forgave us our sins by canceling the debt that stood against us, by nailing it to the cross (v. 14). He also triumphed over and disarmed demonic spirits through the work of Christ at Calvary.

My point is simply that these were obviously *powerful* expressions of divine grace and activity on our behalf. Only God could pull it off, so to speak. If we do not have faith in the fact that God did this in and through Christ we cannot be saved. That may be the sense, then, in which Paul declares that we are saved through faith in the powerful working of God.

Saving faith entails confidence that God and God alone is able and powerful enough to deliver us from spiritual death and the guilt of sin. This isn't separable from faith in Christ as the one who by his death and resurrection made it all possible. But here in Colossians 2:12 Paul wanted to highlight the importance of faith in God's power. That is to say, it's important for us to know and trust in the omnipotence of God, the limitless energy of the divine will, to do for us what we are helpless and hopeless to do for ourselves.

But I wonder if perhaps more is in the apostle's mind when he uses this language. In fact, it reminds me of something found in the gospel records of Jesus' healing ministry.

Jesus took special delight in healing those who trusted in his *power*, people who were open and receptive to his ability to perform a mighty work. In Matthew 9:28–29 Jesus asks the two blind men only if they believe he is "able" to heal them. He wanted to find out what they thought about him, specifically whether or not they trusted his *ability*. "Yes, Lord," came their response. "According to your faith be it done to you," he replied, and they were instantly healed. Jesus regarded their confidence in his power to help them as faith, and he dealt mercifully with them on that basis.

"Jesus, I believe you are able to heal me" is the kind of faith that pleases him. I can almost hear Jesus say: "Yes! I was waiting to hear you say that. It's important that you truly believe that I am capable of doing this." The leper in Matthew 8 said to Jesus, "Lord, *if you will, you can make me clean*" (v. 2). The leper didn't question Christ's ability. He asserts, without hesitation, you "can" make me clean. But he is less certain about the willingness of Jesus to do it. Jesus didn't rebuke him for such doubts, as if it were a shortcoming in his faith that might jeopardize his healing. Jesus healed him because of his confidence that he *could* do it, not that he necessarily *would* do it.

The hemorrhaging woman in Mark 5 was healed when she simply touched Jesus' garment. "Your faith has made you well" (v. 34), said Jesus. In other words, "What I enjoy and respond to is your simple confidence and trust in my ability to make a difference in your life."

So, I ask: is there an extended application of this statement in Colossians 2:12 to the subject of miracles? In other words, I wonder, for example, if the reason we see fewer healings than we do (or any variety of supernatural manifestation) is related to our lack of faith in God's power to perform them? Do we take steps in our study of his Word and in prayer and in conscious dependence on the Spirit to cultivate a more vibrant belief that God can really bring these things to pass? Would God do more in the way of the miraculous if our faith in his power were deeper, more intense, more consistent, and less plagued with hesitation and doubt? I'm not sure, but it's worth pondering.

# 51

# Alive in Him!

## Colossians 2:13–14

And you, who were dead in your trespasses and the uncircumcision of your flesh, God made alive together with him, having forgiven us all our trespasses, by canceling the record of debt that stood against us with its legal demands. This he set aside, nailing it to the cross.

Someone once said that before we get people saved we have to get them lost. There's a lot of truth in that statement. The fact is, our society has virtually lost any sense of sin. What good is it to speak of salvation to those who have no awareness of alienation from God or liability to his righteous wrath?

In Colossians 2:13–14 Paul describes two glorious elements in our salvation—being made spiritually alive and having our sins forgiven. But before those concepts can mean anything to us, he first portrays our condition before and apart from Christ. First, we were dead in our trespasses. Second, we were in debt to God infinitely beyond our capacity to pay.

But before I look at the first of these statements, a word is in order about Paul's description of the Colossians as "uncircumcised in the flesh" (v. 13).

The label "uncircumcised" was used by Jews of Gentiles as an expression of derision and scorn. When Paul refers to the uncircumcision of the flesh of the Colossians, he's not talking about their moral or ethical condition but of their ethnic identity as non-Jews. To be a Gentile meant that you were "separated from Christ, alienated from the commonwealth of Israel and strangers to the covenants of promise, having no hope and without God in the world" (Eph. 2:12). Paul's point here in Colossians 2:13 is that their ethnic identity is no longer a barrier to fellowship with God. God has forever broken down the wall between Jew and Gentile, having created in Christ one new man, the church (see Eph. 2:11ff.).

Now, let's look at his description of the Colossians (and us) as being formerly "dead in trespasses" (v. 13; see Eph. 2:1 for almost identical language).

The word translated "transgressions" means a false step, a blunder, a crossing over a known boundary. Paul says we were dead *in* our transgressions, which is to say because of or by reason of our transgressions. His point is to highlight the state or condition of spiritual death "in" which people languish.

But we have a problem. At first glance, to say that people are "dead" seems to run counter to human experience, for:

> lots of people who make no Christian profession whatever, who even openly repudiate Jesus Christ, appear to be very much alive. One has the vigorous body of an athlete, another the lively mind of a scholar, a third the vivacious personality of a film star. Are we to say that such people, if Christ has not saved them, are dead? Yes, indeed, we must and do say this very thing. For in the sphere which matters supremely (which is neither the body, nor the mind, nor the personality, but the soul) they have no life. And you can tell it. They are blind to the glory of Jesus Christ, and deaf to the voice of the Holy Spirit. They have no love for God, no sensitive awareness of his personal reality, no leaping of their spirit towards him in the cry, "Abba, Father", no longing for fellowship with his people. They are as unresponsive to him as a corpse. So we should not hesitate to affirm that a life without God (however physically fit and mentally alert the person may be) is a living death, and that those who live it are dead even while they are living.[10]

No one said it better than eighteenth-century revivalist George Whitefield:

> Come, ye dead, Christless, unconverted sinners, come and see the place where they laid the body of the deceased Lazarus; behold him laid out, bound hand and foot with grave-clothes, locked up and stinking in a dark cave, with a great stone placed on the top of it. View him again and again;

go nearer to him; be not afraid; smell him. Ah! How he stinketh. Stop there now, pause a while; and whilst thou art gazing upon the corpse of Lazarus, give me leave to tell thee with great plainness, but greater love, that this dead, bound entombed, stinking carcass, is but a faint representation of thy poor soul in its natural state: for, whether thou believest or not, thy spirit which thou bearest about with thee, sepulchred in flesh and blood, is as literally dead to God, and as truly dead in trespasses and sins, as the body of Lazarus was in the cave.

Was he bound hand and foot with grave-clothes? So art thou bound hand and foot with thy corruptions: and as a stone was laid on the sepulcher, so is there a stone of unbelief upon thy stupid heart. Perhaps thou hast lain in this state, not only four days, but many years, stinking in God's nostrils. And, what is still more effecting thou art as unable to raise thyself out of this loathsome, dead state, to a life of righteousness and true holiness, as ever Lazarus was to raise himself from the cave in which he lay so long. Thou mayest try the power of thy own boasted free-will, and the force and energy of moral persuasion and rational arguments (which, without all doubt, have their proper place in religion); but all thy efforts, exerted with never so much vigor, will prove quite fruitless and abortive, till that same Jesus, who said "Take away the stone" and cried "Lazarus, come forth," also quicken you.[11]

Make no mistake. Paul is not saying that people are born alive and gradually, through sinning, experience a slow process of spiritual and moral degeneration that eventually consummates in death. No! All people are born dead and remain dead until such time as God sovereignly infuses life and brings them by his Spirit to faith in Jesus Christ.

God made us alive together with Christ. Were ever more precious words uttered? Spiritually lifeless, morally decayed, in every way insensible to the beauty and sweetness of Jesus . . . until God, in sovereign mercy and grace, made us alive together with his Son. Praise God, from whom all blessings flow!

# 52

# Jesus Paid It All

## Colossians 2:13–14

And you, who were dead in your trespasses and the uncircumcision of your flesh, God made alive together with him, having forgiven us all our trespasses, by canceling the record of debt that stood against us with its legal demands. This he set aside, nailing it to the cross.

Most who are reading this are in some form of financial debt. Blessings to those of you who are not! But the majority of us owe money, either on a car or a home or a student loan, or something of the sort. Although it can be burdensome, most of us can at least see a light at the end of the tunnel. We are energized by the hope that one day it will be paid in full and we will receive from our creditors a piece of paper releasing us from any further obligation.

But to be burdened with a debt from which you will never be set free is simply too much to comprehend. To owe a debt that you know you can never pay off is psychologically devastating. Extend that indebtedness, and the penalty it incurs, into eternity and it becomes horrific beyond words.

Such was the reality of our spiritual indebtedness to God—until Jesus paid it all. This is the imagery Paul employs in Colossians 2:13–14 to describe the reality of having our sins forever forgiven: "And you, who were dead in your trespasses and the uncircumcision of your flesh, God made alive together with him, having forgiven us all our trespasses, by canceling the record of debt that stood against us with its legal demands. This he set aside, nailing it to the cross."

The translation "record of debt" reflects terminology often used with reference to an IOU, that is to say, a signed acknowledgement of indebtedness. It is something similar to our promissory note today in which the debtor affixes his or her signature to a document that binds the individual to pay the full amount by a certain date. Without using the same terminology Paul nevertheless makes the same point in Philemon 17–19 where he says, "So if you consider me your partner, receive him [Onesimus] as you would receive me. If he has wronged you at all, or owes you anything, charge that to my account. I, Paul, write this with my own hand: I will repay it." In other words, Paul was giving Philemon an IOU signed with his own hand, in which he obligated himself to pay in full whatever Onesimus might have owed.

What was this spiritual promissory note in Colossians 2:14? Was it the Mosaic law with its "commandments and ordinances" (Eph. 2:15)? If so (and this is an issue very much in dispute), Paul's point would be that the Jewish people were debtors to obey it in full. In the case of Gentiles, their conscience bound them to keep the moral law (cf. Rom. 2:14–16).

Note well that Paul not only says this record of debt was against us, insofar as we are guilty for having failed to pay it, but that it also poses a very real threat to us (the NASB brings this across with its phrase, "which was hostile to us"). The threat consists of the penalty that we incur for having failed to pay it in full. What was the penalty for nonpayment? Not just a bad credit record. Not the repossession of our property. Not merely imprisonment. The penalty was death.

Here again is the glorious good news of the gospel of God's grace in Jesus Christ. The way God forgave us all our trespasses (v. 13b) was by canceling our indebtedness to him. The word translated "canceling" has the sense of blotting out or erasing. God has wiped clean the slate! "I, I am he," declares the Lord, "who blots out your transgressions for my own sake, and I will not remember your sins" (Isa. 43:25).

But God didn't simply tear up the note, so to speak, and throw it away. He didn't say, "Don't worry folks. We'll just let bygones be bygones." The infinitely righteous One cannot pretend that our indebtedness never existed.

Instead, he cancelled the IOU of our spiritual obligation by nailing it to the cross. Some see here an allusion to the ancient practice of affixing to the cross an inscription of the crimes for which the person was being executed. If so, then God nails the accusation against us to the cross of Christ.

In any case, it is critical that we know there was no magic wand that waved off our guilt and made it disappear. God's justice and holiness are at stake here, no less so than our eternal destiny. That is why the payment must be made in full. We were buried beneath a mountain of spiritual bankruptcy. But God took that signed confession of indebtedness which stood as a perpetual witness against us and canceled it in the death of Christ.

We are no longer in default on the debt because Jesus paid it all! Whatever we owed, he paid. Whatever penalty we incurred, he endured. Well did the hymn writer declare:

> My sin, oh the bliss of this glorious thought,
> my sin not in part but the whole,
> was nailed to the cross and I bear it no more,
> Praise the Lord! Praise the Lord! O my soul.

And again,

> "Whatever curse was mine, He bore;
> The wormwood and the gall.
> There in that lone mysterious hour;
> My cup—He drained it all.

# 53

# Demons: Disarmed, Displayed, Defeated (1)

### Colossians 2:15

> He disarmed the rulers and authorities and put them to open shame, by triumphing over them in him.

I believe in the existence and activity of demonic spirits. I believe that spiritual warfare is all too real, that we must be discerning when it comes to "the schemes of the devil" (Eph. 6:11) and diligent in our efforts to "take up the whole armor of God" as we "stand firm" (Eph. 6:13) in the battle with principalities and powers.

We must take seriously Paul's reminder that our primary battle is not against "flesh and blood, but against the rulers, against the authorities, against the cosmic powers over this present darkness, against the spiritual forces of evil in the heavenly places" (Eph. 6:12). What makes this statement all the more amazing is that in Colossians 2:15 the same apostle declares that these very enemies against whom we fight have been disarmed, displayed, and defeated by the cross of Christ.

These are not contradictory assertions, as if Paul himself were confused about the status of Satan and his minions. It's simply his way of reminding us that we fight a defeated foe. Our enemy has received a deadly blow, his judgment has come, his doom is sealed. Though still prowling about as a roaring lion seeking whom he may devour (1 Pet. 5:8), his authority and power have been checked and his days are numbered.

Yes, we are engaged in a war, the outcome of which, however, has already been decided in our favor. We fight an enemy over whom we have complete authority and from whom we need fear nothing. He has been convicted and sentenced to death, and is but for a season out on bail.

I can't begin to imagine the incalculable spiritual harm that has come from failing to recognize the existence of the demonic realm. Ignorance of Satan's schemes and a reluctance to confront the enemy in biblically appropriate ways have opened the door to untold damage, oppression, and spiritual bondage. In the name of "cultural sophistication" and "intellectual respectability" (code words for pride), the demonic has either been denied altogether or, at best, relegated to a prescientific medieval mentality that is beneath the dignity of forward-thinking folk of the twenty-first century. In doing so, many in the professing church have opened wide the doors to demonic intrusion and are now suffering its debilitating and soul-numbing effects.

On the other hand, there is an equally unbiblical obsession with the demonic that virtually attributes to them a power reserved for God alone. For some believers it isn't the comforting assurance of Christ's gracious presence that thrills them, but the frightful prospect of "a demon behind every bush" that terrifies and paralyzes them (without for a moment denying that there are indeed multitudes of demons).

It isn't to the Lord Jesus Christ that such Christians pray in times of trouble and distress, entrusting themselves to his promised and loving care, but it is the devil whom they proceed to bind and denounce (without for a moment denying that we are commanded to resist the enemy).

It isn't to the Holy Spirit that they turn, to enable them to overcome the lusts of their own fallen, sinful flesh, but some demon on whom they are quick to blame every sin and catastrophe, and from whom they need to be delivered (without for a moment denying that deliverance is often precisely what is needed).

In Colossians Paul makes several important points that must guide our thinking and direct our behavior when it comes to this crucially important issue.

First, Satan and his demonic hosts are among those thrones and dominions and rulers and "authorities" that were created by the Son of God (Col. 1:16). Of course, he did not create them evil. He made all things good, but their rebellion is a well-documented biblical fact. My point is simply that Satan is "God's Devil." All demons are subject to the one who made them and even now upholds and sustains them in being (Col. 1:17).

Second, Satan and his hosts are indeed active and will continue to be until the coming of Christ. Paul warns the Colossians about "the elemental spirits of the world" (Col. 2:8) and elsewhere acknowledges the nefarious designs of Satan himself (2 Cor. 2:11).

Third, and most important of all, the forces of darkness were dealt a fatal blow at the cross of Christ. This is Paul's point in the text before us: "He disarmed the rulers and authorities and put them to open shame, by triumphing over them in him" (Col. 2:15). This glorious truth must govern our faith and undergird all encounters with the enemy.

You will never engage in spiritual warfare in a way that both honors Christ and encourages his people until you are energized by the truth that "he who is in you is greater than he who is in the world" (1 John 4:4b). The words of Jesus to the seventy-two disciples are as true today of you and me as they were then to them: "Behold, I have given you authority to tread on serpents and scorpions, and over all the power of the enemy, and nothing shall hurt you" (Luke 10:19).

One final comment is in order. What Paul describes in Colossians 2:15 was invisible to those standing at the foot of the cross. No one could see this remarkable phenomenon with their physical eyes. All they beheld at the moment of Christ's death was the crucifixion of a man on a Roman gibbet.

But the apostle assures us that in his death a great and glorious victory was achieved. In that cross the enemy of your soul was disrobed and disarmed. By means of that obscene instrument of execution the accuser of the brethren was put to open and public shame. It was at Calvary that our Lord triumphed over every demonic entity. Like those who witnessed this event two millennia ago, we also must accept it by faith, on the authority of Scripture. How this invisible victory was won through the visible agony of a man on a cross is the subject of our next meditation.

# 54

# Demons: Disarmed, Displayed, Defeated (2)

### Colossians 2:15

> He disarmed the rulers and authorities and put them to open shame, by triumphing over them in him.

What an incredibly encouraging passage this is! "He disarmed the rulers and authorities and put them to open shame, by triumphing over them in him" (Col. 2:15). Let's examine it, word by word.

We should begin by determining who the "He" is in verse 15 who is responsible for this remarkable triumph. Is the subject of this disarming God the Father or our Lord Jesus Christ or perhaps, in some sense, both of them? In verses 13 and 14 God the Father was clearly the subject of the saving action described, and it is most likely that such is the case here again in verse 15.

However, many years ago J. B. Lightfoot proposed an interpretation of this text that is not only fascinating and instructive but would also suggest that we view Jesus himself as the one who performed or achieved this disarming or disrobing of the rulers and authorities. But before we look at Lightfoot's theory, we need to be clear on who Paul has in mind when he refers to "rulers and authorities."

Some have argued that by "rulers and authorities" Paul is referring to holy, elect angels who in the Old Testament were portrayed as mediators of the Mosaic law. Thus by means of the cross God has stripped himself of the mediatorial ministry of angels, making a public display of them as inferior to Christ who alone is the mediator between God and man.

This is highly unlikely, though, given the violent terms employed: "disarm" or "strip away," "publicly display," as well as "triumph over." Most are agreed, therefore, that the "rulers and authorities" are fallen angelic hosts, whom we know as the devil and his demons. In fact, the terms Paul uses to describe them ("rulers and authorities") are standard vocabulary in the New Testament for demonic beings (see Eph. 1:20–21; 3:10; 6:10ff.; Rom. 8:38).

What precisely, then, is meant in saying that God disarmed the demonic hosts? The only other place in the New Testament where this verb is used is in Colossians 3:9 where Paul describes Christians as those who have "put off" the old self, which is to say, they have *laid aside* or *stripped themselves* of the old self as if it were a garment to be discarded.

Lightfoot contended that Paul's point is that whereas the powers of evil constantly attacked our Lord, assailing him throughout the course of his earthly ministry, Jesus by means of his atoning death stripped them from himself much as one would disrobe and cast aside an old and filthy garment.

Perhaps an illustration will help. In ancient mythology, Hercules once permitted his wife Deianira to be carried across a flooded stream by a centaur named Nessus. The centaur provoked Hercules by his rudeness and was subsequently shot with a poison arrow. As Nessus lay dying, he told Deianira to save his blood as a love charm. Later, when Hercules fell in love with Iole, Deianira dipped a robe in the blood of Nessus and sent it to her husband. When Hercules put it on, the poison began to eat away his flesh. In agony, he begged his friends to burn his body to end the ordeal.

Thus wrote Bishop Lightfoot: "The powers of evil which had clung like a Nessus robe about His [Christ's] humanity, were torn off and cast aside forever."[12] The demonic powers beset our Lord at every turn of his life and shrouded, as it were, his person with their poisonous hostility, much as the Nessus robe did the body of Hercules. But whereas the mythological hero was defeated by death, our Lord was victorious by means of it. In his crucifixion he stripped the forces of evil from himself as one would a tattered and ragged robe.

Lightfoot's is a vivid and instructive interpretation, but an unlikely one. Whereas the translation "disrobed" is a better rendering of this word than "disarmed," it is God the Father who, in effect, stripped the demons of their power and authority. So, yes, in a sense they have indeed been disarmed and defeated and are unworthy of either our honor or fear.

More than that, God has put them to open shame or made a public spectacle of them. This is a bit unusual, insofar as we humans cannot see or witness such an exposure of these spiritual beings. In what sense, then, were they put to open shame or made a public spectacle of?

There are two ways of answering this question. On the one hand, Paul may be referring to a display or spectacle visible only to the spiritual realm itself. In other words, it is before both the holy angels and the unholy, fallen hosts that this triumph was made known. In Ephesians 3:10 Paul says that it is through the church that the wisdom of God is being "made known to the rulers and authorities in the heavenly places." Clearly, it is important to God's purposes that the demonic realm sees or is aware of his wisdom as it is revealed in the salvation and ministry of the church on earth. Perhaps, then, the disrobing or disarming of the demonic hosts is made public to the unseen world of angels and demons alike as part of God's design to glorify himself in the salvation of sinners.

On the other hand, we may be guilty of pressing Paul's language beyond its proper bounds. It would seem he is making use of a common image in his day to make a theological point. In other words, our problem may be that we are expecting some literal manifestation of a truth that is described in obviously metaphorical terms. Let me explain.

The verse actually says that he "put them to open shame, *by triumphing over them* in him." In other words, the way in which the rulers and authorities were put to open shame was by being subject to the "triumphal procession" of God in Christ. The word translated "triumphing" (used elsewhere in the New Testament only in 2 Corinthians 2:14) was descriptive of a Roman general parading his captives behind him as the spoil and booty of war, all of which was designed to humiliate them and bring public attention to their subjugation.

Thus, Paul's point here may simply be that God's defeat of the demonic hosts is like that of an earthly military commander's triumph over and public display of his enemies. We are not to look for some specific time or event or way in which this "open shame" of the demonic hosts was made known or visible. Rather, we are to rest assured and rejoice in the promise that our spiritual enemies were as thoroughly defeated and stripped of their dignity and power as were those physical enemies who unsuccessfully opposed and were eventually conquered by a Roman general and his army.

But surely the most stunning statement of all is the final phrase of verse 15. It was *in* or *through* or *by* the cross that this victory was achieved. The ESV renders it, "in him," as if referring to Christ. This is certainly possible, but I think it more likely that the antecedent in view is the cross of verse 14, to which God is said to have nailed our sins.

Amazing! The very instrument that to all eyes appeared to seal Christ's doom was his tool of triumph. In a marvelous twist of divine irony, the cross, the emblem of disgrace and death by which the demonic hosts thought they had defeated Christ, is turned on them and becomes the instrument of their humiliating demise. F. F. Bruce writes:

> As our Lord was suspended there, bound hand and foot to the wood in apparent weakness, [the rulers and authorities] imagined they had Him at their mercy, and flung themselves upon Him with hostile intent. But, far from suffering their assault without resistance, He grappled with them and mastered them, stripping them of all the armor in which they trusted, and held them aloft in His mighty, outstretched hands, displaying to the universe their helplessness and his own unvanquished strength.... Now they are disabled and dethroned, and the shameful tree has become the victor's triumphal chariot, before which His captives are driven in humiliating procession, the involuntary and impotent confessors of their overcomer's superiority.[13]

John Calvin put it best: "For there is no tribunal so magnificent, no throne so stately, no show of triumph so distinguished, no chariot so elevated, as is the gibbet on which Christ has subdued death and the devil, nay more, has utterly trodden them under His feet."[14]

The bottom line is this: spiritual authority is in the name of Christ, the balance of power rests with us, and the ultimate outcome has been settled in our favor. We do not fear those who have suffered a decisive defeat, but our faith is in God. Therefore, we stand firm, resisting the enemy with the assurance that he will flee.

# 55
# Legalism Can Be Lethal
## *Colossians 2:16–23*

Therefore let no one pass judgment on you in questions of food and drink, or with regard to a festival or a new moon or a Sabbath. These are a shadow of the things to come, but the substance belongs to Christ. Let no one disqualify you, insisting on asceticism and worship of angels, going on in detail about visions, puffed up without reason by his sensuous mind, and not holding fast to the Head, from whom the whole body, nourished and knit together through its joints and ligaments, grows with a growth that is from God. If with Christ you died to the elemental spirits of the world, why, as if you were still alive in the world, do you submit to regulations—"Do not handle, Do not taste, Do not touch" (referring to things that all perish as they are used)—according to human precepts and teachings? These have indeed an appearance of wisdom in promoting self-made religion and asceticism and severity to the body, but they are of no value in stopping the indulgence of the flesh.

This paragraph is probably the most difficult one in the book of Colossians to interpret. It is also difficult to apply, given the fact that the false teaching that provoked Paul to write what he did doesn't find a perfect counterpart in our day and time. But there are enough parallels between what the Colossians faced in the first century and what we face today to make our study of this text relevant and meaningful.

Perhaps the best way to explain this passage is to provide you with a summary of its argument. I encourage you to carefully read the text above, as it is found in the ESV, and then to prayerfully read through my brief synopsis of what I understand it to mean. In subsequent meditations we will return to this paragraph several times to focus on specific items that are of special concern for us today.

The false teachers claimed that they were able to attain a heightened form of spirituality and holiness independently of Jesus Christ (v. 19). At its heart, then, this false teaching advocated a pathway to fullness and favor with God that refused to rest satisfied in all that we have in Jesus Christ alone (similar to what Paul said earlier in 2:1–10).

In order to achieve this elite status, they insisted that a person must follow a rigorously ascetic approach to life. This entailed abstinence from strong drink, most likely wine, and certain kinds of food, perhaps meat (v. 16a). One was also expected to be meticulous in the observance of certain religious festivals and holy days (v. 16b).

This particular form of asceticism required that one deny himself basic bodily needs and be willing to endure other forms of physical mistreatment (vv. 18, 23; I can't help but think of Silas, the albino Opus Dei monk made [in]famous in Dan Brown's *The Da Vinci Code*).

The leaders of this movement had created a long list of proscribed activities from which one must be diligent to abstain (vv. 21–22). If a person proved faithful in abiding by these extra-biblical and ascetic practices, and engaged in fervent worship of angels (v. 18a), one might expect to receive religious visions in which things inaccessible to the ordinary believer were seen and experienced (v. 18b). All this served to mark them out as spiritually superior when compared to the average individual.

The apostle's response to such alleged "religious" behavior is pointed and unequivocal. He tells us that we should not let such people judge us as inferior or disqualify us from attaining the ultimate prize (i.e., fellowship and acceptance with God) simply because we don't follow their instructions (vv. 16, 18). After all, Old Testament religious festivals and holy days were a mere shadow pointing to Jesus Christ in whom they are all fulfilled (v. 17). In other words, if we have him, we don't need them.

As much as you might think that this sort of "religious" commitment is the height of spirituality, it is in fact the product of fleshly and ungodly thoughts (v. 18) and is the result of refusing to seek strength and guidance and growth from God through the person of Jesus Christ (v. 19).

After all, if you have died with Christ (as verses 11 to 15 indicate you have), why would you want to go on living as if the world and those demonic spirits that seek to control it are in charge of your life (v. 20)? So resist their efforts to enslave you (v. 20)! Fight against the inclination to submit to their demands and decrees (vv. 20–21). They are obsessed with religious activities and material things that will ultimately decay and perish and have no place in the life of the age to come (v. 22a). Furthermore, their approach to godliness is manmade; it didn't come from God (v. 22b). They made it up themselves to promote their own religious agenda (v. 23).

The allure of such behavior is that on the surface it looks so spiritual. It appears wise and effective in gaining control over one's fleshly desires (v. 23). But it does no such thing. Afflicting the body or demanding of oneself practices that the Bible nowhere endorses may make one look uniquely committed to God and on one's way to defeating temptation and conquering the impulses of the flesh, but it is all an illusion (v. 23).

Clearly Paul is addressing a particularly lethal form of legalism that was threatening the life and freedom and joy of the Colossian church. Our next task will be to examine particular items in this spiritually destructive perversion of true Christianity.

# 56

# Don't Let Them Judge You

## Colossians 2:16–17

**Therefore let no one pass judgment on you in questions of food and drink, or with regard to a festival or a new moon or a Sabbath. These are a shadow of the things to come, but the substance belongs to Christ.** Let no one disqualify you, insisting on asceticism and worship of angels, going on in detail about visions, puffed up without reason by his sensuous mind, and not holding fast to the Head, from whom the whole body, nourished and knit together through its joints and ligaments, grows with a growth that is from God. If with Christ you died to the elemental spirits of the world, why, as if you were still alive in the world, do you submit to regulations—"Do not handle, Do not taste, Do not touch" (referring to things that all perish as they are used)—according to human precepts and teachings? These have indeed an appearance of wisdom in promoting self-made religion and asceticism and severity to the body, but they are of no value in stopping the indulgence of the flesh.

There is a sense in which divine grace will always be a threat to human nature. Why a threat, you ask? Because grace undermines our efforts to justify ourselves. Grace runs counter to human pride and that impulse we all feel to boast in our own accomplishments. Grace requires that we defer all praise to God. Grace undermines our best efforts at establishing a list of requirements and prohibitions that we can impose on ourselves and others as the condition on which we gain acceptance with God. Grace demands only one thing: that all glory and honor and credit be given to Jesus

Christ for what he has done, not for what we have done. And human nature instinctively hates that.

That is why wherever the gospel of grace is preached, legalism rears its ugly head. Once you declare that God has graciously provided everything we need in the person and work of Jesus Christ, you can rest assured that fallen human nature will rise up in protest and try to sneak in somewhere a rule or regulation that we, in our strength, can fulfill, or an observance or ritual that we, without God's enabling power, can perform that will enhance our spiritual standing or gain some reward that will put God in our debt.

The Colossians had heard and received, by grace, the gospel of grace. They had turned from self-reliance and prideful self-justification to rest wholly in the all-sufficiency of what God had done for them in Jesus Christ alone. But there were some folk in Colossae, as there are similar folk everywhere in our day, who refused to leave well enough alone. We know what they were up to because of Paul's passionate, indeed heated, exhortation: don't let them judge you! (Col. 2:16a).

The focus of these false teachers was multiple and varied, but in verses 16 and 17 Paul mentions two things in particular. First, the enemies of grace were insisting that the Colossians abstain from certain food and drink. This is probably not a reference to Old Testament dietary regulations, because the Mosaic law contained no significant prohibitions concerning what a person drinks (there were a few exceptions, of course, as in the case of those who took a Nazarite vow).

Rather, these people were probably demanding abstinence from meat and strong wine regardless of the amount of intake. They were most likely convinced that abstinence *per se* was inherently more pleasing to God than participation. In other words, like many today they believed that self-denial was intrinsically more spiritual or an indication of greater fervency for God, regardless of what the activity or experience might be. The self-discipline allegedly required to say no to the offer of something to eat or drink was thought to be a mark of genuine piety and commitment.

Perhaps they feared that by partaking of certain foods and drink or participating in certain practices they would be *spiritually infected* in some way. They might have believed that partaking would diminish their religious fervor and perhaps expose them to even greater evils. Nowhere is this perspective endorsed in the New Testament. It is true, of course, that those who overindulge and drink or eat to excess are rebuked (drunkenness is never permissible). But that is not because partaking is itself inherently less godly than abstinence.

Evidently the heretics in Colossae were declaring that those who enjoyed their freedom in Christ to eat and drink within the parameters established in Scripture stood condemned or were on the threshold of loss of divine approval or some such notion. "No," said Paul. "Don't let them judge you!"

The second feature of this particular brand of legalism indicates there may well have been a Jewish element involved, for the "festival" and "new moon" and "Sabbath" are no doubt a reference to the holy days of the Jewish calendar (specifically, the annual, monthly, and weekly observances). This very language is used often in the Old Testament to describe the sacred times binding on all under the Mosaic covenant (see 1 Chron. 23:31; 2 Chron. 2:4; 31:3; Ezek. 45:17; Hos. 2:11).

These observances, says Paul, were but a "shadow of the things to come" (v. 17a). The phrase "things to come," of course, is not a reference to what is future to Paul, but what was future to those who lived when the obligation to abide by these holy days was in force (cf. 1 Cor. 5:7–8; Heb. 8:5; 10:1). During the time of the Mosaic covenant they certainly had their place and fulfilled a glorious divine purpose. But that purpose was to point to Christ. They were adumbrations of a greater and more substantive reality that is now present in its fullness in Jesus Christ and all that we have by faith in him.

That is why Paul exhorts the Colossians (and us) not to let anyone suggest they are sub-Christian if they choose not to celebrate these festivals or observe the regulations associated with them during the time of the old covenant. Everything they symbolized, everything they foreshadowed, everything they were designed to teach and accomplish has now come to full and final fruition in Jesus.

Are Christians free to abstain from certain foods and drink? By all means, yes, so long as they do not impose their choice on others or suggest that others have fallen short of what is acceptable to God.

Are Christians free to observe those religious holy days mentioned in verse 16b? Yes. But not because they think that God, for that reason, now regards them as more holy or more committed or more acceptable than those who do not observe them.

Indeed, if you now have in Christ everything and more than those days were designed to provide, why would you want to observe them? Would not your observance come perilously close to denying that the fulfillment that is in Christ has come? Would not your observance have the potential to undermine enjoyment of who Christ is and what he has accomplished by continually taking you back to the age of shadows and types?

In any case, we would do well to heed Paul's counsel. Beware the legalists! Beware those who pass judgment on spiritual worthiness based on practices and observances that God does not require. What his grace has provided for us in Christ is enough. Period.

# 57
# Don't Let Them Disqualify You

## Colossians 2:18–19

Therefore let no one pass judgment on you in questions of food and drink, or with regard to a festival or a new moon or a Sabbath. These are a shadow of the things to come, but the substance belongs to Christ. **Let no one disqualify you, insisting on asceticism and worship of angels, going on in detail about visions, puffed up without reason by his sensuous mind, and not holding fast to the Head, from whom the whole body, nourished and knit together through its joints and ligaments, grows with a growth that is from God.** If with Christ you died to the elemental spirits of the world, why, as if you were still alive in the world, do you submit to regulations—"Do not handle, Do not taste, Do not touch" (referring to things that all perish as they are used)—according to human precepts and teachings? These have indeed an appearance of wisdom in promoting self-made religion and asceticism and severity to the body, but they are of no value in stopping the indulgence of the flesh.

Coaches today, at all levels of athletic competition, will often deliberately get themselves kicked out of a game as a way of motivating their team. They may well have to pay a fine and perhaps lose the respect of certain fans, but they regard it as worth the price if it will serve to light a fire in the hearts of otherwise lethargic and apathetic players.

When Paul tells the Colossian Christians, "Let no one disqualify you" (v. 18a), he uses a word that in ancient times often meant something along the lines of, "to render an adverse decision against someone," or "to act as an umpire against you," hence "to declare you disqualified." Paul's point, if I may be permitted to stretch the athletic metaphor, is: "Don't let anyone throw you out of the ballgame for allegedly having violated rules that God has never imposed."

On what basis did these legalists dare suggest that the Christians at Colossae had failed to meet the standards of true discipleship and were therefore spiritually disqualified?

F. F. Bruce answers this question, at least in part, by reminding us:

> Some people love to make a parade of exceptional piety. They pretend to have found the way to a higher plane of spiritual experience, as though they had been initiated into sacred mysteries which give them an infinite advantage over the uninitiated. Others are overprone to be taken in by such people, for this kind of claim impresses those who always fall for the idea of an 'inner ring.' But (says the apostle) don't be misled by such people.[15]

Don't let them disqualify you.

Paul mentions five things characteristic of this sort of "spiritual snobbery." First, they insist on "asceticism" (v. 18a). The word here is the one typically translated "humility" in the New Testament. Obviously, though, Paul employs it in a negative capacity. The NASB renders it "self-abasement," the idea being that people willingly embrace lowliness and even suffering to enhance their appearance of piety. It is, then, a false humility (and is translated this way by the NIV), the kind in which a person proudly wears a medal for being so meek.

A few have argued that the word could also mean fasting and other forms of bodily rigor and self-deprivation that would set them apart as especially committed and thus uniquely worthy of honor and praise. In fact, in Colossians 2:23 Paul again uses the word "asceticism" and associates it with "severity to the body." If that is in Paul's mind, he would be referring to what Jesus denounced in Matthew 6:16: "And when you fast [indicating that he expected his followers to do so], do not look gloomy like the hypocrites, for they disfigure their faces that their fasting may be seen by others."

So, let's be clear on this. If Paul is referring to fasting (and it's by no means certain that he is), he is not denouncing the practice *per se*, but rather its perversion. If fasting, or any bodily discipline, is unduly elevated as an essential mark of true spirituality or is employed as a means of parading our piety before others and asserting our superiority over them, it must be denounced. But if it is pursued for the right reasons and practiced according to biblical guidelines, it can be of immense spiritual benefit.[16]

Second, they are engaged in the "worship of angels" (v. 18b). This is a notoriously controversial statement due to the ambiguity of Paul's words. I'll try to explain briefly the options for its interpretation.

On the one hand, it could refer to the worship that the angels themselves offer to God (cf. Rev. 4–5). If so, the false teachers were claiming to be extraordinarily spiritual because their worship of God was not in association with that of other, merely human, participants, but was an elevated and exceptionally unique experience in which they joined with the angelic hosts in heaven to praise God.

I'm not inclined to accept this view for two reasons. First, although it is grammatically possible, it is not probable. But second, and more important, why would it be regarded as illicit for Christians to join with the angels in the worship and honor of God? On what grounds would a select few claim that they alone had this privilege? We are told in Hebrews 12:22 that we "have come to Mount Zion and to the city of the living God, the heavenly Jerusalem, and to innumerable angels in festal gathering." The latter may well refer to angels engaged in worship. And there is no indication in Revelation 4–5 that John was in danger of sinning were he to have praised God in the midst of the myriads of angelic hosts who were doing so. So, I find it a stretch to say that Paul was denouncing the idea of worshiping with angels. This would be grounds for rebuke only if it were a claim made by an exclusive and elitist inner circle who insisted they had an access to the heavenly celebration that other, lesser saints did not.

Then, of course, Paul could mean that these heretics were worshiping angels, giving to them the praise and honor that only God is due (cf. Rev. 19:10; 22:8–9). However, if this were the case, why didn't Paul more severely and explicitly denounce such a practice as the blasphemous idolatry that it is?

There is another option. David Garland points out that "some have claimed that the Colossian errorists understood these angels to be involved in creation and the government of the world, and they worshipped them as their link to God. These angels could be regarded as malevolent and needing appeasement or as benevolent and bestowing blessing. Their so-called 'worship' may only have involved propitiating them to ward off their evil effects or beseeching them for protection."[17]

In other words, the word translated "worship" could well mean something more along the lines of "invoke" or "conjure." These folk, then, are guilty of engaging in the somewhat magical solicitation of angels to ward off evil or to provide physical protection or to bestow blessing and success on their daily endeavors.

In any case, there was in Colossae (and oftentimes in our own day) an excessive and inappropriate preoccupation with angels and their involvement in human life that Paul regarded as detracting from the centrality and supremacy of Jesus Christ. We would do well to heed his warning!

Third, they made their case for super-spirituality based on alleged visions they had seen (v. 18c). Perhaps they claimed to experience these visions as a result of extensive fasting and bodily self-discipline or even while caught up in the rapturous joy and ecstatic swirl of angelic worship (depending again on what that means, of course). In any case, they perceive themselves to be members of an exclusive club of spiritual elitists on the strength of bizarre and supernatural experiences. Only those who have "been there and done that" are truly "qualified" to stand in God's presence.

Once again, a word of qualification is in order. Paul's denunciation of their visionary experiences is not a blanket indictment of all revelatory encounters. Paul himself had visions (cf. Acts 18:9–10; 2 Cor. 12:1–10), as did Peter (Acts 10:9ff.) and Ananias (Acts 9:10ff.), just to mention a few. Indeed, Peter described revelatory visions to be characteristic of the work of the Spirit in the present age (Acts 2:17ff.). Paul's concern, therefore, is with elitist claims based on alleged visionary experiences that people use to disqualify so-called lesser saints. These are purported supernatural encounters that lead not to godliness but to arrogance, as the next point makes clear.

Fourth, they are puffed up without reason because of a sensuous mind, or more literally, "the mind of the flesh" (v. 18d). I find it instructive that it is possible to be engaged in numerous "spiritual" activities of a profound supernatural orientation and yet be utterly controlled and driven by the flesh. Beware of those who are constantly parading themselves and building their ministries (as well as their bank accounts) on the basis of repeated extraordinary miraculous experiences (again, without denying that the latter occasionally do occur).

Fifth, and finally, their fundamental problem, as verse 19 makes clear, is that they seek their spiritual strength and sustenance and guidance from something other than Jesus Christ. But God has ordained that true growth, authentic godliness, and a life that pleases and praises him is derived from a conscious dependence upon and drawing of nourishment from the head of the church, Jesus.

In conclusion, I believe in fasting, the ministry of angels, and revelatory visions. But when these (or any other religious activities) are pompously cited as signs of a super-spirituality and exploited for personal gain and fame, we would do well to heed Paul's counsel and warning.

# 58

# Don't Let Them Enslave You

## Colossians 2:20–23

Therefore let no one pass judgment on you in questions of food and drink, or with regard to a festival or a new moon or a Sabbath. These are a shadow of the things to come, but the substance belongs to Christ. **Let no one disqualify you, insisting on asceticism and worship of angels, going on in detail about visions, puffed up without reason by his sensuous mind, and not holding fast to the Head, from whom the whole body, nourished and knit together through its joints and ligaments, grows with a growth that is from God. If with Christ you died to the elemental spirits of the world, why, as if you were still alive in the world, do you submit to regulations—"Do not handle, Do not taste, Do not touch" (referring to things that all perish as they are used)—according to human precepts and teachings? These have indeed an appearance of wisdom in promoting self-made religion and asceticism and severity to the body, but they are of no value in stopping the indulgence of the flesh.**

Perhaps the most insidious form of legalism is asceticism. Not all asceticism is bad. Many in the church could do with a little self-discipline and self-restraint. We live in an overly indulgent society in which at times the only sin seems to be abstinence. Paul referred to godly asceticism when he spoke of buffeting his body and making it his slave, preparatory to running a race so that he might win (1 Cor. 9:24–27).

Sinful asceticism, on the other hand, is the sort that he describes in Colossians 2:20–23. Here he has in mind those who impose manmade rules concerning the body and one's behavior as a means for enhancing one's relationship with God. For the ascetic, the body is a thing to be punished, denied, even abused. The body is regarded as evil and the only way to defeat it is to starve it of anything that might spark desire. Steps are taken to diminish the intake of food and drink to an irreducible minimum. In brief, *asceticism is the belief that if you add up enough physical negatives you will get a spiritual positive*. Mere avoidance becomes the pathway to holiness.

The apostle's point here is "that baptism into Christ's death means death to all this 'stuff'—however and whenever it manifests itself. The key defense for Christians against such error is to hold fast to Christ, 'the Head,' and to recognize that we have died with Christ to the elemental spirits reigning over this world with their various rules and ordinances. When we recognize that we are secure in Christ, we will not be bumped off course by the judgments of others who want to disqualify us in some way."[18] Paul's response to the legalistic approach to the Christian life is unmerciful. He faults it on four grounds.

First, all such things "perish as they are used" (v. 22a). The things included in their list of taboos are perishable objects of the material world, destined to dissipate even as they are being used.

Second, such rules are manmade, not divinely given. They are, Paul says, "according to human precepts and teachings" (v. 22b). As noted in an earlier lesson, this is the essence of legalism: the demand that others conform to your conscience when God has remained silent. Such rules come not by divine revelation but by human ingenuity.

Third, this approach to spiritual living only seems to be wise. Says Paul, "these have indeed an appearance of wisdom in promoting self-made religion and asceticism and severity to the body" (v. 23a). When you look at people so dedicated and disciplined denying themselves the ordinary amenities of life, it is easy to be deceived by the appearance of spirituality. Such people look committed and pious and holy. But appearances can indeed be deceiving.

Fourth, and finally, is perhaps Paul's most important statement. Notwithstanding the surface spirituality that such religious activities produce, "they are of no value in stopping the indulgence of the flesh" (v. 23b). Rules and prohibitions and self-denial that spring from man's own religious creativity are utterly ineffective in curbing the desires of the flesh. The flesh mocks any such attempt to inhibit its expression. Asceticism, in and of itself, won't help you keep in check sinful urgings or energize you in the war with temptation.

What will? Surely Paul will do more than merely denounce what is ineffective. Surely he will offer a more biblical alternative. Well, of course he will. Unfortunately, the division made between chapters 2 and 3 in his epistle to the Colossians tends to obscure his point. Paul was not responsible for this division. Like all chapter and verse divisions in the New Testament, it was the work of religious scribes and biblical scholars of subsequent generations.

Paul does indeed have a remedy for fleshly indulgence, a remarkably simple one. It is found in the immediately following verses of chapter 3: "If then you have been raised with Christ, *seek the things that are above, where Christ is,* seated at the right hand of God. *Set your minds on things that are above,* not on things that are on earth" (Col. 3:1–2).

The italicized phrases in these two verses are simply another way of saying what I've already articulated on numerous other occasions: holiness, in this case the ability to say no to fleshly indulgence (2:23b), comes not from rigorous asceticism or self-restraint but from a mind captivated and controlled by the beauty and majesty of the risen Christ and all that we are in him in the heavenlies.

Part 3

*Colossians* 3:1–25

# 59

# Fighting Pleasure with Pleasure

## Colossians 3:1–4

If then you have been raised with Christ, seek the things that are above, where Christ is, seated at the right hand of God. Set your minds on things that are above, not on things that are on earth. For you have died, and your life is hidden with Christ in God. When Christ who is your life appears, then you also will appear with him in glory.

Regardless of where I go or where I speak I can always count on at least one constant reality, one common thread that unites all Christians and all denominations and all churches: they all struggle with the temptation to sin and want to know how to defeat it and break free of its paralyzing grip.

I've said many times and written of it in my books that the church, to a large degree, has failed in its well-meant efforts to equip Christians to wage war against the world, the flesh, and the devil. Typically today (and throughout history) the approach to getting people to do what is right is telling them in a very loud, angry, and threatening voice, "Don't do what is wrong!" We've operated under the assumption that if we portray the horrid consequences of sin in sufficiently graphic and revolting terms, we will succeed in motivating the human will to turn from it.

I'm not suggesting that sin doesn't have horrid and devastating consequences. It most certainly does, now and especially in eternity. Nor am I suggesting that we cease telling people to abstain from sin or that we tone down the urgency with which we warn them concerning its deceitful and destructive ways.

But if all we bring to bear against the incredibly powerful allure of sensual self-indulgence is a "Just Say No!" campaign, we don't stand much of a chance. Any approach to resisting temptation that consists solely (or even primarily) of a teeth-gritting, fist-clenching, will-wracking resolve not to yield will ultimately fail. Or, if it does manage to succeed in the short term, it will produce a joyless and mean-spirited legalism that will hardly prove attractive either to Christians or non-Christians.

What's missing in our battle with temptation? Without intending to be simplistic, it's the failure to understand the source of sin's allure. We sin because it feels good! Sin is hard to resist because it has a remarkable capacity to please. The author of Hebrews spoke of the "passing pleasures of sin" (Heb. 11:25 NASB; the ESV renders it "the fleeting pleasures of sin"). Granted, the pleasure sin brings is passing, transient, and fleeting. But it's still a pleasure! That's why we so readily yield to it.

The bottom line is this: when faced with temptation, the immediate gratification of sin will almost always triumph over the fear of its long-term consequences.

The only way to defeat the power of sin's promise of pleasure is by faith in God's promise of a superior pleasure. Paul concluded chapter 2 of Colossians with an indictment of any attempt to defeat the promptings of the flesh by the imposition of ascetic, legalistic, extra-biblical regulations. If they provide only an illusion of victory over fleshly impulses, what will actually work? Is there an alterative? Yes.

As I said in the previous meditation, Paul will do more than merely denounce what is ineffective in our battle with the flesh. His recommendation is found in Colossians 3:1–2: "If then you have been raised with Christ, seek the things that are above, where Christ is, seated at the right hand of God. Set your minds on things that are above, not on things that are on earth."

These two verses are simply another way of saying what I've already articulated on numerous other occasions: holiness, in this case the ability to say no to "the indulgence of the flesh" and the passionate desire to walk in the way of Christ (2:23b), comes not primarily from rigorous asceticism or self-restraint but from a mind captivated and controlled by the beauty and majesty of the risen Lord and all that we are in him in the heavenlies.

Yielding to fleshly urges is overcome by seeking the things above. Fixing our minds on things above leaves little time or mental energy for earthly fantasies. The heart that is entranced by the risen Christ is not easily seduced by "the things that are on earth" (v. 2b). Paul uses language that requires both the energetic orientation of our will ("keep seeking") as well as the singular devotion of our mind ("set your mind"). This is a conscious and volitionally deliberate movement of the soul to fix and ground itself on, indeed to glut itself in, if you will, the beauty of spiritual realities as opposed to the trivial and tawdry things of this world.

We must seek the things above because that is where Christ is (v. 1). He is the exalted center and supreme sovereign of the eternal and heavenly realm. Why would we want our lives and thoughts and actions fixed anywhere else? The appeal of heavenly things is the presence of Jesus. It is the glory and beauty and multifaceted personality and power and splendor of the risen Christ to which Paul directs our attention.

The apostle is not averse to calling us away from the earthly and transient temptations of the flesh. In fact, in Colossians 3:5–6 he grounds his appeal to abstain from immorality, impurity, and idolatry in the impending reality of divine wrath, but only *after*, and I believe *because*, he has something incomparably more grand and glorious to which he has already called us, namely, Jesus and the grandeur of things above. This, I believe Paul would have us know, is of *great value against fleshly indulgence*.

# 60

# Celebrating Christocentricity!

## Colossians 3:1–4

> If then you have been raised with Christ, seek the things that are above, where Christ is, seated at the right hand of God. Set your minds on things that are above, not on things that are on earth. For you have died, and your life is hidden with Christ in God. When Christ who is your life appears, then you also will appear with him in glory.

Among the many incredible statements in Psalm 16, consider David's declaration in verse 2: "I say to the Lord, 'You are my Lord; I have no good apart from you.'" I fear that if I were honest with myself, I'd be forced to identify a number of things in life I consider "good" that bear no relation to Christ Jesus. I'm grieved by that. It's another way of saying that my life isn't nearly as Christocentric (now that's a word worth memorizing!) as it should be.

This is what makes Colossians 3:1–4 so indescribably important. Let's take a closer look at this stunning statement concerning the centrality of Christ.

The opening statement in Colossians 3:1 ("If then you have been raised with Christ") parallels what Paul said earlier in 2:20 ("If with Christ you died . . ."). Paul's Christocentric focus is unmistakable: for the Christian, everything makes sense only when seen in terms of our identity, relationship, and union with Christ. We are with him in his death and with him in his rising. Indeed, as verse 4 makes clear, we are also destined to be with him in glory when he comes again to this earth to consummate his kingdom.

Dying with Christ points to the definitive and irreversible split with the old life in which we were once immersed (3:2). We are to be as lifeless and insensible to it as a corpse is to the stimuli of the world in which it once existed. Likewise, being raised with Christ points to our new status that requires a new ethic and a new lifestyle (one that Paul will outline in some detail in verse 5ff.).

By virtue of our having died with Christ we have been set free *from* something (namely, the elemental powers; see 2:8, 20). By virtue of our having been raised with Christ we have also been set free *for* something (namely, a new life in him). Our death with Christ severed any links we had with the values and life of the present world order, and our resurrection with Christ united or connected us with the new, heavenly, eternal order. Or again, we died with him to *our old ways* and have been raised with him to *his new ways*.

So let me emphasize the Christocentricity of the apostle once again: we have been raised with Christ in the past (3:1), we are hidden with Christ in the present (3:3), and we will be revealed with Christ in the future (3:4). Not to be connected or united to Christ by grace alone through faith alone ends all hope of a break with the past, a power for the present, or glory in the future.

We have no independent life of our own. We can claim no right in our bodies or minds or souls or possessions. The only life that we now have is actually the life of Christ in us. Therefore our interests must be identical with his. Our goals and aims and vision must be coextensive with his. All that is precious and dear to him should be to us as well. All that is alien and offensive to him should affect us in the same way.

This isn't to suggest that we can attain sinless perfection in this life. Paul makes it clear that our experience of final and full glory comes only at the second advent of Jesus (v. 4; cf. 1 John 3:1–3). But in the light of what has already happened to us (we died, were buried, and now are raised with Christ) and in light of what will happen to us (we will share his glory when he is revealed) our lives must be radically different, radically other-worldly, radically sin-denying and Christ-affirming.

Once again, the only reason, the sole ground, for Paul's exhortation to set our hearts and minds on the things above is that this is "where Christ is, seated at the right hand of God" (v. 1; an allusion to Psalm 110, the most quoted psalm in the New Testament). We don't seek things that are above because that it is where the things are, but because the things are where Christ is.

Things above have no value or appeal except insofar as they reveal Christ, focus on Christ, and bring us more of Christ. We are not to read Paul's words as if he had in view heavenly *stuff*, whether treasures or streets of gold or rewards for earthly obedience. The things that are above, those things that are to be the focus of our concentrated pursuit, are Christological things. Apart from him, they lose their luster. Apart from him, they have no power to please. Apart from him, heavenly things would be no better than hellish torments.

Perhaps we should pause to identify those things below that hinder our focus on the things above. What earthly entanglements exert a downward drag on your soul? What worldly attractions have become distractions and keep your mind off Christ? What fleshly affections compete with passion for him? The power to disengage from and triumph over all such rival pleasures will come only as we see and savor him who is above.

Oh, Father, make known to us the glory of your Son! Oh, Spirit, shine the light of the knowledge of the glory of Christ Jesus into our hearts! Blind us to all but him. Captivate us with his splendor that we, like Moses, might say no to the passing pleasures of sin (Heb. 11:25–26). Help us to rest in Christ alone as the treasure greater than all earthly rewards. Amen.

# 61

# Was Paul (Am I, Are You) a Gnostic?

## Colossians 3:1–4

If then you have been raised with Christ, seek the things that are above, where Christ is, seated at the right hand of God. Set your minds on things that are above, not on things that are on earth. For you have died, and your life is hidden with Christ in God. When Christ who is your life appears, then you also will appear with him in glory.

Gnosticism is an insidious evil. Whata-cism? Gnosticism. Indeed, few things are as great a threat to godly Christian living as the modern manifestations of this ancient heresy. Some of you may not be familiar with the term, so allow me to explain briefly the sense in which I use it here.

One of the more fundamental elements in Gnosticism is its disdain for the material, earthly realm in favor of a spiritual or other-worldly orientation. This is because according to Gnosticism, matter is inherently evil and spirit is good. Salvation comes by a special knowledge (*gnosis* in Greek) of the truth available only to a super-spiritual elite who have been initiated into the mysteries of the world above.

Being averse to the material or physical creation, most Gnostics denied the humanity of Christ as well as his literal, physical death. They also scoffed at any suggestion of a bodily resurrection, whether his or ours.

This perspective invariably led to a disregard for normal, routine responsibilities and relationships in this life. The things on earth are destined to perish. They are irredeemable. Only heavenly, immaterial realities are eternal.

I mention this (in ever so brief description) simply because some might misconstrue Paul's language in Colossians 3:1–4 (and my comments in a previous study) as an endorsement of Gnosticism. After all, he calls on Christians to seek things that are above, not things on the earth. We are to be "heavenly minded," to use the contemporary phrase. Does this perspective contribute to an otherworldliness that treats with contempt, or at best a benign neglect, the earth and nature and normal human endeavors?

Is there in Paul's perspective and language an encouragement to Christians to ignore social injustice today in anticipation of the vindication of righteousness in the age to come? Is Paul suggesting that we carelessly exploit the environment now, knowing that we shall one day live in the pristine glory of a new heavens and a new earth? The answer to these and related questions that reflect a metaphysical dualism between spirit and matter, between heaven and earth, is a resounding no!

The terms used by Paul, "above" and "on the earth," are not spatially literal but point to two opposing ethical realms, indeed two antithetical world systems with corresponding antithetical worldviews. In saying that Christ and God are "above" does not mean they are absent from the earth or uninvolved with what happens in the world in which we live. Far less is our heavenly Father unconcerned with this cosmos, given the fact that his purpose is to redeem it and deliver it from the curse (see Rom. 8:18ff.). Don't ever forget that we will live on a redeemed, new *earth* for all eternity.

To seek and think about things above does not mean we are to ignore and neglect the daily affairs and responsibilities of life in the here and now. Rather, Paul is using directional categories to make a qualitative distinction. The contrast between *below or on the earth* and *above*, and between *down* and *up* or *here* and *there*, corresponds to the distinction between the present age that is in rebellion against God and the age to come in which the lordship of Christ will be fully and finally manifest.

Thus the distinction is not only ethical, it is eschatological. We are to live, says Paul, knowing that the future kingdom has invaded the present. It has been inaugurated through the work of Christ. We live as energized by the powers of the future, even though we still exist in the present. We are to be governed by the principles and values of the reign of God (things above), not the dominion of the devil.

Don't think for a moment that Paul is endorsing the view that the world above is the truly spiritual and pure one whereas nothing in this life is worth working to redeem or preserve. Salvation is not the release of the spirit from the prison of our physical bodies so that we can live unsullied and unsoiled, soaring in some ethereal realm of a distant eternity. He means that the power and principles of the age to come are to energize us now so that we can influence the earth with the truths and values of heaven.

If Paul were Gnostic in orientation, he wouldn't have continued in verse 5 and throughout the remainder of this chapter with strict and specific instructions on how to live well now. In other words, he was not so heavenly minded that he became of little earthly good. Rather he calls on us to live out in earthly relationships the life of heaven that is already within us.

Paul is not suggesting that we should be careless or indifferent toward the earth or our responsibilities in society. In saying that we should neither seek nor set our minds on things on the earth he is not suggesting that we refuse to mow the grass or take out the garbage or play with our kids or be punctual in our appointments. He is denouncing a carnal mindset, a perspective that is fixated on this world system to the exclusion of the kingdom of God.

The Gnostic heresy, in part, would have you believe that a day meditating on a hillside is inherently more pleasing to God than one in which you faithfully fulfill the terms of your contract with an employer in providing an effort deserving of the wage you are being paid. Those who fail to observe minimal standards of common courtesy, neglect their appearance, and refuse to devote time and energy to cultivating healthy interpersonal relationships, all in the name of devotion to God, have bitten the Gnostic apple and fallen into an unbiblical dualism.

In other words, when Paul refers to things below or things on the earth, he has in mind that worldly system under the dominion of Satan, those values and goals and principles that conflict with the revelation of God in Scripture. "Things on the earth" are whatever is driven by pride, greed, lust, and disregard for the glory of God. "Things above," on the other hand, are whatever reflects the beauty of Christ, whether that be the changing of a diaper, sharing a meal with friends, or celebrating the Eucharist.

But what about Paul's description of Jesus as seated at the right hand of the Father? Doesn't that imply that he is remote and far removed from the circumstances of life on this globe? No! To be seated at the right hand was a common way among both Jews and Gentiles of being granted the highest honor and favor. It is a description of unrivaled privilege and exaltation, not geographical distance. Paul is emphasizing the supremacy and lordship of Christ, not his withdrawal from earthly affairs. The apostle in no way intends to suggest that our Lord is spiritually absent from the earth or unconcerned about its plight and problems.

In speaking of the things on the earth he doesn't mean substance, as over against spirit. After all, jealousy, hatred, and lust are immaterial but most assuredly evil, while our bodies, the stars above, and food are material but most assuredly good. Neither does he mean heaven, as a place, over against earth. This isn't a way of referring to the world as a physical reality but to the world as a system of thought and immoral energy. The "things below" are the selfish, fleshly principles that animate this life as it languishes under the influence of the god of this age (2 Cor. 4:4; cf. 1 John 5:19). These lowly, earthbound things run counter to the kingdom of God, whether they be vain philosophies or human endeavors driven by pride and ambition rather than by the glory of God.

Our focus on the things above is Paul's way of emphasizing our love for the truths of God's kingdom, our devotion to the principles of Christ's lordship, our affirmation of and submission to the eternal values that will characterize life in the new heavens and new earth.

The real life of the Christian, the true life in the Spirit is not something we live out in some distant realm, detached from and unconnected with the dirt and sweat and frustrations of trying to cope with other fallen folk and our own obligations to them (however onerous they may be). The real, true, spiritual life of the Christian is right here, right now, empowered by the exalted Christ with whom we are forever identified.

People who are fixated on things above should, more than all others, positively influence life in the here and now. Paul's desire is that we bring to bear on the present the power of the future. He is laboring to raise up people whose heavenly mindset yields a redemptive, earthly impact for the glory of God. He was not a Gnostic. And neither am I. Are you?

# 62

# Hidden in Him

## Colossians 3:1–4

If then you have been raised with Christ, seek the things that are above, where Christ is, seated at the right hand of God. Set your minds on things that are above, not on things that are on earth. For you have died, and your life is hidden with Christ in God. When Christ who is your life appears, then you also will appear with him in glory.

My life is hidden with Christ in God (Col. 3:3). More than that, there is a sense in which it isn't even my life. It's Christ's (Col. 3:4). It's true of you, too, if you believe in the Lord Jesus. What a powerful declaration! Let me catch my breath and I'll try to make sense of these stunning statements.

First, though, we mustn't overlook the fact that your life is "hidden" only insofar as you are with Christ. In other words, if you don't have Christ, your life is very much exposed and vulnerable and precarious. The only way your life can be thought of as in any sense hidden is if you are united by faith with the Son of God. There is safety and security in him alone.

Second, some would fancy their lives to be "in God" but without Christ. "Hidden in God," yes, "but I don't need Christ for that," so they say. They envision themselves as religious, even spiritual, while yet Christless. They speak of spiritual serenity and meaning and value and a sense of well being but care little, if at all, for the Son of God. But don't be deceived by their sincerity or duped by their fervor: whatever it is that Paul has in mind by the word "hidden" and whatever it means to be "in God," is found only in relationship with Jesus Christ.

Now, with that foundational truth settled, we can proceed to ask what it means to be hidden with Christ in God. The best way to unpack this truth is by noting, first, what it doesn't mean.

Jesus called us to be a light to the world. "A city set on a hill," he noted, "cannot be hidden" (Matt. 5:14). Being hidden in this sense, therefore, is bad.

Like virtually every other young boy who grew up in the 1950s, I was an avid follower and admirer of Superman, whether he appeared on TV or in the pages of a comic book. I suppose I was intrigued by the fantasy of his dual existence. When all was serene and safe, he was Clark Kent, mild-mannered reporter with the *Daily Planet* newspaper. At such times he was indistinguishable from the average citizen in Metropolis. But when chaos broke out or crime raised its ugly head, the light grey suit was cast aside to reveal the man of steel.

In a perverse sort of way, many Christians are like Superman. They keep their Christianity concealed beneath their street clothes. Days, perhaps weeks, may pass before some crisis occurs, demanding that they abandon their normal routine and adorn themselves with the costume of Christianity in order to perform some great feat of faith or mercy. But as soon as the crisis passes, they, like Superman, return to their everyday existence as mild-mannered lawyers, mild-mannered teachers, even mild-mannered pastors.

Little wonder that the church today is so ineffective and its presence rests so lightly on our society. There are too many who profess the name of Christ but want their commitment to him to remain hidden until threatening circumstances or some pressing need requires that they take a public stand for truth, justice, and the American way, or more appropriately, for the gospel.

My point is that Paul by no means intends for us to think of our lives as unseen or obscured. As Jesus said, "Let your light shine before others, so that they may see your good works and give glory to your Father who is in heaven" (Matt. 5:16).

Rather, by "hidden" Paul means that the source of our spiritual life is inexplicable to those who don't know Jesus. They can't figure out where we find perseverance when persecuted or why we show mercy when mistreated or what accounts for our praise of God when pain is so obvious and chronic.

There is an element of mystery in the rationale and motivation of the Christian life. Why does one man refuse to exploit an opportunity for financial gain when others so easily justify circumventing the law? Why does one young lady steadfastly resist the sexual advances of a boyfriend when others so quickly yield without a second thought? What accounts for a life that is qualitatively different when that very difference costs so much from a worldly and economic and political perspective?

Paul's use of the word *hidden* is somewhat analogous to what we can and cannot see of a flower. The root system is concealed beneath the surface of the earth. How it derives nutrients from the soil and contributes to the growth of the stem, leaf, and flower is unseen, being something of a mystery. But the beauty of the rose is for all to behold. Its color and fragrance are ever on display for the joy of all people. So it is with the Christian, whose strength and incentive and inner life are hidden from view, but whose kindness, faith, perseverance, and love are a perpetual witness to the glory of God's grace within.

Do you remember the scene in the movie *Chariots of Fire* when Eric Liddell wins the 400-meter run in the Olympic Games in Paris, France? Harold Abrahams, who earlier won the gold medal in the 100-meter dash, is watching him from the grandstands. As Liddell thrusts his head back in characteristic fashion and displays an almost other-worldly determination, Abrahams appears befuddled, unable to grasp what could drive a man in this way. It's as if he's saying to himself, "Something more than physical training alone is at work in this man. What unknown energy accounts for this seemingly inhuman performance?"

Such ought to be the reaction of the unbeliever who bears witness to our most mundane activities. There is a very real sense in which the life of the believer is an enigma to the world. Something in us is under concealment, hidden, inaccessible to the person who doesn't know Jesus as Lord and Savior. "Outsiders may mistake [Christians] for weak, insignificant, dishonored fools for Christ, little knowing that they are tied to the ruler of the universe and destined to reign with him in glory."[1] In such cases we would do well to encourage our souls with the gentle reminder:

> The reason why the world does not know us is that it did not know him. Beloved, we are God's children now, and what we will be has not yet appeared; but we know that when he appears we shall be like him, because we shall see him as he is. And everyone who thus hopes in him purifies himself as he is pure. (1 John 3:1b–3)

Sometimes it's hidden even to other Christians. Paul faced this problem in his relationship with the Corinthians. Nothing they saw in him appeared apostolic. They were inclined to judge him based on externals alone. How could this bruised and battered life, this one with less than impressive physical features, this persecuted and oppressed man, be an apostle of Christ? Paul himself confessed that before he was converted he also judged based solely on outward appearance, on the basis of fleshly standards (see 2 Cor. 5:16).

But he was quick to remind them (and us) that although "our outer nature is wasting away, our inner nature is being renewed day by day. For this slight momentary affliction is preparing for us an eternal weight of glory beyond all comparison, as we look not to the things that are seen but to the things that are unseen. For the things that are seen are transient, but the things that are unseen are eternal" (2 Cor. 4:16–18).

Finally, there is in the word *hidden* an element of security and safety. In fact, the perfect tense of the word stresses the ongoing and permanent effects of what God has done for us in and with Christ. As O'Brien put it, "Your life has been hidden with Christ in God and it remains that way."[2]

Jesus himself said it best when he declared that "no one will snatch them [i.e., my sheep] out of my hand. My Father, who has given them to me, is greater than all, and no one is able to snatch them out of the Father's hand" (John 10:28–29). There it is: our life is with Christ, in his gracious grip. And together with him we are in God, from whose hand no one can snatch us. Oh, blessed safety!

# 63

# Glorified in Him

## Colossians 3:1–4

> If then you have been raised with Christ, seek the things that are above, where Christ is, seated at the right hand of God. Set your minds on things that are above, not on things that are on earth. For you have died, and your life is hidden with Christ in God. When Christ who is your life appears, then you also will appear with him in glory.

I opened the previous meditation by saying, with Paul, that my life that is now hidden with Christ isn't even mine. It's his (Col. 3:4). More than that, this life of Christ within me, though now somewhat concealed, will someday be fully revealed. Listen to Paul once again: "When Christ who is your life appears, then you also will appear with him in glory" (Col. 3:4).

What does it mean to say that Christ is our life? And what are we to expect when he finally appears? In what sense will we appear with him in glory? Let's take each of these questions in turn.

So, what does it mean to say that Christ *is* my life? Certainly it must be said that apart from him I have no life. Life, both physically and spiritually, finds its source in him and is sustained by him (see Col. 1:16–17). Whatever life I now live is not of my own making, for as Paul said to the Athenian philosophers, "He himself gives to all mankind life and breath and everything" (Acts 17:25). The mere fact that there is an *I*, a *you*, and a *we* is because of the creative intent and energy of the Son of God.

Paul also has in mind that vital, irrevocable union we have with him, such that the Christian simply cannot conceive of life in any meaningful way separable from the indwelling, energizing, loving presence of the Lord Jesus. The believer's personal identity is so inextricably wrapped up in who Christ is and what he has accomplished that it simply makes no sense to speak or even conceive of a *me* independently of him.

This is an affront to those infected with a pull-yourself-up-by-your-bootstraps, Western individualism. We are so accustomed to taking full credit for who we are and what we accomplish that any suggestion we might be wholly dependent on another is quickly and defiantly dismissed. We think entirely in terms of rights and entitlements, disregarding the fact that the only thing we truly deserve is death.

Such a mentality does not accord well with Paul's declaration that "Christ is my life!" As painful to my flesh as it may be to admit, the fact is that I am not my own man. I can claim no rights in my body, soul, or spirit. I own nothing. I am but an unworthy beneficiary of divine mercy. Not only physical life comes through him (Col. 1:16) but every impulse of my renewed heart, as well as every choice in obedience to his will. I do not live my life through the independent exertion of my will in the pursuit of my goals. My life, if I dare even use such terms, is thoroughly through him and sovereignly sustained by him.

Most important of all, this life that he gave me and now upholds and energizes by his good will has value only so far as it is lived for his glory. To say that Christ is my life is to say that my life exists ultimately to make him look great and glorious. I don't make him great or glorious, but I do exist to reveal and display that greatness and glory in all he does through me. John Piper, in commenting on Romans 11:36, put it this way:

> Do you love the thought that you exist to make God look glorious? Do you love the thought that all creation exists to display the glory of God. Do you love the truth that all of history is designed by God to one day be a completed canvas that displays in the best way possible the greatness and beauty of God? . . . Do you love the truth that you personally exist to make God look like what he really is—glorious? I ask again: Do you love the fact that your salvation is meant to put the glory of God's

grace on display? Do you love seeing and showing the glory of God? This is why God created the universe. This is why he ordained history. This is why he sent his Son. This is why you exist. Forever to see and savor and show the glory of Christ, who is the image of God. The question at the end of Romans 1–11 is, *Do you embrace this calling as your treasure and your joy?*[3]

Paul also declares that this glory or beauty or manifest splendor of all that Jesus Christ is will one day be made inescapably visible. According to our text, Christ, who is our life, will one day appear. That is typically taken for granted among Christians. We refer to it as the Second Coming. But we fail to consider that "when" he appears, "then" (note the explicit temporal connection in Paul's language) we also will appear with him in glory.

Paul has much the same thing in mind in Romans 8:17–18. There he reminds us that we are "fellow heirs with Christ, provided we suffer with him in order that we may also be glorified with him. For I consider that the sufferings of this present time are not worth comparing with the glory that is to be revealed to us."

Yes, we will see that glory (Rom. 8:18). But in another sense we will be that glory. But in what sense? And in being that glory how do we keep the focus on him and not ourselves? Look again at Colossians 3:4.

*When Paul says we will appear with him "in glory,"* he is not referring to a place but to an experience. This is the promise of sharing in the glorified life of Christ. It is the promise of the eradication of evil and every fleshly impulse. It is the promise of everlasting deliverance from greed and pride and lust and envy and unforgiveness. It is the promise that our whole being: body, soul, mind, spirit, and affections will experience and forever live in the power and purity of God himself.

It's somewhat akin to what Paul had in mind in 2 Thessalonians 1:10 where he declares that Christ is coming to be glorified "in" his saints. John Stott explains it this way:

> So how will the coming Lord Jesus be glorified in relation to his people? Not "among" them, as if they will be the theatre or stadium in which he appears; nor "by" them, as if they will be the spectators, the audience who watch and worship; nor "through" or "by means of" them, as if they will be mirrors which reflect his image and glory [although, in a sense all those

are true]; but rather "in" them, as if they will be a filament, which itself glows with light and heat when the electric current passes through it.[4]

Stott's point is that we will not only witness Christ's glory, but we will be enveloped within it, engulfed by its surging splendor and made experiential participants of it. One day, oh glorious day, our lives will no longer be hidden with Christ in God (Col. 3:3), but fully and finally and forever seen as we glow with the brightness of his glory, for his glory.

# 64

# Ruthless or Reckless?

## Colossians 3:5–11

> Put to death therefore what is earthly in you: sexual immorality, impurity, passion, evil desire, and covetousness, which is idolatry. On account of these the wrath of God is coming. In these you too once walked, when you were living in them. But now you must put them all away: anger, wrath, malice, slander, and obscene talk from your mouth. Do not lie to one another, seeing that you have put off the old self with its practices and have put on the new self, which is being renewed in knowledge after the image of its creator. Here there is not Greek and Jew, circumcised and uncircumcised, barbarian, Scythian, slave, free; but Christ is all, and in all.

The Puritan theologian John Owen (d. 1683) once wrote, "Be killing sin, or it will be killing you!"[5] Good advice or melodramatic overreaction? Sadly, many professing Christians opt for the latter, at least in terms of how they live.

How radically different is Paul's attitude toward sin from that of the world and, tragically, a great many in the church. In this age of seeker-sensitivity one does not often hear the word *sin* spoken in our pulpits, or if it is spoken it is followed by a quick apology to those who may be offended by such language. It comes as no surprise, then, that people feel free to toy with sin, to tease it, to pet it, and are careless and indifferent toward its devastating effects. They regard it as inconsequential and secondary, something to be tasted and tested in nothing short of moral bravado.

Paul's attitude is of a different sort: Kill it! Put it to death. Execute it. Don't let it live another second. Take whatever steps are necessary to eliminate it from your life. Tolerate no compromise. Take no prisoners. Deal ruthlessly and radically with it, no matter how small or seemingly insignificant it may appear.

And this is the advice of a man who only moments before (in Col. 3:1–4) insisted that we focus on "things above." Our heavenly life that finds its source and strength in the risen and exalted Jesus must be expressed in the concrete rigors and responsibilities of life on earth. The former is never grounds to justify exemption from the latter. Throughout chapters 3 and 4 of Colossians, Paul will explain how the "Christ-is-our-life" reality works itself out not only in our war with the flesh but also in the church, at home, in marriage, at work, indeed in every conceivable human relationship.

There are only two options when it comes to dealing with sin: you are either reckless or ruthless. There is no middle ground. To opt for some third possibility is itself a reckless choice. Either we are ruthless in our commitment and efforts to kill sin (lest it be killing us) or we are reckless by default. One doesn't have to make deliberate choices to commit specific sins to be reckless. All one need do is fail to take calculated and precise steps to avoid temptation, flee sin at first sight, and treat it as one's mortal enemy. Not to do so is to be reckless (defined by Webster's as "lacking proper caution, careless of consequences, negligent"[6]), regardless of intent, regardless of stated hatred for sin.

There is no cease-fire in our war with sin. There are no demilitarized zones to which we can flee. The flesh never takes a sabbatical. To live as if one might let down one's guard for a second is to recklessly expose one's soul to almost certain defeat.

If we are to grasp Paul's perspective on this point, we must take note of the word "therefore" with which verse 5 begins. This clearly links the urgent ethical injunctions beginning at verse 5 to the glorious truths concerning the identity of the believer and his or her union with Christ in verses 1 to 4. Biblical scholars have often referenced to this as the "indicative/imperative" dynamic in Christian living. Paul's imperatives, that is to say, his ethical commands and admonitions, follow upon the assertion of certain theological indicatives. The exhortations that articulate what we are to do and not do flow out of and are based on the indicative truths, the accomplished facts if you will, of our salvation.

It is because we have died with Christ and are buried with him, even now raised together with him and are hidden in him in God, that we are to be ever so diligent to obey the commands that follow. The indicative does not undermine or eliminate the imperative. One cannot say, "Well, since I'm hidden in Christ in God, I hardly need to be overly concerned with what happens when I'm confronted with temptation." God forbid (cf. Rom. 6:1–2)!

Others have been inclined to think that because Christ is our life (3:4) we need not exert ourselves or diligently fight or strive for holiness of life. "Christ will do it for you," so we are told. "He is your life now, so stop trying to live out of any other source or power." Well, yes, he is our life. Yes, of course all our efforts are energized by his presence and power (see Col. 1:29). But that doesn't call for passivity or carelessness or a reckless "let go and let God" approach to confronting sin.

Rather, the theology of the New Testament is that the indicative mandates the imperative, undergirds our efforts to fulfill it, and makes it reasonable to heed. "You have died with Christ; act and speak and think therefore so as to make it plain that this 'death' is no mere figure of speech but a real event which has severed all the links which bound you to the dominion of sin. In short, be (in actual practice) what you now are (by divine act)."[7]

In order to make this clear, Paul builds his case around two vivid metaphors. First, in verses 5 to 7, he portrays sin as if it were a living enemy that must be destroyed. Second, in verses 8 to 11, he describes it as a filthy garment that must be discarded. Or again, when it comes to sin, put it to death and lay it aside. We must *slay* it. We must *strip* it.

The literal rendering of verse 5a would be, "Therefore, put to death the members which are upon the earth." The ESV translates it, "Put to death therefore what is earthly in you," while the NASB has the following: "Therefore consider the members of your earthly body as dead to . . ." David Garland comes right to the point:

> This forceful image means that Christian renewal is not some cosmetic overhaul of our sinful propensities. We do not simply add on a veneer of Christian values that only laminates our old nature and its value system. Paul does not tell us to put on new clothes over the old; the old must be stripped off and thrown away. We need more than a few minor adjustments and cannot skip over the key element of dying with Christ.[8]

What are "the members which are upon the earth"? Paul uses this language in Romans 6:13 and 19 to refer to the faculties of our earthly, physical existence. His warning is that our members can be offered up either to God for a life of righteousness or to sin as instruments of wickedness. Here in Colossians 3 Paul practically identifies certain sins with those bodily members through which they are committed. He is thus calling for the radical and ruthless termination of the immoral and disobedient use of our physical faculties.

Of course, he isn't recommending literal mutilation, as if to suggest that the way to fight sin is by amputation of certain bodily parts. You can lop off an arm, gouge out an eye, and cut out your tongue, but the wickedness of the soul remains. Paul's point, rather, is that we must take unequivocal steps to kill the sin that finds expression through our bodily members. As O'Brien reminds us, "True 'mortification' in the context of Colossians 3:5 has to do with a transformation of the will, a new attitude of the mind."[9]

And how does one deal ruthlessly with sin (cf. Matt. 5:29–30)? Think of it in terms of a man working on a massive machine who suddenly finds that his left hand has been caught in the gears. In only a moment his entire body will be crushed, unless he takes drastic steps to prevent it. Without hesitation he grasps a nearby axe and hacks off his hand at the wrist. It's a graphic and unpleasant picture, but such is the only alternative to death.

The point of the analogy is this: eliminate from your life, as much as is possible, anything that will cause you to stumble. If it's a place, don't go there. If it's an image, turn away. If it's a song, don't listen. If it's a book, don't read it. If it's a liquid, don't drink it. If it's a person, part company. The sacrifice may be uncomfortable, even painful. It will most certainly be unpopular, but "it is better that you lose one of your members than that your whole body be thrown into hell" (Matt. 5:29).

And where do the energy and incentive come from for such a life? From meditating on the majesty of being raised with Christ (Col. 3:1). From fixing our souls on the splendor of his exaltation (Col. 3:2). From celebrating our "concealment" in Christ in God (Col. 3:3). From the joyful expectation of experiencing his glory when he comes (Col. 3:4). In sum: Enjoyment empowers effort. Pleasure in God is the power for purity.

# 65

# Sexual Impurity: A Warning

## Colossians 3:5

*Put to death therefore what is earthly in you: sexual immorality, impurity, passion, evil desire, and covetousness, which is idolatry.*

If I were asked to identify the two most dominant features of our society today, I may well opt for (1) unbridled sexual self-indulgence and (2) greed. If there is any justification for that selection, Colossians 3:5 is uniquely relevant for our day.

In this verse Paul gives us the first of two lists of five sins that we are to slay. I want to say a few words about the first four sins, leaving the fifth for our next lesson.

One thing that makes this sequence of sins especially significant is that Paul, writing under the inspiration of the Spirit, clearly believed that one can exercise control over one's desires. One need not slavishly and passively yield to them. Note well: Paul does not say that we should refrain merely from the outward expression of those desires (although that is surely included). Rather, we are exhorted to kill the desire itself. Put to death passion. Put to death evil desire. Put to death covetousness.

Secular theorists find this untenable because they don't believe a person has any power on which to rely other than the strength of one's own will. One simply cannot resolve or determine or will oneself to cease desiring. This is especially relevant given the current debate over homosexuality. Many argue that a person is powerless over his or her "sexual orientation." Such desires, they say, are a given of human nature and cannot be altered or overcome.

But Paul's counsel is based on his belief that the Christian is energized, animated, and empowered by the Holy Spirit (cf. Col. 1:29). No desire or passion or urge is so entrenched in the human soul that a person indwelt by the Spirit cannot conquer it. This is confirmed again in verse 7 where Paul reminds the Colossians that they "once walked [in these sins]," when they "were living in them" (see also 1 Cor. 6:11). Although they have been delivered from the enslaving power of that lifestyle, they are not yet invulnerable to the temptation to revert to their former ways, hence Paul's urgency in commanding them to "slay" and to "strip" (v. 8) such desires from their hearts.

Many contend that you can't simply choose to suppress certain passions. In fact, they argue that it is psychologically dangerous to attempt any such thing. Venting our desires, giving them full and fetterless freedom, is the counsel we most often hear. "Be yourself! Embrace your longings!" And above all else, never judge or condemn someone for expressing or attempting to find fulfillment of these inward urges.

I'm speaking only for myself when I say that I don't want to "be myself"! I want to be like Christ. When I look within myself, I see evil passions and uncleanness and covetousness and I want nothing of them. These are violations of my true self. These are invasive enemies from which I long to be delivered and over which I am committed to triumph, by the grace of God. I have no desire to affirm all that is within me. I rather choose to oppose it, defeat it, and live in true freedom from its enslaving power. That said, let's look briefly at the first four sins.

We are all familiar with the first term, translated "sexual immorality." It is the Greek *porneia*, from which we have derived our word "pornography." This word has a prominent place in the New Testament. It is the first of the many works of the flesh in Galatians 5:19 and is a practice from which we are commanded to abstain, in 1 Thessalonians 4:3. We are to flee from it (1 Cor. 6:18) and are told, in no uncertain terms, that no individual who is given to the unrepentant practice of it will inherit the kingdom of God (1 Cor. 6:9; cf. Eph. 5:5). Here in Colossians 3:6 Paul declares that it is because of such things as *porneia* that the wrath of God is coming.

"Sexual immorality" (*porneia*) refers to any and every kind of illegitimate sexual intercourse. Yes, dear friend, there are certain kinds and expressions of sexual activity that are illegitimate. With all due apologies to my politically correct readers (but no such apologies, in fact, are due), any sexual intercourse under any and all circumstances outside of marriage between a man and a woman is illegitimate, out of bounds, and is one of those things on account of which God's wrath is most assuredly revealed.

The second sin, "impurity" (cf. 1 Thess. 4:7–8), obviously means sexual uncleanness, given its place in the immediate context. Whereas it is from the first term that we get our word *pornography*, it is this word that more appropriately encompasses that contemporary phenomenon (although it cannot be restricted to it).

Pornography is defiling. It stains the soul. It imprints on the mind images that corrupt, pervert, and twist one's sexuality, as well as one's perception of the opposite gender. Its addictive and destructive power has been well documented.

"Ah, Sam, you've been reading the Puritans too long! You need deliverance from your Victorian, outmoded, and unenlightened views of human sexuality!" Really?

If we are justified in making application of this word to modern expressions of pornography, whether in magazines, videos, Internet web sites, television, or so-called gentlemen's clubs (what a pathetically twisted use of the word *gentleman*), and I think we are, this is a matter of eternal importance (see below).

The third word in Paul's list, translated "passion," together with the fourth, "evil desire," give added weight to the point I'm making. Needless to say, we use the word *passion* today, as well as *desire*, to refer to good and honorable and godly yearnings. But in this context, and in view of the adjective *evil* that qualifies the kind of desire Paul has in mind, clearly these are all related and most likely have in mind sexual longings that are altogether inappropriate for those who bear the image of God.

Worse than inappropriate, it is "on account of these [that] the wrath of God is coming!" (Col. 3:6). Is that serious enough for you?

These are not casual impulses or experiences to be coddled or ignored or justified because "that's simply part of what it is to be human." Such behavior merits divine and eternal judgment.

No, I'm not saying that a person who has ever fallen prey to such sexual impurity is going to hell. Rather, Paul has in mind those who have given themselves over to the persistent practice and cultivation of sexual impurity. He is not talking about the man (or woman) who falls but is broken, contrite, and devastated by the affront that such sin has caused to the purity and dignity of God. He has in view unrepentant, cold-hearted, calloused commitment to a life of sexual impurity.

I have known and ministered to a number of men who are devastated by their addiction to pornography and are determined, with God's help, to break free of their bondage and are willing to make whatever practical sacrifice is necessary to walk in purity of thought and deed, no matter how inconvenient or unpleasant that sacrifice may be. Their conscience has been pricked by the Spirit and they are quick to confess and repent when they sin.

But to those who choose to live in sexual immorality, impurity, passion, and evil desire, and somehow justify or find excuse for it, Paul promises only divine wrath. Yes, it's a hard word. No, we can't afford to ignore it.

# 66

# Idolatry without Idols

## Colossians 3:5

> Put to death therefore what is earthly in you: sexual immorality, impurity, passion, evil desire, and covetousness, which is idolatry.

Where does one draw the line between a legitimate longing and covetousness? It's not a razor's edge, that's for sure. The line is often fuzzy. The boundary between the two is not always as objectively discernible as we might wish.

The problem is that we don't always understand our own motivation. Why do I long to possess that new car? What accounts for my desire to have more than what I currently own? Would more stuff serve a utilitarian purpose and aid me in the pursuit of legitimate spiritual goals? Or do I use that as an excuse to justify the hoarding of goodies? Does having more simply stroke my ego or does it provide me with an opportunity to serve others for the glory of God? Would that we all might know the answer to these obviously difficult questions.

In any case, it's vitally important that we continue to examine our souls and subject our motives to the searchlight of Scripture and the convicting ministry of the Holy Spirit. Why? Because covetousness is a serious sin (see Rom. 1:29; 1 Cor. 5:10–11; 6:10–11; Eph. 5:3). Here in Colossians 3:5 covetousness is the last of five in Paul's first list of sins that we are to put to death. It breaks the sequence from a focus on sexual sins and turns our attention to the issue of greed. It even made God's Top Ten list (see Ex. 20:17—"You shall not covet").

The most basic definition of covetousness is "an inordinate desire for more and more, well beyond any reasonable assessment of what is needed." It is the insatiable longing to lay up stuff simply for the sake of having it. Jesus couldn't have been clearer when he warned his disciples, "Take care, and be on your guard against all covetousness, for one's life does not consist in the abundance of his possessions" (Luke 12:15).

How might we know if our life consists of our possessions? How do we gauge or measure such a phenomenon? At what point have we gone over the top in terms of what we own or desire to own? There's certainly no mathematical formula or other means to calculate the answer. In fact, although there is often great danger in wealth, there is no reason to think that if a person has a great deal of money he or she must, of necessity, be guilty of covetousness. Some of the least covetous and most generous people I know are quite wealthy.

Perhaps the key to our dilemma is found in the qualifying statement that Paul makes about covetousness: "Put to death . . . covetousness, which is idolatry" (Col. 3:5). Idolatry? That must mean I'm not guilty of covetousness! After all, I've never bowed down before wooden idols or worshiped the stars. I'm not in the least inclined to burn incense to a golden calf or swear allegiance to a false god. Needless to say, this betrays a woefully inadequate understanding of what constitutes idolatry.

Idolatry need not entail a statue of Buddha or genuflecting in a pagan temple. Idolatry is any tendency in the human heart to dethrone God for the sake of something else, whether that be money, sex, ambition, power, pride, or something as seemingly innocuous as respectability. To the extent that we give our affections to anything other than God on the assumption that it can do for our souls what he can't, we are guilty of idolatry.

John Piper defines covetousness as "desiring something so much that you lose your contentment in God."[10] Thus the opposite of covetousness is resting satisfied with God. Covetousness is idolatry "because the contentment that the heart should be getting from God, it starts to get from something else."[11] Covetousness, simply put, "is a heart divided between two gods."[12]

When we begin to lose our contentment in Christ, that is to say, when we say that Christ isn't altogether adequate, we start to long for other things to satisfy our souls. We begin to say, "I must have something more or other, an experience, event, or possession that I can't trust God to provide." In effect we elevate something above God in our esteem. We put our confidence in the promise of "things" and "stuff" and whatever money can purchase, believing the lie that there is a depth of joy and quality of life in something that can't be found in God.

Anytime our pursuit of more stuff is driven or energized by the belief that it can fulfill the longing of our souls in ways and means that God cannot, we are guilty of idolatry. Granting any object or possession such a powerful place in our hearts, or to elevate it to a position of highest value, deserving of our utmost effort and attention, is to deify it. We in effect are bowing the knee to another master. Our hearts are captive to a different lord. We have, quite simply, violated the first commandment: "You shall have no other gods before me" (Ex. 20:3).

I think I understand why Jesus spoke so urgently in Luke 12:15: "Take care, and be on your guard against all covetousness." Covetousness is sneaky. It's hard to detect. Worst of all, it often looks so much like the legitimate desire to enjoy the good gifts of God and celebrate life in all its beauty and lavish provisions.

So, no, I don't know where to draw the line. I do know that I'm responsible before God for the state of my own heart. I do know that I'm accountable to Jesus to be extremely careful not to let down my guard lest covetousness creep in unawares and seduce my soul away from single-minded, wholehearted devotion to him alone.

"Search me, O God, and know my heart! Try me and know my thoughts! And see if there be any grievous way in me, and lead me in the way everlasting!" (Ps. 139:23–24).

# 67

# Is a God without Wrath a Good God?

## Colossians 3:6

**Put to death therefore what is earthly in you: sexual immorality, impurity, passion, evil desire, and covetousness, which is idolatry. On account of these the wrath of God is coming.**

Among the many distortions of biblical truth in our world today, few are more egregious than that of Joel B. Green and Mark D. Baker in their horribly mistitled and misleading book, *Recovering the Scandal of the Cross: Atonement in New Testament & Contemporary Contexts*.[13] The focus of the book is their repudiation of Christ's death on the cross as a penal substitutionary sacrifice. My primary concern in this lesson, however, is less with their view of the atonement (which is barely existent in the book) and more with their denial of divine wrath that would warrant Christ's death as a propitiatory offering (see Rom. 3:25; 1 John 2:1–2).

I'm reluctant even to quote from the book, given the distorted and prejudicial language used to describe the wrath of God. But here are a few statements that should give you a sense of what they have in mind.

"Paul's portrait of God," they argue, "is not that of an angry deity requiring mollification. Divine wrath is not an affective quality or 'feeling' on the part of God. Rather, it is a means of underscoring how seriously God takes sin. . . . Whatever else can be made of Paul's understanding of the death of Jesus, his theology of the cross lacks any developed sense of divine retribution."[14]

They ridicule penal substitution as advocating the idea that Christ was punished "by execution on the cross so as to satisfy the rancor of God."[15] Penal substitution, they contend, is based in large measure on "the perceived necessity of placating an emotion-laden God ever on the verge of striking out against any who disobey his every will."[16] They portray the traditional view of divine wrath as God lashing out "in frustration or vengeance" against sinners.[17]

Divine wrath, say Green and Baker, is not a divine property or essential attribute of God. Indeed, the wrath to come (1 Thess. 1:9–10; Col. 3:6) simply "refers to the climactic, end-time scene of judgment when those who prefer to worship idols rather than the living God receive the fruits of their own misplaced hopes and commitments."[18] If you are thinking carefully, you will want to ask of them: Whose judgment? Indeed, why judgment? Receive from whom? What fruits?

There's really nothing new in what Green and Baker say, other than they claim to say it as evangelical Christians (which is why it so egregious; were they theological liberals, one might expect such a perspective). New Testament scholar C. H. Dodd is well known for having argued that the concept of wrath is archaic and beneath the dignity of God. Paul's terminology, said Dodd, refers to no more than *an inevitable process of cause and effect in a moral universe*. In other words, divine wrath is an impersonal force operative in a moral universe, not a personal attribute or disposition in the character of God.

This runs directly counter to the way in which the two Greek words for wrath (*thumos* and *orge*) are used in the New Testament. The former, *thumos*, is said to be "of God" in Romans 2:8 and six times in the book of Revelation (14:10, 19; 15:1, 7; 16:1; 19:15). Here in Colossians 3:6, however, and in most other cases, the word *orge* is used and suggests the idea of a settled disposition arising out of God's nature. It is specifically said to be "of God" in John 3:36 (on the lips of Jesus) as well as in Romans 1:18; Ephesians 5:6; Colossians 3:6; and Revelation 19:15. We read of the "wrath of the Lamb" in Revelation 6:16 (see also Rev. 6:17; 11:18; 14:10; 16:19). In Revelation 19:15 John speaks of "the winepress of the fury of the wrath of God the Almighty," where "fury" is a translation of *thumos* and "wrath" is a translation of *orge*.

Clearly, then, Dodd, Green, and Baker misunderstand divine wrath. It is not the loss of self-control or the irrational and capricious outburst of anger. Neither should it be conceived as a celestial bad temper or God lashing out at those who rub him the wrong way. Divine wrath is *righteous antagonism toward all that is unholy*. It is the revulsion of God's character to that which is a violation of God's will. Indeed, one may speak of *divine wrath* as a function of *divine love*. For God's wrath is his love for holiness and truth and justice. It is because God passionately loves purity and peace and perfection that he reacts angrily toward anything and anyone who defiles them.

J. I. Packer put it best by asking, "Would a God who took as much pleasure in evil as He did in good be a good God? Would a God who did not react adversely to evil in His world be morally perfect? Surely not. But it is precisely this adverse reaction to evil, which is a necessary part of moral perfection, that the Bible has in view when it speaks of God's wrath."[19] Leon Morris agrees:

> Then, too, unless we give a real content to the wrath of God, unless we hold that men really deserve to have God visit upon them the painful consequences of their wrongdoing, we empty God's forgiveness of its meaning. For if there is no ill desert, God ought to overlook sin. We can think of forgiveness as something real only when we hold that sin has betrayed us into a situation where we deserve to have God inflict upon us the most serious consequences, and that is upon such a situation that God's grace supervenes. When the logic of the situation demands that He should take action against the sinner, and He yet takes action for him, then and then alone can we speak of grace. But there is no room for grace if there is no suggestion of dire consequences merited by sin.[20]

Why have I focused on the reality of divine wrath? Because it is on account of such things as "sexual immorality, impurity, passion, evil desire, and covetousness" (Col. 3:5) that "the wrath of God is coming" (Col. 3:6; see also Eph. 5:5–6; 1 Thess. 4:3–6; 1 Cor. 6:9–10; Gal. 5:19–21).

The translation "is coming" is a bit misleading, for Paul may well have in mind a more timeless notion that wrath always *comes* on account of these things, not only in the future but throughout the course of human history. This is certainly the case in Romans 1:18ff. where Paul indicates that the wrath of God is *presently* seen in the way he has given over humanity to its sin and the consequences it invariably yields. In other words, divine wrath is not simply reserved for a future day of judgment (although it will most certainly be revealed then in its consummate fury), but is actively present now as God "gives up" men and women to their chosen course of corruption and wicked behavior (see esp. Rom. 1:24, 26, 28).

Cranfield is surely correct in saying that "the wrath which is being revealed is no nightmare of an indiscriminate, uncontrolled, irrational fury, but the wrath of the holy and merciful God called forth by, and directed against" men's ungodliness (sin is an attack on God's majesty) and unrighteousness (sin is a violation of God's will).[21]

Divine wrath is real. It is both operative now and will come in its full and final manifestation. Thanks be to God that "there is therefore now no condemnation for those who are in Christ Jesus" (Rom. 8:1).

# 68

# Changing Clothes

## *Colossians 3:8*

Put to death therefore what is earthly in you: sexual immorality, impurity, passion, evil desire, and covetousness, which is idolatry. On account of these the wrath of God is coming. In these you too once walked, when you were living in them. **But now you must put them all away: anger, wrath, malice, slander, and obscene talk from your mouth.**

Okay, Paul, we agree with you about slander and obscene talk. Those are verbal actions over which we can exercise a measure of control. We can choose not to speak ill of someone or to use inappropriate language. Whether or not we do so is up to us. We can just keep our mouths shut!

But how can you tell us to put away anger and wrath and malice? Those don't feel like choices. They are simply states of mind, passions of the heart. Are you really telling us to stop being angry, to cease feeling wrath, to terminate malicious thoughts?

If I may be allowed to speak for the apostle, yes, that is precisely what he's commanding us to do. As was the case earlier in Colossians 3 when it came to sexual desires (v. 5), so now with anger and wrath and malice, we are responsible before God to do whatever is necessary to eliminate these affections or emotions from our souls. Again, it isn't simply the outward expression of anger or certain physical actions that reveal our wrath and malice. *We must confront and conquer the inner impulse.*

This is the point Jesus was making when he said, "You have heard that it was said to those of old, 'You shall not murder; and whoever murders will be liable to judgment.' But I say to you that everyone who is angry with his brother will be liable to judgment; whoever insults his brother [or more literally, says to him, "Raca!"] will be liable to the council; and whoever says, 'You fool!' will be liable to the hell of fire" (Matt. 5:21–22).

By "insult," i.e., by saying "Raca," an Aramaic term meaning "empty(headed)," Jesus refers to the mocking of an individual's intelligence. This isn't merely a casual reference to a person's IQ or the equivalent of our calling someone a nitwit or a blockhead or a boneheaded dufus. He has in mind an angry and dismissive belittling that is designed to embarrass and humiliate. Worse still is the word translated "fool" (Gk. *moros*), which is an attack on the dignity or metaphysical value of the person. It's bad enough to call someone an idiot, but something worse to call them a worthless idiot.

Jesus isn't saying that people aren't fools or that there is never occasion on which we are justified in saying so. He himself called people fools or foolish (Matt. 7:26; 23:17; cf. Luke 11:40; 12:20), as did several Old Testament authors (see Ps. 14:1; 49:10; Prov. 1:7, 22, 32) who warned us to be cautious of our involvement with them. But in these texts the person is a fool because of his stubborn rebellion against God. In Matthew 5 Jesus has in mind the deliberate and angry undermining of a person's dignity. He is describing a demeaning, denigrating disdain and malicious contempt for another human being.

Now let's return to Colossians 3. The metaphor Paul employs is vivid and to the point. Earlier he instructed us to slay sin (3:5). Here he tells us to strip it off (v. 8). We must not only destroy it, but discard it. We are to put it to death and put it aside. The verb translated "put away" was often used of disrobing or removing garments (see Rom. 13:12; Eph. 4:22, 25; Heb. 12:1; James 1:21; 1 Pet. 2:1). Thus, we are to put aside or strip off old sinful habits like a set of tattered, worn-out clothes.

The words Paul uses are instructive. "Anger" (*orge*) is the same term used in verse 6 to describe divine wrath. What is appropriate for God, it would appear, is inappropriate for humans. "Wrath" is the translation of *thumos*, a more passionate and spontaneous outburst of anger, as over against the chronic, settled seething or brooding that *orge* suggests. Some argue there is no substantive difference between the two; but if Paul meant only one thing, why did he use two terms?

"Malice" may refer to the conscious desire to harm another that is subsequently expressed in evil speech such as slander and abusive language. The word "slander," although commonly translated "blasphemy," most likely refers to the "defamation of human character"[22] rather than a cursing of God (cf. Titus 3:2). The word translated "obscene talk," found only here in the New Testament, isn't so much curse words as it is the sort of speech that ridicules and embarrasses others.

Paul isn't suggesting there is no place for anger at sin or injustice or cruelty. Nor is he saying that we should immediately forgive and forget apart from repentance. Given what he wrote in numerous texts, it goes without saying that he is by no means undermining the importance of church discipline. Rather, he is talking here about the anger that erupts and lingers within interpersonal relationships in the body of Christ.

Although Paul doesn't address the underlying cause of these emotions, it's important that we understand our own motivation. Why do we feel such things in the first place? In most instances, it's because of an entitlement mentality. Someone defrauded us or failed to respect our rights. Things haven't gone our way and we blame them for it. Or we have been violated or treated unjustly. That may well be true, but does it justify anger, wrath, or malice?

Paul isn't talking about psychological repression but spiritual mortification. So, how does one "put to death" and "lay aside" anger, wrath, and malice? I know of only one way: by meditating on the magnitude of mercy shown us in the cross of Christ. We must ponder deeply what Christ endured for us rather than fixate on what others have done to create discomfort or pain. That is to say, focus on what Christ has done *for* you and not on what others have done *to* you. As we labor to saturate our minds with what Christ has done on the cross, it will gradually, ever so progressively, swallow up and erase the pain of what others have done to us. This is the power of grace. This is the power of Spirit-anointed truth.

The "example" (1 Pet. 2:21) Christ set for us, according to Peter, was precisely in his refusal to retaliate in anger at those who unjustly inflicted harm. "When he was reviled, he did not revile in return; when he suffered, he did not threaten, but continued entrusting himself to him who judges justly" (1 Pet. 2:23).

You may be wondering whether there is legitimacy in what we call "righteous indignation." Is anger ever justified or warranted? We must account for Paul's counsel in Ephesians 4:26–27: "Be angry and do not sin; do not let the sun go down on your anger, and give no opportunity to the devil."

Some argue that Paul's exhortation is conditional or concessive: *If* (or, when) you get angry, don't sin (however, this is grammatically unlikely[23]).

Another view is that the command and prohibition that follow are both to be taken at face value. There are occasions in the life of the church when righteous indignation is called for. But be careful. Don't let your anger simmer and seethe and lead you into other sins such as pride, spite, malice, or a longing for revenge.

The exhortation not to let "the sun go down on your anger" (v. 26b) is not to be taken literally. If it were, "it would mean that those who lived in the Arctic or Antarctic would at certain times of the year have no temporal limitation on their anger!"[24] In the Old Testament, sunset was viewed as the time limit for a number of activities (see Deut. 24:13, 15).

Paul's point is that we must be brief in our anger; we mustn't brood in it or nurse it or let it settle and harden before addressing its cause. Reconciliation, if possible (see Rom. 12:18–19), must be pursued promptly.

# 69

# The Destructive Power of Deception

## Colossians 3:9a

Put to death therefore what is earthly in you: sexual immorality, impurity, passion, evil desire, and covetousness, which is idolatry. On account of these the wrath of God is coming. In these you too once walked, when you were living in them. But now you must put them all away: anger, wrath, malice, slander, and obscene talk from your mouth. **Do not lie to one another**, seeing that you have put off the old self with its practices and have put on the new self, which is being renewed in knowledge after the image of its creator.

Following the other sins of the tongue, and somewhat singled out from them, is this brief but crucial command: "Do not lie to one another" (Col. 3:9a). So easily written. So easily recited. So easily ignored.

I don't want to commit another sin of the tongue by giving myself to overstatement, but it's hard to imagine a more destructive force in the body of Christ (or in marriages or in routine relationships) than lying. Virtually everything else we do to and against one another can be healed, but deliberate, conscious, premeditated deception is perhaps the most devastating of all.

Something truly sacred is shattered when we lie to one another. The confidence we have in another person, so essential for life in the body of Christ, cannot be easily repaired. The safety we feel because of a shared commitment to the truth is violated when deceit is embraced. It makes us feel vulnerable and tentative in our relationship with others.

The phrase "to one another" (Col. 3:9a) shows that "the exhortation has particular reference to believers in their relations within the Christian community. This, of course, in no way suggests that Christians could take the question of truth less seriously when speaking to outsiders."[25] But Paul specifically has in mind our obligations toward one another in the church. In Ephesians 4:25, the reason for this exhortation is not simply because lying is sinful and thus an offense against God, but because "we are members one of another" (v. 25b). We must remember that "fellowship is built on trust, and trust is built on truth."[26]

When someone lies to us, we feel abandoned by them, even abused. Someone can be guilty of any number of sins and we can forgive them when they repent. But rebuilding trust in someone who has deceived and misled us is a monumental task.

So, why do we lie? What makes lying such a powerful temptation? What do we hope to accomplish by means of a lie that seems to trump all the reasons why we should tell the truth? There are countless answers, no doubt, but I want to focus on three.

One reason we lie is that we simply don't trust the truth to get us what we want. In fact, telling the truth may be costly and painful and lead to hardships we'd rather avoid. Perhaps the underlying problem is greed, and telling the truth will cost us business or lead to the loss of a job. Lying on one's tax return is certainly one example of this and, in the minds of some, so easily justified.

A related factor is power. People frequently lie to gain an advantage over others that would rarely if ever occur had they chosen to be honest, forthright, and humble. This power-grab may be in the form of authority in the local church or a promotion at work or prestige among one's peers, regardless of age or context. And why is such power so appealing that it would prompt one to lie to gain it? Simply because we've bought into the false belief that personal value and worth is based on the perception of others and the sort of achievement that wins the applause and approval of society at large. If our identity were more wholly wrapped up in Christ and who we are in him, we would be less tempted to lie to gain from people what only he, ultimately, can give.

Perhaps the most powerful energy behind lying is pride. We lie to protect ourselves from whatever embarrassment the truth might bring. The truth would expose us in our weakness and sinfulness and failures. So we lie to make ourselves appear to others different from what we really are. People are terrified that if those whose respect and acceptance they can't live without were to see them stripped of every façade, they would suffer irreparable loss. Not so much financial loss, or even of power, but loss of status, respect, honor, praise, and the simple enjoyment we want people to have whenever they are in our presence.

The thought of people knowing the truth about us or seeing what we know but are ashamed to confess, drives us to lie in any number of ways, whether by direct verbal prevarication or by the creation of a public image that bears little correspondence to our true, inner selves.

Tragically, even the church has created a value system in which being perceived as competent, right, highly favored by the leadership, and most important of all, "anointed," is prized more than humility and brokenness and service and poverty of spirit. In this sort of atmosphere, telling the truth becomes an obstacle to advancement. Authenticity and honesty threaten the image we project to those whom we want to impress or whose favor we desire.

Related to this point is the powerful temptation to lie to cover our sin. We want to be thought of by others as spiritual, as truly committed, as lovers of God, and the truth would reveal that we aren't quite what we promote ourselves to be.

But is it really all that serious? Well, yes. In Revelation 21:8 (cf. also 21:27), John provides a partial list of those whose "portion will be in the lake that burns with fire and sulfur, which is the second death." They include "the cowardly, the faithless, the detestable, . . . murderers, the sexually immoral, sorcerers, idolaters, *and all liars.*"

As if to make the point even more pointedly, John virtually repeats himself in Revelation 22:15. Those who are outside the gates of the New Jerusalem, who will never gain admittance, include "the dogs and the sorcerers and the immoral persons and the murderers and the idolaters, *and everyone who loves and practices lying*" (NASB).

So, how important is speaking and living the truth? Eternally important!

# 70

# "To Life" versus "From Life"

## Colossians 3:9–10

Put to death therefore what is earthly in you: sexual immorality, impurity, passion, evil desire, and covetousness, which is idolatry. On account of these the wrath of God is coming. In these you too once walked, when you were living in them. But now you must put them all away: anger, wrath, malice, slander, and obscene talk from your mouth. **Do not lie to one another, seeing that you have put off the old self with its practices and have put on the new self, which is being renewed in knowledge after the image of its creator.**

Put to death sexual immorality. Avoid covetousness. Stop lying. Do this. Don't do that. Taboos. Prohibitions. Commandments. Rules. Enough already!

At least, that's how some feel when they read Colossians 3. The fact is, Paul does provide in quite some detail a list of proscribed activities. Later in the chapter he will insist on a display of compassion and kindness and humility and any number of other moral virtues to govern our relationships with one another, with our spouse, with our kids—with just about everyone.

So, here's the rub. What's the difference between what Paul commends in chapter 3 and what he condemns at the end of chapter 2? You may recall that he spoke harshly of those in Colossae who insisted on strict behavior when it came to such matters as eating and drinking, as well as the observance of certain religious festivals. The false teachers insisted on a rigorously ascetic life, always quick to say, "Don't handle that! Don't taste these! Don't touch those!" (see Col. 2:21).

What makes Paul's rules different? How is his perspective on the Christian life an improvement on theirs? He has commandments and taboos, as do they. So how does one avoid falling prey to the legalistic mentality that Paul so roundly denounced? How do we pursue holiness without reducing Christianity to being moral?

The answer is found in something Paul repeatedly emphasizes in chapter 3 that is noticeably absent from the manmade philosophy threatening the church in Colossae. Legalists, of whatever variety, typically argue *to* life. That is to say, they identify the good one must pursue and the bad one must avoid as a means to gain favor with God or as a condition on which he may be disposed to grant life.

Paul, on the other hand, together with other New Testament writers, argues *from* life. Holiness is portrayed as the fruit of acceptance with God, not the root. We already are the favored and beloved of God, made such by sovereign grace alone, and it is on the basis of this glorious truth that we are inwardly impelled (rather than outwardly compelled) to express life, not earn it.

We are not encouraged to do this or avoid that in order to gain Christ. Rather, it is because we have already died with Christ (Col. 2:20) and have already been raised with Christ (Col. 3:1) that we avidly seek after holiness. We pursue purity and eschew evil not in order to be hidden with him but because we already are (Col. 3:3).

Nowhere is this more clearly seen than in Colossians 3:9–10 where Paul explicitly mentions the basis on which he issues his ethical imperatives. Look closely: "Do not lie to one another, seeing that you *have put off the old self* with its practices and *have put on the new self*, which is being renewed in knowledge after the image of its creator." As was the case earlier in chapter 3, so also here the ground for his exhortation is the accomplished truths of salvation. And it doesn't stop here. It is also *because* we are "God's chosen ones, holy and beloved" (Col. 3:12), that we are to be compassionate and kind and humble, etc. And it is *because* we have already been fully and freely forgiven by Christ that we also must forgive one another (Col. 3:13).

So, the reason for this choice to "put to death" and "put off" such practices is that you have already discarded the old man and his ways and have put on the new. We put off the old man in our baptism with Christ in his death and we put on the new man when we were raised with Christ in baptism to newness of life.

The contrast between the old man and the new man is not simply an individual one, as if the old referred to my personal bad behavior and the new to my good, Christian conduct. Yes, that is involved, but there's more. There are corporate and historical-redemptive overtones in Paul's language. Peter O'Brien explains it best: "Just as the 'old man' is what they once were 'in Adam,' the embodiment of unregenerate humanity, so the 'new man' is what they now are 'in Christ,' the embodiment of the new humanity."[27] In other words, "the renewal refers not simply to an individual change of character but also to a corporate recreation of humanity in the Creator's image. Christ is the 'new man' whom the Colossians have put on. He is the second Adam, the head of a new creation."[28]

Interestingly, Paul has a different, but entirely compatible, emphasis in the parallel passage in Ephesians. There he commands the believer "to put off your old self" and "to put on the new self" (Eph. 4:22, 24). Thus, whereas in Colossians 3:9 and Romans 6:6 the break with the old is portrayed as having already occurred in the past, most likely at the moment of conversion, in Ephesians Paul calls on his readers "to continue to live out its significance by giving up on that old person that they no longer are. They are new people who must become in practice what God has already made them, and that involves the resolve to put off the old way of life as it attempts to impinge."[29] Here again we see the tension between the *already* and the *not yet* in Paul's theology. We have already put off the old man but we have not yet grown into a life of consistency with that new identity.

The bottom line, then, is this: There is a world of difference; indeed it is the difference between heaven and hell, between working *to* or *for* life, as if to put God in your debt, and working *from* and *because of* a life that God has already graciously and mercifully bestowed.

# 71

# To Be Like Jesus

## Colossians 3:10

Do not lie to one another, seeing that you have put off the old self with its practices **and have put on the new self, which is being renewed in knowledge after the image of its creator**.

Have you ever found yourself asking the question, "What is God doing in me, why is he doing it, and how?" Sadly, we often respond to that question with simplistic and unbiblical answers that cater to personal preferences and conform to what we want the Christian life to be.

There are, in fact, a number of different but compatible images, models, and metaphors in the New Testament that account for and explain the Christian life: it's a war, it's a walk, it's a washing; it's a romance, it's a race, it's a renovation. We are exhorted to fight against sin and be filled with the Spirit, to submit to our leaders and serve our Lord. The list could go on endlessly.

But there are certain common elements and themes that hold it all together and make sense of what we call sanctification. Three of them are found in Colossians 3:10 and are deserving of our attention. Forgive the alliteration and observe how Paul speaks of the process, the purpose, and the pattern of every Christian's life.

This new self that we put on when we came to faith in Christ and were identified with him in water baptism "is being renewed in knowledge after the image of its creator" (Col. 3:10). All three elements are found in this passage.

Let's begin with the *process*. It is, after all, a process and not a singular or momentary event. That is why we speak of "progressive" sanctification. Becoming what God desires of us is incremental, not instantaneous. I'd actually prefer it be the latter, but God knows better than I (surprise!). Divine wisdom dictates that we grow by fits and starts, by trial and error, by three steps forward and two back. This is suggested by Paul's use of the present passive, "is being renewed" (Col. 3:10). The only other place where Paul uses this verb in the present passive is in 2 Corinthians 4:16 where he says that in spite of outer decay "our inner nature is being renewed day by day."

Although we certainly have a responsibility to avail ourselves of the means of grace, God is always antecedent. Were he not first to work for us, there would be no work by us (cf. Phil. 2:12–13). The renewal is ultimately his doing, hence Paul's use of the passive. He is the ultimate and efficient cause of all change from selfish to selfless, from rebellious to repentant, from bondage to our fleshly impulses to the freedom of being like Jesus.

As Garland points out, "Paul does not urge the Colossians to amend their lives for the better, to reform their ways, or to make minor modifications in the direction of their lives.... [Rather] it is a matter of a new creation (cf. 2 Cor. 5:17), not just giving up a few vices and accepting a few virtues. One's whole nature must be exchanged, not just revamped."[30] Paradoxically, this experience, says Moule, requires "a continual 'mortification' of what is, in fact, already dead, a continual actualization of an already existing new creation."[31]

The *purpose* or goal of this process of renewal is "knowledge" (3:10), or perhaps "ever-increasing knowledge" would be more accurate. But knowledge of what? Of whom? Most likely it is either of God (Col. 1:10), of his will (Col. 1:9), or even of Christ (Col. 2:2; cf. Eph. 1:17; 4:13).

This is virtually synonymous with what Paul wrote in Romans 12:2: "Be transformed by the renewal of your mind." Christian growth is not the result of the crucifixion of the mind or the suspension of its exercise in deference to the spirit. Progressive renewal, that daily putting to death of fleshly behavior, only comes as the mind is renewed, not repressed or rejected. The mind, far from being the obstacle to Christian growth, is the object of the Spirit's daily renovation, cleansing, informing, and illumining.

Ignorance is the mortal enemy of sanctification and a Christlike life. There is certainly more to the Christian life than knowledge, but there is no Christian life without it. Knowledge may not be sufficient in itself, but it is absolutely necessary, and apart from it all other expressions of alleged conformity to Christ ring hollow and useless.

There is also a *pattern* or standard or measure in accordance with which this process unfolds. It is "after the image of its creator" (3:10). We could as easily render this "according to the image of its creator" or "in conformity with the image of its creator" (cf. Eph. 4:24).

In the New Testament, God is typically the subject of the verb *create*. However, since Christ is consistently portrayed as the image of God (see Col. 1:15; also Rom. 8:29; 1 Cor. 15:49; 2 Cor. 4:4; Phil. 2:6), Paul probably means that our re-creation is "after the pattern of Christ" who is God's perfect image. In other words, "God created 'the new person/humanity' and is now renewing it after the pattern of Christ, who is God's image."[32] This ongoing process of renewal, of re-creation, "continues until a full knowledge of God is acquired and Christians finally bear 'the image of the heavenly man' [cf. 1 Cor. 15:49] . . . as the result of a resurrection transformation."[33]

As I suggested in an earlier lesson, I don't want to grow into the fullness of who I am, but into the fullness of who Christ is. All my aspirations are submissive to his in me. He is the paradigm for life. He is the model for living. He is the standard of my sanctification.

The image of the Creator himself, who is preeminently Jesus Christ, serves as the archetype for the renewal of the believer. Christlikeness, comprehensively conceived, is the goal of renewal and our progressive transformation. God's aim in us and our aim through him is to think like Jesus, to love like Jesus, to feel and act and speak like Jesus. This is the essence of Christian living. Whatever other image or metaphor or model we use to explain "what God is doing in me, why he is doing it, and how," at its center and core is conformity to Christ.

# 72
# "All That Matters Is You, O Lord!"

## Colossians 3:11

> Here there is not Greek and Jew, circumcised and uncircumcised, barbarian, Scythian, slave, free; but Christ is all, and in all.

We who happily call ourselves evangelicals are good at proclaiming the gospel and insisting on the doctrine of justification by faith. We defend the inerrancy of Scripture and look forward to the Second Coming of Christ. In a word, we excel in our emphasis on the theological fundamentals of Scripture and the vertical dimension of our relationship with God.

But we don't do nearly as well when it comes to the horizontal implications of what Christ has accomplished. By "horizontal" I have in mind our ethical and social obligations to those around us, such as the pursuit of justice, opposition to racial discrimination, ministry to the poor and homeless, etc.

Sadly, many Christians view such things with more than a little suspicion, fearful that too much involvement outside the four walls of the church building will eventually undermine or dilute our commitment to the centrality of saving souls. But the apostle makes it inescapably clear that our new life in Christ must issue not only in personal purity but also in public righteousness. Often we pride ourselves on having conquered the sins in Colossians 3:5, 8, and 9, all the while harboring prejudice and disdain for people of another color, another race, a lower social status, an inferior educational degree, a less affluent economic stature.

Paul simply won't stand for it. "Here," that is to say, within this new humanity, this new life, this new identity that we have in Christ, "there is not Greek and Jew, circumcised and uncircumcised, barbarian, Scythian, slave, free; but Christ is all, and in all" (Col. 3:11). How so? Because "in one Spirit we were all baptized into one body—Jews or Greeks, slaves or free—and all were made to drink of one Spirit" (1 Cor. 12:13). Again, and yes, it needs to be stated again and again lest we dismiss it as secondary or unimportant, "there is neither Jew nor Greek, there is neither slave nor free, there is neither male nor female, for you are all one in Christ Jesus" (Gal. 3:28).

Paul's point is quite simple. He isn't saying that Gentiles literally become Jews or vice versa. Nor is he suggesting that slaves are no longer bound to their masters or that women are now men (Gal. 3:28). These ethnic, cultural, sexual, and social distinctions don't automatically disappear. They just don't matter anymore when it comes to our spiritual standing with God or the blessings and promises we inherit from him. In the body of Christ, ethnicity is irrelevant. In the church, economic achievement is irrelevant.

All these folk are now brothers (Col. 1:2) because they are united in Christ. Paul denounces all such discrimination on the single ground that the only thing that matters anymore is Christ. The same Jesus with whom you died and were raised and who now enables you to live as the new man that you are, indwells both Greek and Jew, both educated and barbarian, both slave and master, both male and female.

Let's be clear about one thing. Paul isn't talking about our merely believing this to be true. You can say that we are all one in Christ while you retain prejudice against a person of another race or fail to fight against efforts to perpetuate the old stereotypes. Our responsibility, indeed our joy, isn't just to declare this truth but to work diligently in the church and in society to embrace and affirm and liberate those who've suffered from the lingering effects of these divisions and the discrimination that energizes them.

Again, we evangelicals grew up singing, "Jesus loves the little children, all the children of the world: red and yellow, black and white, they are precious in his sight; Jesus loves the little children of the world." At the same time, many still wonder if perhaps he loves some more than others. Perhaps the red are more precious than the yellow. Maybe the white get spiritual perks withheld from the black. Paul's not talking about singing a song but living a life, perhaps demanding, sacrificial, and painful, that reflects the truth of what has been accomplished in the work of Christ.

So, if these factors don't matter anymore, what does? Jesus! This is the apostle's point in saying that "Christ is all and in all." The latter phrase, "in all," is not an affirmation of divine omnipresence, nor a declaration that Christ is in all circumstances providentially speaking (although he certainly is). Rather, Christ is in all who know him, regardless of ethnicity or social standing; he is no less in believing Gentiles and Scythians than he is in believing Jews; he indwells and abides fully with slaves no less than he does with the freeman.

The phrase "Christ is all" is not an endorsement of pantheism, as if Christ were indistinguishable from what he has made. Rather, Paul is stating in no uncertain terms that Christ is all that matters, something along the lines of our saying, "You're everything!" "You're the tops!" Jesus Christ, wrote Murray Harris, "amounts to everything and indwells all—without distinction—who belong to his new people."[34]

My good friend Daniel Brymer once wrote a song entitled, "All That Matters Is You, O Lord!" He's right. Can you honestly say that? Or does the pigmentation of people's skin matter more? Or their ancestry? Or the year and make of the car they drive? Or where they work? Or the size and diversity of their portfolio?

Let us never be so arrogant as to say that we know and embrace the gospel of Jesus Christ if we cannot also say that in him there is neither Jew nor Gentile, slave nor free, male nor female, rich nor poor, American nor Russian. And we will never be able to say it, or be happy about doing so, until we can fully grasp that "Christ is all, and in all." All that matters is you, O Lord. Really!

# 73

# Changed by His Choice

## Colossians 3:12

**Put on then, as God's chosen ones, holy and beloved, compassion, kindness, humility, meekness, and patience**, bearing with one another and, if one has a complaint against another, forgiving each other; as the Lord has forgiven you, so you also must forgive.

What does it mean to be "God's chosen ones, holy and beloved" (Col. 3:12a)? We'll get to that, but right now it may be more important and instructive to take note of the context in which these terms are found.

Don't think for a moment that Paul wasn't keenly aware of what had preceded in chapter 3 and what would immediately follow. He's been talking, rather forcefully and graphically, about our ethical responsibility, our moral obligations as Christian men and women to avoid sexual immorality, covetousness, anger, and lying, just to mention a few (see Col. 3:5–10). Beginning with 3:12 he will turn to more positive expressions of Christian behavior, such as compassion, kindness, humility, forgiveness, and love—again just to mention a few.

Some would argue that the worst possible thing you can do in such a setting is remind your readers of their privileges. They fear that to do so would undermine the urgency with which they respond to the many exhortations and moral imperatives that follow. "If you tell people that God has already chosen them and already consecrated them and already loves them, don't you rob them of any incentive to be holy?

Shouldn't such blessings be held forth as the reward for obedience, as the proverbial 'pot of gold' at the end of the rainbow of diligence and effort and meticulous observance of God's rules?" No!

Far from undermining holiness of life, the apostle believed that such glorious blessings undergird it. It is precisely because you are chosen of God and beloved that you must heed Paul's exhortations. It is "as" God's elect, sanctified, beloved people that Paul now commands we put on compassion and humility and love.

Anyone who might reason otherwise knows little, if anything, of God's grace. To tell yourself, "As God's elect people we are exempt from excessive concern with behavior," is to betray a massive distortion of the nature of saving grace, indeed, of the very nature of Christianity itself. To think that privilege and status and security somehow release the soul from moral accountability is directly contrary to everything Paul has written and will write in this letter.

The grace of God has appeared in the person and work of Christ precisely to train us "to renounce ungodliness and worldly passions, and to live self-controlled, upright, and godly lives in the present age" (Titus 2:12). Our having been sovereignly selected by God for salvation, set apart unto himself by his mercy (this is the sense in which we are here called holy), and being made the focus and object of his affection and love, are the reason for righteous behavior, not an excuse for sinful self-indulgence or a badge of honor that elevates one above the responsibilities of less-favored folk.

Paul's design in describing the Colossians (and us) with such exalted language isn't to lull them into spiritual slumber and moral indifference but to shock them, so to speak, with the stunning realization of who they are in Christ. He's determined to awaken them to the awesome task of living a life that honors the Lord and distinguishes them from the ways of the world. I can almost hear him shouting: "People! Do you have any idea who you are? Elect! Holy! Beloved! And do you know who's responsible for this? God, not you! Here, then, is how you are to live: be compassionate, kind, humble, meek, patient, bearing with one another, forgiving one another."

Are you suffering from an identity crisis? Do you struggle to know who you are? If so, let's put it to rest here and now. If you know Jesus Christ as your savior, you are one of "God's chosen ones, holy and beloved" (Col. 3:12). Do you really need to know anything else? Is it not enough to know you are the object of the saving, sovereign love of an infinitely righteous and powerful and holy God?

You are, literally, "elect of God." The ESV renders this "God's chosen ones," emphasizing the notion of possession or ownership. That's certainly involved, but I think Paul's emphasis is on the fact that it is God who has made this choice. You are the elect of God in the sense of being chosen by God (the NASB renders it "as those who have been chosen of God"). This decision emanated from him and him alone. It wasn't your choice or mine. It was his.

Not everyone likes the doctrine of election, but God does. We were chosen according to his "will." God didn't predestine us unwillingly, grudgingly, or reluctantly. He *wanted* to do it. He *delighted* to do it. Choosing hell-deserving sinners to spend an eternity with him as his beloved children is uniquely joyful and pleasing and exciting and satisfying to the heart of God. It pleased the Lord to set his love upon you. It made him happy.

We must never think of election as a dispassionate choice on God's part, as if it meant little to him or was discharged without feeling or thought or joy. According to Deuteronomy 10:14–15, although both heaven and earth belong to God, he "*set his heart in love* on your fathers and chose their offspring after them, you above all peoples, as you are this day."

Jesus "rejoiced in the Holy Spirit" as he contemplated the Father's electing love, and declared: "For such was *your gracious will*" (Matt. 11:26; Luke 10:21), or perhaps more accurately, "your good pleasure." God enjoys election, and so must we.

So what should be our response to all this? How does it make you feel to know that you are his "beloved"? What should you do, knowing that you are the recipient of his infinite affection, joy, and favor? Paul's answer: Change clothes! Strip off immorality and idolatry and malice. Put on compassion and purity and forgiveness. That's a start anyway.

# The Seamless Garment of Christian Godliness

## Colossians 3:12

**Put on then, as God's chosen ones, holy and beloved, compassion, kindness, humility, meekness, and patience**, bearing with one another and, if one has a complaint against another, forgiving each other; as the Lord has forgiven you, so you also must forgive.

The garment of Christian godliness is seamless. It isn't a patchwork of virtues sewed together and therefore just as easily pulled apart. The life that truly reflects the beauty and goodness of Jesus is unified in its display of the many, interrelated qualities that he embodied.

Nowhere is this better seen than in Colossians 3:12 where Paul lists several of the characteristics of that garment of godliness with which we are to adorn ourselves. "Put on, as God's chosen ones, holy and beloved, compassion [literally, "bowels of mercy"], kindness, humility, meekness [or "gentleness," as in the NASB], and patience." There's simply no way to have one of these without having them all. To forego one is to undermine the integrity of the others.

Before I go any further, note again how Paul envisions the Christian living in holiness: "put on" compassion and kindness, etc. As noted before, the verb often means "get dressed with" or "adorn" and "clothe" yourself. These virtues and qualities are portrayed as a beautiful, glorious floor-length garment that envelops the believer. "Deck yourself out in that garment," says Paul.

In yet another passage Paul doesn't even bother to enumerate or list the characteristics and qualities. He simply says, "Put on the Lord Jesus Christ, and make no provision for the flesh, to gratify its desires" (Rom. 13:14). All the features of a godly life were embodied perfectly in our Savior. Therefore, all one need do is put on Jesus! Clothe yourself with Christ.

But wait a minute. I'm already dressed. How can I put on Christ over what I'm already wearing? You can't. That's why both in Romans 13 and here in Colossians 3 Paul first tells us to get undressed, metaphorically speaking, of course. Strip off the garments of unrighteousness and sin; disrobe yourself of your former ways and then put on Jesus.

That these many virtues are interrelated, if not inseparable, is evident from a consideration of *humility* and *meekness* as just one example. It's not easy to differentiate between what these two words have in mind. We often use them interchangeably and rightly so.

Jesus spoke of the meek in the Beatitudes when he promised to them that they would inherit the earth (Matt. 5:5). The word used there is *praus* (cf. the use of *prautes* here in Col. 3:12 as well as in Gal. 5:23; 6:1). What is the essence of meekness?

Bobby Knight, boisterous basketball coach at Texas Tech University, once said: "The meek may well inherit the earth, but they rarely get rebounds!" This comment reveals the common misconception of meekness: that it entails indolence, laziness, weakness of heart, a sort of mental and emotional flabbiness, perhaps a fear of expressing oneself forcefully, a lack of aggression when called for, a tendency to compromise when the truth is at stake. Others would identify meekness with a docile, dependent personality. This is most assuredly not what Paul has in mind. What, then, does he mean?

Although meekness is not weakness, let's not lose sight of an essential element: tenderness and sensitivity, or a capacity to deal gently and compassionately with others. Thus we see immediately that to be "compassionate" (Col. 3:12a) one must first be "meek" (Col. 3:12d). You simply can't be merciful and mean-spirited at the same time.

Another essential element in meekness is the willingness to allow others to say about oneself the very things one readily acknowledges before God. Thus again, to be meek, one must first be "humble" (Col. 3:12c). Meekness, together with humility, is living in accordance with the abilities God has given us, neither as if we had more nor less, neither pressing ourselves into situations we are not equipped to handle (for fear that if we don't, people will lose respect for us), nor shying away from those we can.

The key to meekness and humility is a healthy acknowledgement of and submission to the sovereign grace of God. In 1 Corinthians 4:7, Paul writes: "For who sees anything different in you? What do you have that you did not receive? If then you received it, why do you boast as if you did not receive it?" Meekness should always be in direct proportion to one's grasp of grace. Pride is the fruit of the lie that what I have I didn't receive. Meekness or humility is the fruit of the truth that everything is of God (see also John 3:22–30, esp. vv. 27, 30).

The meek person is also, necessarily, "patient" (Col. 3:12e), in that he or she is not easily provoked: "A meek spirit, like wet tinder, will not easily take fire." And again: "Those who seek my life lay their snares; those who seek my hurt speak of ruin and meditate treachery all day long. But I am like a deaf man; I do not hear, like a mute man who does not open his mouth" (Ps. 38:12–13). Meekness, reflecting patience, is therefore the antithesis of hastiness, malice, and revenge.

Perhaps most of all, meekness is being like Jesus: "I am gentle [or meek] and lowly in heart" (Matt. 11:29; cf. Phil. 2:5–11). The measure of Christ's humility was his "compassion" (Col. 3:12a). Proud people don't love the unlovely very well. The measure of your humility is the degree to which you happily embrace the unembraceable, touch the untouchable, and love the unlovable.

So there it is: to be compassionate one must be kind, to be kind one must be humble, to be humble one must be meek, to be meek one must display patience. Such Jesus was. Such we ought to be.

# 75

# Forgive, as the Lord Has Forgiven You (1)

## Colossians 3:13

Put on then, as God's chosen ones, holy and beloved, compassion, kindness, humility, meekness, and patience, **bearing with one another and, if one has a complaint against another, forgiving each other; as the Lord has forgiven you, so you also must forgive**.

I once heard it said that much of the ground that Satan gains in the lives of Christians may be traced to unforgiveness. I couldn't agree more. It isn't hard to figure out why, once we realize that unforgiveness breeds bitterness, resentment, anger, unkindness, and even despair.

The apostle Paul certainly knew this, which explains his emphasis in Colossians 3:13 where he exhorts us to bear "with one another, . . . forgiving each other; as the Lord has forgiven you, so you also must forgive."

Nothing is more important for us than to know what forgiveness is as well as what it isn't. So what I propose in this meditation is to look at five myths about forgiveness, that is to say, five lies many of us have embraced about what it means to forgive another person. In the subsequent lesson I'll turn to five truths about forgiveness, or five essential elements apart from which true forgiveness will never take place.

First, contrary to what many have been led to believe, forgiveness is not forgetting. "Forgive and forget," we have been told by so many through the years. It's a nice saying, but highly misleading. Why?

God does not forget, notwithstanding your interpretation of Jeremiah 31:34, which says, "For I will forgive their iniquity, and I will remember their sin no more." This language of the prophet is a metaphor, a word picture, designed to emphasize God's gracious determination and resolve not to hold us liable for our sin. He has canceled the debt and will never demand payment. If God could literally forget, it would undermine the truth of his omniscience. God always has and always will know all things, but he has promised never to use our sin against us or treat us as if the reality of our sin were present in his mind.

Additionally, "forgive and forget," quite simply, is psychologically impossible. As soon as you make up your mind to forget something you can be assured that, in most instances, it is the one thing that will linger at the forefront of your conscious thinking. We all forget things, but we do it unintentionally over the course of time. Life and experience and old age work to erase certain things from our memory, but that is rarely if ever the case with sins committed against us and the wounds we have suffered.

To think that forgiving demands forgetting can be emotionally devastating. Let's suppose that Jane succeeds for two months in forgetting Sally's betrayal of her. She's getting along well and hasn't given a second thought to Sally's sin. Then Jane is told that Sally did the same thing to Mary and she immediately remembers the offense she herself endured. She is suddenly riddled with guilt for having failed to forget. What she thought she had forever put out of her mind now comes rushing back involuntarily and she feels like an utter failure for not having truly forgiven her friend. Worse still, she now feels like a hypocrite for having promised to forget only once again to feel anger and resentment toward Sally. Not only is Jane emotionally devastated, she now realizes how impossible it is to literally forget something so painful. This makes her extremely reluctant ever to forgive anyone again, knowing in her heart that she is incapable of forgetting.

Second, forgiving someone does not mean you no longer feel the pain of the offense. In most cases, the only way you can stop hurting is to stop feeling, and the only way you can stop feeling is to die emotionally. But passionless robots can truly love neither God nor others. This may be the primary reason people are reluctant to forgive. They know they can't stop feeling the sting of the sin against them, and they don't want to be insincere by saying they forgave when deep down inside they know they didn't.

Let's suppose that Barbara discovers that her husband Bill has had an affair. The agony and deep feelings of betrayal are intense. Although Barbara seeks extensive counseling, she eventually separates from her husband for a season. Upon their reconciliation, she forgives him, but she is under the assumption that in so doing she must never again feel the pain of his adultery. Then one evening she sees Bill smiling and talking to another woman at church. Although it was nothing more than innocent friendliness, the anguish and suspicion of his betrayal come rushing back into her soul. She berates herself and questions her own sincerity: "What's the matter with me that I can't get over this?" Barbara has to learn that the pain of her husband's adultery will probably never entirely dissipate, but that doesn't mean she hasn't truly forgiven him.

Third, forgiving someone who has sinned against you doesn't mean you cease longing for justice. Be certain of this: vengeance is not a bad thing. If it were, God would himself be in a bit of trouble, for as Paul tells us, "Beloved, never avenge yourselves, but leave it to the wrath of God, for it is written, 'Vengeance is mine, I will repay, says the Lord'" (Rom. 12:19). To long for justice is entirely legitimate, but to seek it for yourself is not. Let God deal with the offender in his own way at the appropriate time. He's much better at it than you or I.

The point is that forgiveness does not mean you are to ignore that a wrong was done or that you deny that a sin was committed. Forgiveness does not mean that you close your eyes to moral atrocity and pretend that it didn't hurt or that it really doesn't matter whether the offending person is called to account for his or her offense. Neither are you being asked to diminish the gravity of the offense or to tell others, "Oh, think nothing of it; it really wasn't that big a deal after all." Forgiveness simply means that you determine in your heart to let God be the avenger. He is the judge, not you.

Often we refuse to forgive others because we mistakenly think that to do so is to minimize their sin. "And that's not fair! He really hurt me. If I forgive, who's going to care for me and take up my cause and nurse my wounds?" God is. We must never buy into the lie that to forgive means that sin is being whitewashed or ignored or that the perpetrator is not being held accountable for his or her actions. It simply means we consciously choose to let God be the one who determines the appropriate course of action in dealing justly with the offending person.

Fourth, forgiveness does not mean you are to make it easy for the offenders to hurt you again. They may in fact hurt you again. That is their decision. But you must set boundaries on your relationship with them. The fact that you establish rules to govern how and to what extent you interact with such people in the future does not mean that you have failed to sincerely and truly forgive them. True love never aids and abets the sin of another. The offenders may themselves be offended that you set parameters on your friendship to prevent them from doing further harm. They may even say, "How dare you? This just proves that you didn't mean it when you said you forgave me." Don't buy into their manipulation. Forgiveness does not mean you become a helpless and passive doormat for their continual sin.

Fifth, forgiveness is rarely a one-time, climactic event. It is most often a life-long process. However, forgiveness has to begin somewhere at some point in time. There will undoubtedly be a moment, an act, when you decisively choose to forgive. It may well be highly emotional and spiritually intense and bring immediate relief, a sense of release and freedom. But that doesn't necessarily mean you'll never need to do it again. You may need every day to reaffirm to yourself your forgiveness of another. Each time you see the person, you may need to say, "Self, remember that you forgave _____!"

There may well be other myths concerning forgiveness, but those are probably the most important ones. In our next study we'll turn our attention to the essence of true forgiveness.

# 76

# Forgive, as the Lord Has Forgiven You (2)

## Colossians 3:13

Put on then, as God's chosen ones, holy and beloved, compassion, kindness, humility, meekness, and patience, **bearing with one another and, if one has a complaint against another, forgiving each other; as the Lord has forgiven you, so you also must forgive**.

*I*n the previous lesson we looked at five myths about forgiveness that many people, sadly, embrace as truth. We now need to look at what forgiveness actually is. What does it mean and how do we do it?

The apostle Paul said in our text that we are to forgive as the Lord has forgiven us (Col. 3:13b; cf. Eph. 4:32). The word "as" points to two things. We are to forgive *because* God forgave us. But we are also to forgive *as* or *like* or *in the same manner* that he forgave us. So, how did God in Christ forgive us? This leads us to the five truths about forgiveness.

First, God in Christ forgave us by absorbing in himself the destructive and painful consequences of our sin against him.

Jackie Pullinger is a missionary and church planter in Hong Kong whose remarkable life story is told in her autobiography, *Chasing the Dragon*.[35] (Get it! Read it!) One particular incident occurred in the early years of Jackie's ministry that illustrates the point I'm making here. A young man named Ah Ping had joined the Triads, gangs that controlled crime in Hong Kong, when he was only twelve years old. He soon came to be supported financially by a fourteen-year-old prostitute. When Jackie showed up and began to reach out in mercy and kindness to Ah Ping and his associates, he told her in no uncertain terms: "You'd better go. Just get out of here. We're no good. Go find some people who will appreciate what you're doing and be grateful for your kindness. We will only hurt you and exploit you and kick you around. Why do you stay? Why do you care?" Said Jackie, "I stay because that's what Jesus did for me. I didn't want him either. But he didn't wait until I got good and wanted him. He died for me while I was his hateful enemy. He loved me and forgave me. He loves you, too."

"No way," shouted Ah Ping. "Nobody could love us like that. We rape and fight and steal and stab. Nobody could love us." She explained how Jesus didn't love what they did, but that he still loves sinners and is willing to forgive them. Ah Ping was shattered. He sat down on the street corner and received Christ as his savior. Not long after his conversion, Ah Ping was attacked by a gang of youths and was beaten mercilessly with bats. When his friends vowed revenge, Ah Ping said, "No. I'm a Christian now and I don't want you to fight back."

What transformed Ah Ping? What accounted for his readiness to forgive his enemies? It was his realization that Jesus Christ had absorbed in himself the consequences of Ah Ping's sins.

So what is forgiveness? It is deciding to live with the painful consequences of another person's sin. You are going to have to live with it anyway, so you might as well do it without the bitterness and rancor and hatred that threaten to destroy your soul.

Second, God forgave us in Christ by canceling the debt we owed him. That is to say, we are no longer held liable for our sins or in any way made to pay for them.

The way we cancel the debt of one who has sinned against us is by promising not to bring it up to the offender, to others, or to ourselves. We joyfully resolve never to throw the sin back into the face of the one who committed it. We promise never to hold it over their head, using it to manipulate and shame them. And we promise never to bring it up to others in an attempt to justify ourselves or to undermine their reputation. And lastly, we promise never to bring it up to ourselves as grounds for self-pity or to justify our resentment of the person who hurt us.

Third, forgiving others as God has forgiven us means we resolve to revoke revenge.

As noted earlier, this doesn't mean we cease desiring that justice be served. It does mean we refuse, by God's grace, to let the anger and pain energize an agenda to exact payment from those who wrong us, whether that payment be emotional, relational, physical, or financial. It also means we refuse to use our past suffering to justify present sin.

Fourth, forgiving others as God has forgiven us means that we determine to do good to them rather than evil. Read especially Romans 12:17–21.

This may entail doing simple acts of kindness, like greeting them warmly, from the heart, or providing a meal when they are sick, or other routine acts of compassion or mercy. What will it accomplish? It will both surprise and shame them (in a redemptive way).

Usually people who deliberately sin against you expect that you will respond in like fashion. If you do, it justifies in their mind their initial sin against you. The last thing they expect is sustained kindness and strength. Thus when evil is met with goodness it disarms them; they are stunned with incredulity. According to Dan Allender, it is goodness that breaks the spell the enemy tries to cast and renders him powerless.[36] Hopefully, this will open a door in your relationship that will lead to a genuine life change.

Responding this way also shames them. I'm not talking about a bad sense of shame, as if you are seeking to humiliate them. Rather, your hope is to expose the condition of their heart, to lay bare their motivation, and to enable them to see the wickedness of their deed. Responding to evil with good compels those who offend you to look at themselves rather than at you. When the light of your kindness shines back in the face of their darkness, the latter is exposed for being what it really is. The shame they feel on being "found out" will either harden or soften their heart, depending on how they choose to respond.[37]

Fifth, God forgave us in Christ by reconciling us to himself, by restoring the relationship that our sin had shattered.

Often we avoid forgiveness because we want to avoid conflict. Going to the offender and saying, "I forgive you," carries the potential for an explosion. He or she may even deny having sinned against us. But true forgiveness pursues relationship and restoration. True forgiveness is not satisfied with simply canceling the debt. It longs to love again.

It's important to remember two things here. First, the offenders may refuse your overtures of kindness and resist any efforts on your part to reconcile. But that's ultimately out of your control. As Paul said in Romans 12:18, your responsibility is to do whatever you can within your power to be at peace. If they refuse to be at peace with you, the fault is theirs. You will at least have fulfilled your responsibility before God.

Second, oftentimes when the reconciliation or restoration is successful, the relationship never fully returns to what it was before the offense was committed. It takes a long time to regain trust and confidence and delight in another person after a serious sin has been committed. But even without such delight, it doesn't mean you haven't fully forgiven the person.

In conclusion, none of this will make sense to someone who has not experienced and received and tasted the joy of the forgiveness of God in Christ Jesus. If we do not forgive as the Scriptures command, perhaps the problem is with our ignorance of what God has done for us in Christ. That is why the key to forgiveness is the cross.

# The Crowning Glory of Christian Godliness

## Colossians 3:14

Put on then, as God's chosen ones, holy and beloved, compassion, kindness, humility, meekness, and patience, bearing with one another and, if one has a complaint against another, forgiving each other; as the Lord has forgiven you, so you also must forgive. **And above all these put on love, which binds everything together in perfect harmony.**

You may be tired of hearing about it, but there's simply no escaping the centrality of love in the community of God's people. We must consciously resist any temptation to diminish its importance or casually set it to the side simply because it's overused and abused.

I certainly understand why there is a reaction to the concept of love. I've seen countless instances where truth has been compromised or altogether sacrificed in the name of preserving and promoting some vague ideal that goes by the name of love. We've all witnessed the emergence of "sloppy agape," in which love has been cited to trump righteousness or discipline or justice. And who can deny that in our society at large love has become virtually synonymous with lust. So, yes, the temptation to shake our heads in frustration and ignore the biblical mandate to love is all too real.

But make no mistake: the centrality and supremacy of love among all Christian virtues is pervasive in the biblical record. One need only think of Paul's declaration in Romans 13:8–9 that "the one who loves another has fulfilled the law," and that "the commandments . . . are summed up in this word" (cf. Gal. 5:14). We must never forget that whereas "faith, hope, and love abide . . . the greatest of these is love" (1 Cor. 13:13). It is "in Christ Jesus," Paul reminds us, that "neither circumcision nor uncircumcision counts for anything, but only faith working through love" (Gal. 5:6).

The supremacy of love among all Christian qualities and virtues is reinforced here in Colossians 3:14, where Paul writes, "And above all these put on love, which binds everything together in perfect harmony." To fully appreciate Paul's point, we need to analyze this translation (ESV).

Does he mean "above all these" (or "upon all these") in the sense that love is the crowning grace with which we are to adorn ourselves? In other words, is love the hat, so to speak, which tops off the clothing of Christ which we are to "put on" (Col. 3:12) and wear daily? Or should we render this phrase "beyond all things," the point being that love is the greatest and most important of all virtues? I don't think there's much need for a choice, for the two notions certainly overlap and each assumes the other.

More challenging is the latter part of the verse in which Paul describes love as that which "binds everything together in perfect harmony" (Col. 3:14b). The single word translated "perfect harmony" has the sense of perfection or maturity or completeness. Its only other occurrence in the New Testament is in Hebrews 6:1. I actually prefer rendering the phrase something like, "the bond that produces (or results in) perfection."

But what exactly is love envisioned as binding together in perfection or completeness? Is it the many and varied virtues that Paul has just described in verses 12 and 13? In other words, is Paul saying that love is the grace or power that holds all the others together? There is certainly a sense in which love is the catalyst that empowers and energizes all other fruit of the Spirit. And who could deny that love is also the spiritual lubricant, so to speak, that minimizes relational friction and makes the rest of the virtues function smoothly? It is the glue that unites all Christian qualities. It is the mortar that holds the bricks of Christian behavior in place. Without love, knowledge is but a selfish and arrogant acquisition; without love, purity is self-righteousness; without love, zeal is an aimless endeavor; without love, hope is a fool's deception. Love, as it were, holds them all together in a single coherent package.[38]

Whereas that is all quite true and can be defended from any number of other texts, I'm not certain that is what Paul has in mind here in Colossians 3:14. Given the emphasis in 3:8–11 on the importance of harmony amidst the diversity in the body of Christ, I think Paul envisions love as that which ultimately binds together the Christian community itself. In other words, it isn't so much the virtues of individual Christians that are bound together by love (as true as that may be in its own right) as it is the many fellow-believers themselves who are united by this remarkable affection.

David Garland agrees. "Paul's main concern," he suggests, "is not that these virtues be joined together in a perfect unity. Instead, he is concerned about diverse individuals—Greek, Jew, barbarian, Scythian, slave and free—being joined together in one community. . . . Love bonds the community of believers together into the one body where peace reigns (3:15) and leads to their perfection (see Eph. 4:13)."[39] Dunn agrees, that "at the end of the day it is this love (and only this love) which is strong enough to hold together a congregation of disparate individuals."[40]

Whatever the case, and however we choose to translate verse 14, let no one deny the indispensable role that love plays in our lives individually and corporately as God's people. And just as our forgiving one another (Col. 3:13) is based on Christ's having forgiven us, so too must our love be modeled after the love wherewith he loved us.

# 78

# The Peace of Christ

## Colossians 3:15

And let the peace of Christ rule in your hearts, to which indeed you were called in one body. And be thankful.

One undeniable thing about the New Testament is its often brutal honesty. There is no whitewashing of human weakness or the hardships of life. The apostle Paul is especially open and forthright about the struggles of being a Christian as well as the realities of existence in the church. We are not yet perfect. Heaven is still to come.

Nowhere is this better seen than in Colossians 3. Paul recognizes that, notwithstanding the grace of conversion, Christians still fight against fleshly impulses to sexual immorality and impurity and anger and unforgiveness, just to mention a few. He knows that believers are capable of exasperating behavior and that sinning against one another (cf. 3:13) is a very real threat that must be addressed.

Disputes are inevitable. Schisms occur. Theological disagreements and relational friction are ever present. Threats to the unity and tranquility of church life are all too real. This is why Paul includes this crucial word of counsel on how to resolve such problems when they arise: "And let the peace of Christ rule in your hearts, to which indeed you were called in one body" (Col. 3:15a).

The first order of business is determining what Paul means by "the peace of Christ." He earlier stated that Christ made "peace by the blood of his cross" (Col. 1:20). That is to say, he removed the hostility of God toward sinners by absorbing it in himself on the tree. Thereby he established a relationship of peace, tranquility, harmony, love, and fellowship between God and the Christian.

Then there is the "peace" Jesus had in view in John 14:27 when he reassured his disciples with this promise: "Peace I leave with you; my peace I give to you." This is a peace he both embodies and gives. It is the peace that characterizes Christ himself, a peace that he in turn graciously imparts to his people.

Clearly, then, Paul is saying that in making decisions in the corporate assembly we must give consideration "in our hearts" to what will preserve and promote the peace that Christ died to achieve. It is in the realm of the "one body" (3:15b), the church, where this "peace of Christ" comes to effect and exercises its authority.

Although the "peace of Christ" in other contexts may well refer to the personal and individual experience of spiritual tranquility (cf. the "peace of God" in Phil. 4:7), I don't think that is Paul's primary concern here in Colossians 3. The context of this passage is the corporate body of Christ and relations among the many and varied members of the church. This is obvious from a careful reading of verses 11, 12, 13, and 14 (note the emphasis in these verses on how we interact with others in the church).

This is reinforced, I believe, by the word Paul uses that is here translated "rule" (found only here in the New Testament). This word was used to describe the responsibility of an umpire in the athletic games who directed the competition and rendered decisions concerning the winners of each contest. He also awarded the competitors their prizes. It later came to have the more general meaning of "to arbitrate, give a verdict, preside, rule, control, and hold sway."

Thus, contrary to the way many have used this passage, Paul is not telling us to make personal decisions in our individual lives based on whether or not we "feel peace" in our hearts. "I'm at peace with this course of action" is something I often hear people say as a way of declaring their conviction that they are in the will of God. This may well be legitimate in another context, but it is not what Paul is addressing here.

We should also take note of the reference to the "one body" (i.e., the unified corporate life of the church) to which we "were called" (3:15b). Whether or not we should take "in one body" as expressing purpose or perhaps result (hence, "so that you might be united in one body" or "so that you form one body"), or simply "as members of one body," the point is the same: pay close heed to what maintains the unity of the church.

This, then, is Paul's point: "In making your decisions, in choosing between alternatives, in settling conflicts of will, a concern to preserve the inward and communal peace that Christ gave and gives should be your controlling principle."[41] A decisive factor in how you should conduct yourselves in relation one to another is whether or not the peace that Christ died to achieve and impart is preserved and promoted. When you are faced with tensions and potentially divisive decisions in the community of faith, give strong consideration to what will most effectively sustain the "peace of Christ."

The apostle said much the same thing in Ephesians 4:3. There he called on Christians to be "eager to maintain the unity of the Spirit in the bond of peace." There is an obvious urgency in Paul's exhortation to be "eager." That is to say, spare no effort, make it a priority, be urgent about it, make haste! Peace has a bonding effect. It is that which enables us to get along and support and sustain one another. Thus, "the bond of peace" is the means by which we demonstrate to the world that unity which the Spirit has created among us. This unity already exists by virtue of what the Spirit has done, but we must be diligently committed to preserving it.

One final comment is needed. Paul is not saying that peace, precious though it be, is preeminent. Unity in the church is certainly important, but it doesn't come at any price. We must never sacrifice the fundamental truths of Christian faith simply to avoid conflict. One cannot appeal to this passage to justify the termination of all theological disputes in the church. Paul is not suggesting that "peace trumps truth" and that we should compromise on what we know to be biblical lest we offend those who disagree.

Some things are actually worth fighting for. One thinks immediately of Galatians 1:6–10 and Paul's commitment to the purity of the gospel. We cannot negotiate when it comes to the foundational principles of God's work in Christ in saving souls. Any so-called "peace" that comes at the expense of gospel truth is not "of Christ," no matter how pleasant it may feel or effective it may appear.

# How Rich the Word of Christ!

## Colossians 3:16

Let the word of Christ dwell in you richly, teaching and admonishing one another in all wisdom, singing psalms and hymns and spiritual songs, with thankfulness in your hearts to God.

Yes, all Scripture is God-breathed and profitable for our instruction and growth in Christ. No text is any more inspired than another. At the same time, some passages seem to have been written in bold print, in a different font, so to speak. They come across as if highlighted at every turn with exclamation points. One feels as if they are crying out more loudly than others, demanding our undivided attention and analysis.

"Don't just read me," they seem to say. "Feast on me! Meditate! Ruminate! Saturate your spirit! Let my words wash over your soul like the refreshing waters of a cool mountain stream. Hear them again and again. May they be permanently embedded in your brain, shaping how you think and live and relate to one another. Don't be satisfied with a surface scan. Dig deeply. Explore me, word upon word, line upon line."

For whatever reason, Colossians 3:16 has this effect on me. Perhaps it's because this is one of the rare passages in the New Testament that provides us with a glimpse of how the early church worshiped. Given the controversy today over how to "do church," as well as the "worship wars" that continue to rage, this passage is remarkably relevant for us in the twenty-first century. Then there is its literary and theological complexity. The grammatical options are numerous, and the consequences of our decisions on how to render it in English are far-reaching.

Needless to say, I'm compelled to spend several lessons meditating on its truths. I do run the risk, however, of focusing so precisely on the many words and phrases that we lose sight of the forest for having analyzed the trees. I don't want to break it up into so many individual parts that we lose sight of the majestic whole or lose sight of its place in the larger context of the epistle. So the task ahead is a difficult one, but ever so important.

Here again is the passage before us: "Let the word of Christ dwell in you richly, teaching and admonishing one another in all wisdom, singing psalms and hymns and spiritual songs, with thankfulness in your hearts to God." For the sake of our study, I would like to suggest an alternative rendering to the ESV translation that I believe more accurately reflects what Paul is saying. The differences are minor in appearance, but not insignificant: "Let the word of Christ dwell in you richly, teaching and admonishing one another in all wisdom by means of psalms, hymns, and spiritual songs, singing in your hearts to God with thanksgiving."

My translation is to some extent shaped by the parallel passage in Ephesians 5:18–19. There Paul exhorted the church, "Do not get drunk with wine, for that is debauchery, but be filled with the Spirit, addressing one another in psalms and hymns and spiritual songs, singing and making melody to the Lord with all your heart." What Paul meant by "addressing" or "speaking" in Ephesians 5:19 is defined as "teaching and admonishing" in Colossians 3:16.

As a way of getting started, let's focus on what Paul means by the phrase "the word of Christ." Although some have said it means "the word spoken by Christ," I'm not convinced. I don't think Paul is referring to words that Jesus might speak directly into the hearts of individual Christians. Rather, this is "the word about Christ," that is to say, all the truth that has been revealed and is now in Scripture concerning him.

Most likely "the word of Christ" is identical to what Paul wrote in Colossians 1:5 where he spoke of "the word of the truth, the gospel." The "word of Christ," therefore, is the totality of biblical revelation concerning Jesus: who he is, his mission, his life, his redemptive work, his character and will and ways.

At the core of our individual and corporate experience as God's people must be the person and work of Jesus. The importance of this for today is easily seen with a quick glance at the predominant themes in our pulpits and on our platforms. Christ is largely absent! That's not an overstatement. Obsessive preoccupation with self has usurped the place of Jesus in the life and ministry of countless churches.

If you listen closely to what is being proclaimed on Sunday mornings, you will discern two dominant themes: conquering and coping. How can I conquer my world? How can I enter into my destiny? How can I triumph over my enemies and claim my inheritance? How can I better cope with life's daily struggles? How can I relate more effectively with my peers and co-workers? If Christ is mentioned, and he usually is, he exists to aid us in our search for significance. He is important only so far as he awakens us to our importance. We talk about him so that we can feel good about ourselves. Need I go on?

No, I'm not saying that conquering and coping are unimportant or should be ignored in the ministry of the church. In fact, Paul will address a number of these practical issues in the latter half of Colossians 3. But in virtually every instance he grounds the responsibility or task in our prior relationship with Christ. If wives are to submit to their husbands it is because such "is fitting in the Lord" (Col. 3:18). Although not explicit in Colossians, in Ephesians 5 the responsibility of husbands to love their wives is patterned after the love Christ has for his church and his sacrifice in giving "himself up for her" (Eph. 5:25). Slaves are to obey their masters, "fearing the Lord" (Col. 3:22). They are to work heartily, "as for the Lord" (Col. 3:23). Indeed, they are "serving the Lord Christ" and will receive their inheritance "from the Lord" (Col. 3:24). Masters must treat their servants justly, knowing that they "also have a Master in heaven" (Col. 4:1).

Paul's point is that every human relationship, every human responsibility, whether it entails conquering some obstacle or enemy or coping with yet another problem or person, must be seen in light of the person and work of Christ and be governed by it as a controlling principle. The redemptive suffering of Christ for his church, his dominion as Lord, and his authority as the judge of all things all have a direct and practical impact on how we function on a daily basis. If the "word of Christ" is not allowed to exert this formative influence on our beliefs and behavior, whatever conquering and coping skills we develop will not be pleasing to God or honoring of Christ himself.

This word of Christ, says Paul, must dwell in us richly. The word Paul uses, translated "dwell," should not be taken as some sort of inert or static presence. It has a dynamic force and envisions an operative and transformative and powerful force within and among us. I say "within and among us" because Paul likely has in view more than simply an individual experience. Given the contextual emphasis on the corporate reality of the one body" and our obligations one to another (see vv. 11–15), the word of Christ must dwell "among us," that is to say, in our midst as the body, exercising its authority and power within the life of the gathered community of God's people.

Thus, Paul's point is that we must grant the word of Christ the highest priority and place in the corporate experience of the church. It must be preached, proclaimed, explained, and applied. Whatever use is made of drama, multimedia displays, or other forms of communication, "the word of Christ" should be the focus. It should dwell "in us" individually and "among us" corporately (by the way, either of these is a legitimate rendering of the Greek), not haphazardly or insignificantly, but richly! In other words, let the truth about Jesus be taught and known and obeyed in all its glory and beauty and richness. Give it full sway. Let its intrinsic power and splendor do its work in and for you.

Would that we might leave every church service and every small group gathering saying, "The word of Christ dwelt richly among us here today! All that we know of him governed what we said and sang and did by way of ministry." To the extent that we do reveals how clearly we understand Paul's counsel and how committed we are to implementing it in church life.

# 80

# Singing Truth

## Colossians 3:16

Let the word of Christ dwell in you richly, teaching and admonishing one another in all wisdom, singing psalms and hymns and spiritual songs, with thankfulness in your hearts to God.

The translation of Colossians 3:16 in the ESV is slightly different from the NASB. According to the former, our responsibility is one of "teaching and admonishing one another in all wisdom, singing psalms and hymns and spiritual songs, with thankfulness in [y]our hearts to God." As you can see, "psalms and hymns and spiritual songs" are to be sung by Christians. Well, of course one sings them! But I don't think that's what this verse is saying. Rather, I would opt for the NASB rendering, in which we are envisioned as "teaching and admonishing one another with psalms and hymns and spiritual songs." Did you notice the difference?

Whereas both views are grammatically possible, I'm swayed by the parallel passage in Ephesians 5:18–19. There Paul exhorted the church, "Do not get drunk with wine, for that is debauchery, but be filled with the Spirit, addressing one another in psalms and hymns and spiritual songs, singing and making melody to the Lord with all your heart." Clearly, and indisputably, Paul envisions believers communicating truth and knowledge and instruction by means of these various forms of singing. It seems quite reasonable, therefore, that the same point is being made in Colossians 3:16. The "addressing" or "speaking" in Ephesians 5:19 is now defined as "teaching and admonishing" in Colossians 3:16.

Thus, in the NASB translation, Paul's point is that the way to let the "word of Christ richly dwell" in our midst is by our teaching and admonishing one another *with* or *by means of* psalms and hymns and spiritual songs. I realize that sounds odd to modern ears. The first question you may be tempted to ask is, "How does one teach someone else by singing to them? How can singing psalms and hymns and spiritual songs admonish another believer?"

Those are excellent questions and ones that I think Paul wants us to ask. But before we give an answer, let us ask, what's the difference, if any, between psalms and hymns and spiritual songs? Some insist there is no difference among these items. But if he meant only one thing, what is the point of employing three different words? More likely Paul had a distinction in mind that's important for us to note.

"Psalms" most likely refers to those inspired compositions in the Old Testament book of that name. Luke uses the word in this way in his writings (Luke 20:42; 24:44; Acts 1:20; 13:33), and Paul encouraged Christians to come to corporate worship with a psalm to offer (1 Cor. 14:26). The word literally meant "to pluck" or "to strike or twitch the fingers on a string" and thus could possibly have referred to singing with instrumental accompaniment (although we shouldn't restrict it to that).

The word "hymns" would be any human composition that focuses on God or Christ. Hannah's song in 1 Samuel 2 or the Song of Moses in Exodus 15 would qualify, as would Mary's Magnificat in Luke 1. Perhaps the most explicit examples would be the so-called Christ Hymns in Philippians 2:6–11, Colossians 1:15–20, and 1 Timothy 3:16.

Why is the third expression of singing designated as "spiritual" (although some contend that this adjective applies to all three)? Could it be Paul's way of differentiating between songs that were previously composed as over against those that are spontaneously evoked by the Spirit himself? Yes, I think so. In other words, "spiritual songs" are most likely unrehearsed and improvised, perhaps short melodies or choruses extolling the beauty of Christ. They aren't prepared in advance but are prompted by the Spirit and thus are uniquely and especially appropriate to the occasion or the emphasis of the moment. I agree with Dunn that these may well be "songs sung under immediate inspiration of the Spirit."[42] He believes there was, in all probability, "a lively, spontaneous, charismatic worship (including glossolalia?) [that] continued to be a feature of the Pauline churches . . . , at least for the full length of his own ministry."[43]

If these distinctions are valid, Murray Harris would be correct in calling them, respectively, "songs from Scripture, songs about Christ, and songs from the Spirit."[44] This possibility strikes many as strange for the simple fact that, outside of charismatic churches, there are virtually no opportunities for expressions of spontaneous praise. The only songs permitted are those listed in the bulletin or liturgy. Singing is highly structured, orchestrated, and carefully controlled (but not for that reason any less godly or edifying). There is typically a distinct beginning and ending without the possibility of improvisation or free vocalization. People are expected to sing what is written in the hymnal or projected on a screen, nothing more and nothing less.

But Paul seems to envision a singing in which the individual is given freedom to vocalize his or her own passions, prayers, and declarations of praise. Although this may strike some as chaotic and aimless the first time it is heard (it certainly did me!), it can quickly become a beautiful and inspiring experience as the Spirit is given free reign in the hearts of Christ's people. As the instrumentalists play a simple chord progression or perhaps even the melody of a familiar song, the people spontaneously supply whatever words are most appropriate to their state of mind and heart. As Dunn noted, this may well have involved singing in tongues (without being restricted to it), or what Paul describes in 1 Corinthians 14:15 as "singing in the Spirit."

On countless occasions I have been blessed and edified by what some have called "prophetic singing" (so called because it is believed the Spirit reveals something to the person who in turn puts it to music). Typically an individual who is part of a worship team is led by the Spirit into a spontaneous song that may well evoke another to respond antiphonally. Such "spiritual songs" can last a few seconds or several minutes. Often, what one person sings will stir up yet another with a similar refrain, which on occasion will lead back into a verse or the chorus of a hymn previously sung.

I can only hope and pray that those of you who have never been exposed to this form of worship will have opportunity to experience it first hand.

More important still is the fact that such singing, whether psalms, hymns, or spiritual songs, is designed not simply to extol God but to educate his people. By means of psalms, hymns, and spiritual songs we "teach" and "admonish" one another. Clearly Paul envisioned songs that were biblically grounded and theologically substantive, songs that both communicated truth and called for heartfelt consecration, repentance, and devotion to the Lord. It's possible, as O'Brien has pointed out, that if Paul "had in mind antiphonal praise or solo singing for mutual edification in church meetings . . . then mutual instruction and exhortation could well have been possible."[45] Let's also not forget that Paul is describing a situation far in advance of the printing press and hymnbooks. Thus these various expressions of singing were an invaluable means for transmitting and inculcating Christian truth.

Although many today may never experience a worship service that incorporates these elements in the way I described, the educational and convicting power in music and song cannot be denied. Wrote Warren Wiersbe:

> I am convinced that congregations learn more theology (good and bad) from the songs they sing than from the sermons they hear. Many sermons are doctrinally sound and contain a fair amount of biblical information, but they lack that necessary emotional content that gets hold of the listener's heart. Music, however, reaches the mind and the heart at the same time. It has power to touch and move the emotions, and for that reason can become a wonderful tool in the hands of the Spirit or a terrible weapon in the hands of the Adversary.[46]

All the more reason for us to be conscientious and biblically accurate in what we sing.

# 81

# Wholehearted Worship

## Colossians 3:16

> Let the word of Christ dwell in you richly, teaching and admonishing one another in all wisdom, singing psalms and hymns and spiritual songs, with thankfulness in your hearts to God.

Here again is my translation of this remarkable passage: "Let the word of Christ dwell in you richly, teaching and admonishing one another in all wisdom by means of psalms, hymns, and spiritual songs, singing in your hearts to God with thanksgiving." I would like to conclude our study of this text with four brief observations.

First, although one can surely worship without singing, we can't ignore the emphasis in Scripture on this expression of praise and joy in God. I encourage you to take the time to read the following representative texts that highlight the centrality of singing in worship: Exodus 15:1, 20–21; Judges 5:2–5; 1 Chronicles 16:9; Psalms 47:6–7; 66:2, 4; 69:30–31; 96:1–2; 105:2; 1 Corinthians 14:15; James 5:13. Eighty-five times in the Old Testament alone God's people are exhorted to sing their praises to God.

But why singing? Why not just speak your praise to God? In my book *The Singing God*, I tried to answer this question as follows:

> Singing enables the soul to express deeply felt emotions that mere speaking cannot. Singing channels our spiritual energy in a way that nothing else can. Singing evokes an intensity of mind and spirit. It opens the door to

ideas, feelings, and affections that otherwise might have remained forever imprisoned in the depths of one's heart.

Singing gives focus and clarity to what words alone often make fuzzy. It lifts our hearts to new heights of contemplation. It stirs our hope to unprecedented levels of expectancy and delight. Singing sensitizes. It softens the soul to hear God's voice and quickens the will to obey.

I can only speak for myself, but when I'm happy I sing. When my joy increases it cries for an outlet. So I sing. When I'm touched with a renewed sense of forgiveness, I sing. When God's grace shines yet again on my darkened path, I sing. When I'm lonely and long for the intimacy of God's presence, I sing. When I need respite from the chaos of a world run amok, I sing.

Nothing else can do for me what music does. It bathes otherwise arid ideas in refreshing waters. It empowers my wandering mind to concentrate with energetic intensity. It stirs my heart to tell the Lord just how much I love Him, again and again and again, without the slightest tinge of repetitive boredom.[47]

Second, the singing Paul has in mind is neither random nor aimless. It is "to God." He is the focus of our faith, the object of our praise, the audience of One to whom we lift our hearts in wonder and awe. I suspect this is one reason certain people are uncomfortable with singing. It requires of them vulnerability, openness, and honesty as they direct their most heartfelt adoration, hopes, and desires to God. They are fearful of the depth of commitment and devotion that singing to God entails. But sing to God we must.

Third, all our singing to God must be bathed in gratitude, a consistent theme in Colossians (see 1:3, 12; 2:7; 4:2). In fact, it is mentioned three times here in the span of three verses: "be thankful" (3:15b); "singing . . . with thankfulness in your hearts to God" (3:16b); and "giving thanks to God the Father through him" (3:17b).

Gratitude is to characterize our corporate relations with one another, as evident from its use in verse 15. It is also to characterize our worship and singing, as verse 16 makes clear. And finally, as if to cover all his bases, Paul instructs us in verse 17 to give thanks in whatever we do in whatever circumstance. It reminds me of something Matthew Henry wrote in his diary after being robbed: "Let me be thankful: first, because I was never robbed before; second, because although he took my money, he did not take my life; third, because although he took all I possessed, it was not much; fourth, because it was I who was robbed, and not I who robbed."

Fourth, and finally, this grateful and glorious singing unto God is to take place "in our hearts." In referring to our hearts, Paul does not mean that worship is to be silent or secretive. The heart is here a reference to the whole being: mind, spirit, soul, will, affections—everything we are in the core of our personality. Thus, worship must be "rooted in the depths of personal experience and springing up from that source—heart worship and not merely lip worship."[48]

This passage in Colossians 3 reminds me of one of the most frightening texts in all of Scripture. In Matthew 15:7–9, Jesus denounced the scribes and Pharisees with these words: "You hypocrites! Well did Isaiah prophesy of you, when he said: 'This people honors me with their lips, but their heart is far from me; in vain do they worship me, teaching as doctrines the commandments of men.'"

Just think of it: you can worship God by singing and shouting and dancing and loud declarations of loyalty and love and have it all be vanity! If the heart is not engaged, worship is a sham. You can be orthodox and honored among men, as the religious leaders in that day certainly were, fervent and faithful in your vocalized praise of God, quite pious by all outward indications, and at the same time your heart is distant and cold and lifeless.

Whatever else our worship may entail, regardless of the style we prefer, no matter the form or freedom in which it is expressed, let us labor by the grace of the Holy Spirit (1) to "sing" (2) "to God" (3) "with thanksgiving" (4) "in our hearts."

"My heart and flesh sing for joy to the living God" (Ps. 84:2b).

# 82

# Comprehensive Christianity, or, Doing All in the Name of Christ

## Colossians 3:17

Let the word of Christ dwell in you richly, teaching and admonishing one another in all wisdom, singing psalms and hymns and spiritual songs, with thankfulness in your hearts to God. **And whatever you do, in word or deed, do everything in the name of the Lord Jesus, giving thanks to God the Father through him**.

Some Christians are really good at compartmentalizing their faith. By that I mean they pick and choose when and where and in what ways their Christian values and beliefs are expressed. There are certain sacred arenas, so to speak, in which being a Christian is for them the thing to do. But there are also secular venues in which they check their Christianity at the door and live almost as if they know nothing of Jesus Christ.

Paul won't have it! As far as he's concerned, there is no such thing as "secular space." There is no event, activity, endeavor, or goal that is exempt from the lordship of Jesus. There is no idea, aspiration, dream, or belief that does not come under his sovereign sway. There is no achievement, accomplishment, work, or word that does not exist for the glory of the Son of God.

If you doubt this, consider the comprehensive, all-encompassing, universal scope of Paul's language in Colossians 3:17. He writes: "Whatever you do, in word or deed, do everything in the name of the Lord Jesus, giving thanks to God the Father through him" (Col. 3:17). He said virtually the same thing in 1 Corinthians 10:31: "So, whether you eat or drink, or whatever you do, do all to the glory of God."

Note carefully the language he employs: "word or deed" (Col. 3:17), "eat or drink" (1 Cor. 10:31). These are what we call *spectrum* terms, which is to say, they are designed to be all-inclusive of every conceivable option. They cover the spectrum. One cannot say in response to Colossians 3:17, "Well, there are some things in my life that are technically neither 'words' that I speak nor 'deeds' that I perform." By "word or deed" Paul is spanning the spectrum of all possible activities, whether physical, mental, spiritual, vocal, or whatever.

Likewise, one cannot say in response to 1 Corinthians 10:31, "Well, I'm happy to 'eat' and 'drink' to the glory of God, always diligent to give thanks for the sustenance he provides, but my sex life and my career and my hobbies are something else altogether." No! By "eating" and "drinking" Paul means all human endeavors, all human experiences, no exceptions allowed.

Some folks don't like that. They want to hold back something for themselves. They want to lay hold of money or power or certain pursuits that they conceive as outside the dominion and lordship of Jesus, something over which they exercise independent and autonomous authority.

But again, Paul won't have it. Don't try to evade the force of this passage by saying it only applies to the subject of worship in the preceding verse (Col. 3:16). Yes, of course all the words and deeds that are utilized in the singing of psalms, hymns, and spiritual songs are done in the name of the Lord Jesus. But Paul refuses to compartmentalize Christian discipleship by restricting the lordship of Jesus to something so obviously "spiritual" in nature. Note again: whatever you do, do all in the name of Jesus. There are no exceptions. End of argument.

The phrase "in the name of the Lord Jesus" is found frequently in the New Testament. It is in the name of the Lord Jesus that we are baptized in water (Acts 10:48). Salvation itself is available only in that name (Acts 4:12). It is in his name that forgiveness of sins is found (Acts 10:43; 1 John 2:12), as well as eternal life (1 John 5:13), the presence of the Holy Spirit (John 14:26), dominion over demons (Luke 10:17), and miraculous healing (Acts 3:6, 16)—and the list could go on and on. "In the name of the Lord Jesus" thus means "for the sake of the Lord Jesus" or "in open and explicit acknowledgement that he alone is Lord and Sovereign over all" or "to the glory of the Lord Jesus" or "in humble admission that he is the source of all good things" or "because of who Jesus is and all that he has accomplished in his life, death, and resurrection."

So, what would your life look like if it were actually the case that literally everything you did or said or thought or even dreamed was "in the name of the Lord Jesus"? Let's take our speech, as one example. How often, before we speak, do we think: "What I am about to utter should reflect the fact that I'm a Christian, that Christ died for me, that he is worthy of glory and honor"? How might that affect what we actually end up saying?

How often, before we act, do we think: "What I am about to do ought to conform perfectly with what Jesus did and should make clear to everyone who watches that I am his and he is mine"?

The great Dutch statesman and theologian, Abraham Kuyper, once said, "There is not one square inch in all the universe over which Jesus Christ does not say: 'Mine!'" (paraphrased). Well, that includes the thoughts in our heads, the words on our lips, the steps we take, the books we read, the things on television we watch, the food we eat, the music we hear. It is all to be placed in submission to him and made subservient to his glory.

In conclusion, and on a practical note, consider for a moment all the many decisions we face in life for which the Bible does not provide explicit guidance. I have in mind those so-called gray areas in which the scales of balance appear to be evenly weighted. How are we to proceed when a choice is unavoidable? Perhaps we should apply the principle of this passage and ask the questions: "Can it be done in the name and for the glory of Christ? Is this a decision that will encourage and facilitate thanksgiving to God? Will it honor the

Savior? What choice or direction will most readily display Christ as the treasure of my life and as the glorious and beautiful God that he is?"

Do you compartmentalize the lordship of Jesus, confining him to activities typically discharged on Sunday? Or is your view of his authority and dominion as utterly comprehensive and all-consuming as Paul envisions in this passage? May we joyfully consecrate all to him, in his name, and for his sake.

# 83

# Wives Who Submit to Their Husbands

## Colossians 3:18

**Wives, submit to your husbands, as is fitting in the Lord.** Husbands, love your wives, and do not be harsh with them.

There is a sense in which I address the issue of submission with a measure of reluctance and hesitation. It isn't because I'm in doubt about what Scripture says on the subject or because I'm uncertain about my own beliefs. It has to do with the widespread misunderstandings about the nature of headship and submission.

Many think that headship and submission mean that a wife must sit passively and endure the sin or the abuse of the husband, as if submission means she has no right to stand up for what is true and good or to resist her husband's evil ways. Perhaps some of you come from families in which the husband was an insensitive bully and where it was assumed that it was the wife's duty to tolerate this silently. God's word does not call upon a wife to acquiesce to brutality or thievery or abuse.

Some of you may think that a husband can get away with whatever he wants in the name of headship, as if that word or concept endorses and encourages his sinful behavior, such that the wife has no recourse but to submit to his dictatorial and destructive ways. I utterly reject and grieve over such a terrible distortion and misapplication of these biblical concepts.

I know there are both men and women who look at someone like me or other complementarians and say to themselves, or perhaps to others, "My dad is a mean and abusive bully who belittles my mom and ignores her needs, and those complementarians hold to a view that says it's okay or that there's nothing she can do but quietly submit and put up with it; after all, he's the head of the house." It's hard not to be offended by such a horrible distortion of the truth. I assure you of this one thing: that is *not* biblical headship; that is *not* biblical submission.

On more than one occasion I've had women tell me horrible stories of neglect, tyranny, abuse, abandonment, and even adultery on the part of the man, the husband, and then ask: "How could you possibly embrace complementarianism, a view that permits and perhaps even encourages such sinful behavior?" Let it be said once and for all: I don't! Can complementarianism and the notion of male headship be perverted and distorted by selfishness and sinful oppression? Yes. Even as egalitarianism and the denial of male headship can be perverted and distorted into a rejection of any differences between male and female.

My prayer is that if nothing else is accomplished in our study of this passage, perhaps I may be of some help in clarifying the meaning of these ideas and how they actually work within a marriage.

The verb translated "submit" (Col. 3:18; Gk. *hupotasso*) carries the implication of voluntary yieldedness to a recognized authority. Biblical submission is appropriate in several relational spheres: (1) the wife to her husband (here and in Eph. 5:22–24); (2) children to their parents (Eph. 6:1); (3) believers to the elders of the church (Heb. 13:17; 1 Thess. 5:12); (4) citizens to the state (Rom. 13); (5) servants (employees) to their masters (employers) (1 Pet. 2:18); (6) each believer to every other believer in humble service (Eph. 5:21). So what does it mean? First, let's note what it doesn't mean.

Submission is not grounded in any supposed superiority of the husband or inferiority of the wife (this is clear from Gal. 3:28 and 1 Pet. 3:7). The concept of the wife being the *helper* (Gen. 2:18–22) of the husband in no way implies her inferiority. In fact, the Hebrew word translated "helper" is often used in the Old Testament to refer to *God* as the helper of mankind. Surely *he* is not inferior to us. Rather, this passage means that the husband, even before the fall into sin, was *incomplete* without his wife, and that the husband will never reach his full potential apart from the input and support of his wife.

Submission does not mean that a wife is obligated to follow should her husband lead her into sin. The biblical principle that we owe obedience to God first and foremost applies to Christian wives as well. If there must be a choice between obedience to God and obedience to the state, God is to be obeyed (Acts 5:29). The same would apply in a marriage.

Submission does not mean the wife must suppress her creative energy or adopt a passive approach to life in general. One need only read Proverbs 31 to put this myth to rest. Note especially the emphasis in that paragraph on her initiative, creativity, and tireless industry. There is no biblically prescribed "personality" for wives, anymore than there is one for husbands. Husbands who exercise godly leadership can be introverts, and wives who submit can be extroverts.

Neither does submission entail silence. Many mistakenly think a wife is not submissive if she ever (1) *criticizes* her husband (constructive criticism that is lovingly motivated and corrective in nature is not inconsistent with godly submission); or (2) *makes requests* of him (in particular, that her husband and family act responsibly in private and public; submission of the wife is not an excuse for sin or sloth or sloppiness in the husband); or (3) *teaches* her husband (cf. Prov. 31:26; Acts 18:26; it is not inconsistent with godly submission that a wife be more intelligent or more articulate than her husband. On a personal note, I've probably learned more from my wife than from any other living soul).

Finally, submission does not mean that everything a wife does must be directly dependent upon or connected to her husband. Submission does not mean the wife can never do anything for her own benefit or for the benefit of others or that she should never become involved in activities or ministries outside the home. It simply means that nothing she does should bring harm to her husband or undermine her primary responsibility to her family.

What, then, does submission actually mean or entail? The following is by no means exhaustive, but here are a few suggestions. First, submission is the disposition to honor and affirm a husband's authority and an inclination to embrace his leadership. When that leadership is lacking, it forces the wife to assume a responsibility God never intended her to carry. She flourishes most when his initiative awakens in her a spontaneous and joyful response to his headship.

Second, submission is fundamentally an attitude and act of obedience to the Lord Jesus Christ. This is clear both from Colossians 3:18 and especially Ephesians 5:22.

Third, submission is a commitment to support one's husband in such a way that he may reach his full potential as a man of God. This may involve several things: making the home a safe place, free from the sinful influence of the world; striving to be dependable and trustworthy (Prov. 31:11–12); providing affirmation and encouragement; building loyalty to him in the children (differences of opinion about discipline should be settled in private, away from the children, lest she be seen as taking sides against her husband); and showing confidence in his decisions.

But what happens if the husband is not a Christian? Is a believing wife still obligated to submit to him? Before you read my answer, be sure to read 1 Peter 3:1–7. This passage suggests that submission does not mean she must agree with everything her husband says. First Peter 3:1 indicates that she is a believer and her husband is not. Thus she disagrees with him on the most important principle of all: God! Her interpretation of ultimate reality may well be utterly different from his.

This indicates that submission is perfectly compatible with independent thinking. The woman in 1 Peter 3:1–7 has heard the gospel, assessed the claims of Christ, and embraced his atoning work as her only hope. Her husband has likewise heard the gospel and disobeyed it. There's no indication that Peter expected her to rescind her commitment to Christ simply because it was a decision at odds with that of her husband.

Submission does not mean giving up all efforts to change her husband. The point of the passage is to tell a wife how she might "win" her husband to the Lord. Strangely enough, Peter envisions submission as the most effective strategy in changing the husband.

It bears repeating that submission does not mean putting the will of one's husband above the will of the Lord Jesus Christ. Peter in no way suggests a wife should abandon her commitment to Christ simply because her husband is an unbeliever. This wife is a follower of Jesus before and above being a follower of her husband.

Submission to an unbelieving husband does not mean a wife gets her personal spiritual strength from him. When a husband's spiritual nurturing and leadership is lacking, a Christian wife is not left helpless. She is to be nurtured and strengthened by her hope in God (v. 5).

In conclusion, the wife should submit to her husband, which "is fitting in the Lord" (Col. 3:18b; "in the Lord" is the same as "for those who belong to the Lord," i.e., "as Christians," or "according to the way of Christ"). This should forever put to rest any suggestion that godly submission is inherently oppressive or offensive or contrary to the spirit and life and teachings of Jesus.

Obeying any biblical command, whether it be a wife's submission to her husband or a husband's love for his wife, is an appropriate, indeed a beautiful, thing. It is fitting or proper not because it conforms to the culture of that day but because that is what God has ordained for our marital relations (Eph. 5:23–24; cf. 1 Cor. 11:3, 7–9). In the final analysis, it is the Lord Jesus himself who determines what is and is not fitting or proper for his people.

And what of headship on the part of the husband? That's next.

# 84

# Husbands Who Lovingly Lead Their Wives

## Colossians 3:19

Wives, submit to your husbands, as is fitting in the Lord. **Husbands, love your wives, and do not be harsh with them**.

Although the word *headship* does not appear in this text, it is found in the parallel passage in Ephesians 5 and thus calls for extensive comment. Perhaps the best place to begin, as I did with submission, is by dispelling the myths about the nature of biblical headship.

First, husbands are never commanded to rule their wives, but to love them. The Bible never says, "Husbands, take steps to ensure that your wives submit to you." Nor does it say, "Husbands, exercise headship and authority over your wives." Rather, the principle of male headship is either asserted or assumed and men are commanded to love their wives as Christ loves the church.

Second, headship is never portrayed in Scripture as a means for self-satisfaction or self-exaltation. Headship is always other-oriented. I can't think of a more horrendous sin than exploiting the God-given responsibility to lovingly lead by perverting it into justification for using one's wife and family to satisfy one's lusts and thirst for power.

Third, headship is not the power of a superior over an inferior. Human nature is sinfully inclined to distort the submission of the wife into the superiority of the husband. That some, in the name of male headship, have done precisely this cannot be denied, but it must certainly be denounced. We must also remember that the abuse of headship is not sufficient justification for abandoning it. Rather, we must strive, in God's grace, to redeem it and purify it in a way that honors both Christ and one's spouse.

Fourth, headship is never to be identified with the issuing of commands, nor does it mean that the husband must make every decision in the home. Unfortunately, some men have mistakenly assumed that it undermines their authority for their wives to take the initiative in certain domestic matters. This is more an expression of masculine insecurity and fear than it is godly leadership. So let's try to identify the essence of male headship.

First, headship is more a responsibility than a right. A right is something we tend to demand or insist upon as something we are owed. This can all too often make for an authoritarian and self-serving atmosphere in the home. When headship is viewed as a sacred trust in which the husband is called by God to lead and honor and sacrifice for his wife, the tone and mood of the home are radically improved.

Second, headship is the authority to serve. John Stott explains: "If headship means 'power' in any sense, then it is power to care, not to crush; power to serve, not to dominate; power to facilitate self-fulfillment, not to frustrate or destroy it. And in all this the standard of the husband's love is to be the cross of Christ, on which he surrendered himself even to death in his selfless love for his bride."[49]

Third, headship is the opportunity to lead. If Jesus is our example of biblical leadership, it will help to take note of how he led his disciples. Among other things, he led by *teaching* his disciples, by setting an *example* for them (John 13:15), by spending *time* with them (Acts 4:13), and by *delegating authority* to them (Luke 10:1–20).

Fourth, headship is scripturally circumscribed. Husbands have never been given the right to be wrong or the authority to lead their families in ways that are contrary to the Bible. On a related note, if a wife is ever asked or told by her husband to do something that violates Scripture, she is not only free to disobey him, she is obligated to do so.

Fifth, headship does entail the responsibility to make a final decision when agreement cannot be reached. This final decision, however, may on occasion be to allow his wife to decide. Contrary to what you may think, this latter option does not undermine the husband's authority.

Sixth, headship entails gentleness and sensitivity, as our text in Colossians 3:19 makes clear. Paul's exhortation not to be harsh or embittered toward one's wife has in view "friction caused by impatience and thoughtless nagging."[50]

Seventh, headship means honoring one's wife (see 1 Pet. 3:7). What a powerful word! Men, pause for a moment and reflect on what you feel, do, and say when you honor something: whether an idea, an event, your country, the flag, or a person. Is that how you treat your wife?

Eighth, headship means loving and caring for one's wife as much as we love and care for ourselves (see Eph. 5:28–29).

Ninth, and finally, headship means loving and caring for one's wife as much as Christ loves and cares for us (see Col. 3:19; Eph. 5:25–27). Christ's love for us is unconditional (Rom. 5:8), eternal (Rom. 8:39), unselfish (Phil. 2:6–7), and sacrificial (Eph. 5:25), among countless other characteristics. John Stott put it best:

> Christ "loved" the church and "gave himself" for her, in order to "cleanse" her, "sanctify" her, and ultimately "present" her to himself in full splendour and without any defect. In other words, his love and self-sacrifice were not an idle display, but purposive. And his purpose was not to impose an alien identity upon the church, but to free her from the spots and wrinkles which mar her beauty and to display her in her true glory. The Christian husband is to have a similar concern. His headship will never be used to suppress his wife. He longs to see her liberated from everything which spoils her true feminine identity and growing towards that "glory," that perfection of fulfilled personhood which will be the final destiny of all those whom Christ redeems. To this end Christ gave himself. To this end too the husband gives himself in love.[51]

# 85

# Focus on the Family

## Colossians 3:20–21

Wives, submit to your husbands, as is fitting in the Lord. Husbands, love your wives, and do not be harsh with them. **Children, obey your parents in everything, for this pleases the Lord. Fathers, do not provoke your children, lest they become discouraged.**

Although his comments are brief, Paul cared deeply for the welfare of the family and the relational dynamics that governed it. Having addressed both husbands and wives (Col. 3:18–19), he now turns his attention to the parent/child relationship. "Children, obey your parents in everything, for this pleases the Lord [literally, 'this is pleasing in the Lord']. Fathers, do not provoke your children, lest they become discouraged" (Col. 3:20–21).

I consider myself incredibly blessed. I was born and raised in a free land with indescribable physical, spiritual, and social blessings. No one has ever threatened me for attending church or suggested I be jailed or persecuted for my Christian faith. The educational and vocational opportunities in the United States are staggering, especially when compared with most other countries around the globe. But all such blessings pale in comparison to what God has given me in my family.

My father died in 1983 at only sixty-two years of age. My mother recently turned eighty-six and is in remarkably good health. I have one sister whom I love dearly. Being obedient in our home came easily, not because my sister and I were free from sin (far from it, especially in her case!), but because my father and mother were Christians who consecrated and committed our home to the glory of Christ in all things. Neither of my parents was perfect, and I'm sure they made their fair share of mistakes, but I can never recall feeling discouraged or disheartened by their discipline and authority.

That's what I mean when I say that obedience came easily. Their love and patience and constant affirmation made obeying their rules a joy. As much as was possible throughout the course of growing up, I never doubted that their guidelines and restrictions were designed for my welfare. If it could be said they were strict (and I suppose some might have thought they were), I never felt it. Even when I disagreed with their decisions, I never questioned their love for me.

In a time when "dysfunctional" families have become something of the norm, my sister and I praise God that we were "functional," at least as far as four sinners saved by grace can be. But I realize that perhaps most who are reading this can't say the same thing. That deeply grieves me. God is grieved even more. It's obviously too late to change how you were raised, but it's only the beginning of how you choose to live from this point on, whether you are a child or a teenager still at home or a parent trying to figure out how to glorify God in your family.

To the children, Paul says: "Obey your parents in everything, for this pleases the Lord" (Col. 3:20). Given the fact that Paul addresses these children directly indicates that they are old enough to understand and respond to his exhortation. And one can only assume that they are young enough to still be living at home and are under the authority and oversight of their parents. Paul appears to have the Christian family in view, for he says that such obedience is well pleasing "in" (not "to") the Lord; i.e., "in that sphere in which the Christian now lives, that is, in the new fellowship of those who own Christ as Lord."[52]

When Paul says their responsibility extends to "all things," he's reminding us that children are not the judges of what they should or should not obey in terms of parental precepts. In the parallel passage in Ephesians Paul declares that obedience to one's parents "is right" (Eph. 6:1). He doesn't contemplate the situation where parental orders may be contrary to Scripture, but as is true with the submission of the wife, the law of Christ must take precedence.

There is something to learn from the fact that disobedience to one's parents is included among the pagan vices that indicate a refusal to acknowledge and honor God (Rom. 1:30). Paul also mentions disobedience to one's parents as a mark of the last days when wickedness will abound (2 Tim. 3:2). Needless to say, this is no small or insignificant matter!

But parents beware: the obedience your children must render to you in no way excuses or justifies insensitivity, brutality, or an overbearing authoritarianism that crushes their spirit. "Fathers," says Paul, "do not provoke your children, lest they become discouraged" (Col. 3:21). Although fathers are here singled out as being primarily responsible for discipline—even though this Greek word means "parents" in Hebrews 11:23—in homes where there is no father (due to divorce or death) the mother assumes that role. Of course, a wife also must be a partner with her husband, and the two of them, ideally, will be of one mind when it comes to establishing the moral and spiritual guidelines by which the family will be shaped.

To "provoke" or "exasperate" refers to the result of undue severity in the exercise of discipline. Firmness is necessary, but it should always be tempered with purity of motive and a loving spirit, lest "they become discouraged" (the NASB says, "that they will not lose heart").

This is crucial: an overly obsessive and exacting posture in parenting leads to emotional and spiritual irritation in the child. An inflexible, judgmental, and demanding temperament creates despondency in a child's heart. Faced daily with this harshness, children often simply give up, convinced that nothing they ever do will be quite right or good enough to please their parents. When it comes to motivating your children, the threat of punishment, while often necessary, is less successful than the promise of reward.

Although his prose is a bit dated, John Eadie's comments are deserving of our attention: "If children . . . never please their father, if they are teased and irritated by perpetual censure, if they are kept apart by uniform sternness, if other children around them are continually held up as immeasurably their superiors, if their best efforts can only moderate the parental frown, but never are greeted with the parental smile, then their spirit is broken, and they are discouraged."[53]

Parents, let me highlight one critically important principle mentioned by Eadie. One of the worst things we as parents can do is constantly talk about how beautiful, competent, successful, and smart other kids are without being as complimentary of our own. If we are always quick to laud others without praising, affirming, and expressing our heartfelt pride in our own children, they can easily become disheartened and discouraged.

Parenting is undoubtedly the most difficult, yet rewarding, endeavor any of us will ever experience. We need the wisdom of the Word and the patience of Job and the kindness of Christ and the authority of the Father and the power of the Spirit, and, well, just about all the help we can get!

# 86

# Is All Scripture Profitable?

## Colossians 3:22–4:1

Slaves, obey in everything those who are your earthly masters, not by way of eye-service, as people-pleasers, but with sincerity of heart, fearing the Lord. Whatever you do, work heartily, as for the Lord and not for men, knowing that from the Lord you will receive the inheritance as your reward. You are serving the Lord Christ. For the wrongdoer will be paid back for the wrong he has done, and there is no partiality. Masters, treat your slaves justly and fairly, knowing that you also have a Master in heaven.

I believe, like you (I trust), that "all Scripture is breathed out by God" (2 Tim. 3:16a). Although Paul originally had in mind the Old Testament when he wrote this to young Timothy, his statement surely extends to all Scripture, inclusive of the New Testament and his own writings (see 2 Pet. 3:15–16).

But how can a passage giving instructions to slaves and masters be "profitable for teaching, for reproof, for correction, and for training in righteousness" (2 Tim. 3:16b)? What can this passage possibly say to us in the twenty-first century when slavery no longer exists in the United States and everyone (well, most everyone) acknowledges that it is a moral reproach? Are there ethical ideals that can be gleaned from Paul's instructions to slaves and masters in the first century that are relevant, even binding, on us in the twenty-first? In other words, once we've conceded that Paul is addressing a situation that no longer obtains in our society, are there moral principles in his counsel that we might discern in the text and apply to circumstances that bear some degree of resemblance to the slave/master relationship?

There is no easy answer to that question. When I first preached through Colossians in the early 1980s I rather naïvely transferred Paul's counsel concerning ancient slaves to modern employees and his counsel for ancient masters to modern employers. But the correspondence between the two is far from exact, making application in this instance a more difficult task than interpretation. Still, there appear to be certain principles in Paul's instruction that apply to a number of contexts today, the workplace being one.

But before I go any further, we need to address a sticky issue. Many have argued that it is inconsistent to insist upon the submission of the wife to the headship of the husband (Col. 3:18) while setting aside the slave/master relationship as antiquated and morally intolerable. In other words, is not the argument for why wives should submit to husbands the same as the argument for why slaves should submit to masters? If we insist on the abolition of the latter, should we not also insist on the abolition of the former? Craig Keener, for example, contends that "modern writers who argue that Paul's charge to wives to submit to their husbands 'as to Christ' is binding on all cultures must come to grips with the fact that Paul even more plainly tells slaves to 'obey' their masters 'as they would Christ' (Eph. 6:5). If one is binding in all cultures, so is the other."[54]

There are several reasons why we can (and should) insist on the abolition of slavery while retaining the submission of wives to their husbands.

First, Scripture is known to regulate undesirable relationships without condoning them as permanent ideals (see Matt. 19:8; 1 Cor. 6:1–8). Paul's recommendation for how slaves and masters relate to each other does not assume the goodness of the institution. Wayne Grudem explains:

> The Bible does not approve or command slavery any more than it approves or commands persecution of Christians. When the author of Hebrews commends his readers by saying, "You joyfully accepted the plundering of your property, since you knew that you yourselves had a better possession and an abiding one" (Hebrews 10:34), that does not mean the Bible supports the plundering of Christians' property, or that it commands theft. It only means that *if* Christians have their property taken

through persecution, they should still rejoice because of their heavenly treasure, which cannot be stolen. Similarly, when the Bible tells slaves to be submissive to their masters, it does not mean that the Bible supports or commands slavery, but only that it tells people who are slaves how they should respond.[55]

Second, the institution of slavery is not grounded in creation but is a distortion resulting from the fall. Marriage and male headship, on the other hand, are part of the original created order that antedates the fall. As Grudem has noted, "People who abolished slavery, *based on an appeal to biblical principles* . . . were abolishing something evil that God did not create. But Christians who oppose male headship in marriage and the church are attempting to abolish something good, something that God did create. The examples are simply not parallel."[56]

Third, on several occasions in the New Testament the seeds for the dissolution of slavery are sown. This is especially seen in Paul's words to Philemon (vv. 12–16; see also Eph. 6:9; Col. 4:1; 1 Tim. 6:1–2). Nothing in the New Testament, however, suggests that the same was envisioned for the relationship between husbands and wives.

Fourth, no permanent moral command is used with reference to the institution of slavery in Paul's writings. He is obviously adapting to a temporary and ultimately repugnant social construct, but such is not the case with his instruction to husbands and wives which is consistently grounded not in culture but in creation (see 1 Cor. 11:8–12; 1 Tim. 2:13–14) or in the relationship of Christ to the church (see Eph. 5:22–33).

Fifth, and finally, Paul explicitly envisions and endorses the possibility of a slave's obtaining freedom (1 Cor. 7:21). He never says anything comparable to this with regard to wives and submission to their husbands.

Well, enough on that issue. In the next meditation we'll return to this passage and determine what, if any, application it has for us today.

Part 4

## Colossians 4:1–18

# 87

# You Are Serving the Lord Christ!

## Colossians 3:22–4:1

Slaves, obey in everything those who are your earthly masters, not by way of eye-service, as people-pleasers, but with sincerity of heart, fearing the Lord. Whatever you do, work heartily, as for the Lord and not for men, knowing that from the Lord you will receive the inheritance as your reward. You are serving the Lord Christ. For the wrongdoer will be paid back for the wrong he has done, and there is no partiality. Masters, treat your slaves justly and fairly, knowing that you also have a Master in heaven.

Let me say again, as I did in the previous meditation, that it would be a mistake to think there is a one-to-one correspondence between the slave/master relationship in the first century and the employee/employer relationship today. I won't take time to point out the obvious differences, but common sense alone would call for caution in our movement from the ancient context to a modern one.

Still, though, there are spiritual and ethical truths that inform and shape Paul's counsel to both parties. These principles may well have application in a variety of contexts and relationships today, and we would do well to take note of them.

Let's begin by observing how Paul envisions the service slaves are to render to their masters. They are to obey them in "everything" (language similar to what we saw in v. 20 with regard to children and their parents). It goes without saying, of course, that this assumes the master does not require his servant to sin or to deny Jesus.

His work is not to be done "by way of eye-service" (v. 22b), an interesting phrase that translates one word in the Greek text. Paul has in mind an approach to one's work designed either to attract attention or to avoid punishment (or both). Perhaps he has in mind work discharged only when one's master (employer?) is present and observant, together with the tendency to trifle and piddle when he's absent, hoping that one's sloth won't be detected.

A television commercial from several years ago beautifully illustrates what Paul has in mind. It portrayed an office where several employees took advantage of the boss's absence: they played games, took naps, and generally shirked their responsibilities. They received advanced warning of his return to the office from the smell of an obviously unpleasant aftershave, providing them with time and opportunity to resume their duties and give the impression of having been diligently at work all along. When the boss switched to Mennen's Skin Bracer, he returned unannounced and caught them in the act.

The point is this: Christians are to fulfill their responsibilities, whatever they may be and to whomever they are obligated, based on principle, not pragmatism. We work regardless of who may be present, conscious that another eye is upon us. Or as Paul says, "you are serving the Lord Christ" (v. 24b). He is always watching. And whatever wage you may or may not receive from another human, remember that "from the Lord you will receive the inheritance as your reward" (v. 24a). It's important to remember that under Roman law a slave could never inherit anything.

We labor and serve and discharge our obligations ultimately to please Christ, not people (v. 22b). We must avoid a merely perfunctory and mechanical performance and do all things "with sincerity of heart." Reverence, or fear, for the Lord, says Paul, must govern our actions. Yes, even work is worship!

As difficult as it may be, we must labor in God's grace to look beyond mere earthly payment or praise as the motivation for our efforts. There is something inherently spiritual in all that a Christian does, whether that be the digging of a ditch, the preaching of a sermon, or the changing of a diaper. It is for Christ that we work. It is from Christ that the reward will come.

John Eadie well sums up the point of verse 24: "Your masters on earth have no absolute right over you: the shekels they may have paid for you can only give them power over your bodies, your time and your labour, but the Lord has bought you with His blood, and has therefore an indefeasible claim to your homage and service."[1] That certainly applies to all of us, regardless of social or economic status.

Is verse 25, "for the wrongdoer will be paid back for the wrong he has done, and there is no partiality," addressed to slaves or masters? Probably both. Together they should remember that God takes no note of cultural achievement or fame or fortune when it comes to assessing right and wrong. Class distinctions are irrelevant.

Finally, Paul is quick to point out that if slaves have duties, so also have masters: they must treat their servants justly and fairly (Col. 4:1). They may have the upper hand in this life, but Christ is their master too! Therefore, let them treat their servants with the same consideration and equity they themselves hope to receive from the Lord Jesus.

So what's the ultimate takeaway from a passage that seems so irrelevant to conditions in the twenty-first century? Simply this: all of life, whether in work or family or ministry, be it immensely significant or utterly mundane, all of life, I repeat, is subject to the sovereignty and governed by the lordship and ultimately lived to the glory of Jesus our Lord.

Christ Jesus is your master in heaven (4:1). Fear the Lord, not man (3:22b). All you do is ultimately for the Lord (3:23a). It is he whom you serve (3:24b). It is from him that your eternal reward is coming (3:24a).

Whatever our lot in life, wherever we may live, for whomever we may work, to whomever we owe allegiance, let us never forget that we do it all for Christ.

# 88

# The Easiest Thing about Prayer

## Colossians 4:2

> Continue steadfastly in prayer, being watchful in it with thanksgiving.

The easiest thing about praying is quitting. Giving up seems so reasonable, so easy to justify. It's always been that way, which is why Paul wrote in Colossians 4:2, "Continue steadfastly in prayer, being watchful in it with thanksgiving." Persevering in prayer when no one seems to listen strikes many people as a sign of fanaticism, if not mental instability.

Not long ago I received an e-mail from a friend who was facing the impending deaths of several people in his church. Soon after, I learned of the untimely passing of an incredibly godly Christian man who left behind a grieving wife and two young children. In any given week I hear the same stories you do: a loved one dies, a job is lost and another not found, bills go unpaid, relationships are shattered, dreams fail to materialize. Rain does not fall and crops fail. A teenager is loved and cared for, yet rebels and abandons God.

What makes such incidents especially disturbing is that they all occur notwithstanding persistent and fervent prayer that they not. Why is it that a man or woman prays for relief or deliverance or some essential blessing to alleviate intense aggravation, but hears nothing? In humble faith, with sincerity of heart, not for a moment doubting that God is able both to hear and answer their prayers, they pray. But heaven is silent, or so it seems.

I recently saw the film *The Island* (that's not a recommendation!) in which unsuspecting clones are nourished and sustained to serve as organ donors for their wealthy sponsors who aspire to live as long as possible. These "folk" know virtually nothing of the outside world or its ways. Two have escaped and are in conversation with a rather strange man who happens to mention "God."

"What's 'God'?" asks one of the clones.

"Oh, well, you know when you close your eyes and ask for something?"

"Yeah."

"Well, God's the one who doesn't answer you."

It's a bad joke, but for many people it rings all too true. People in Paul's day faced the same temptation to quit that we do. But too much was at stake. Though defeated at the cross, Satan and his demons are still active. The weakness of the flesh abides. The threat of schism in the body of Christ is ever present. Great opportunities to share the gospel are at every turn. So, don't quit, says Paul. Continue steadfastly in prayer. Keep watch at all times lest you despair. Be thankful for all God has done and will do in response to your petitions.

Much has already been said in Colossians concerning perseverance in prayer, so I won't repeat myself here (see the lessons on Col. 1:3, 9, 29; 2:1). Instead, I want to briefly address the reasons why a good God who can help often seems not to, or at least not to in accordance with our schedules. There are surely reasons other than these, but here are a few suggestions that I hope will encourage you to "continue steadfastly in prayer" (Col. 4:2a).

First, we are a presumptuous people. We just assume that God ought always to do what we ask, when we ask, precisely in the way we ask. By delaying his response, God awakens us to the gracious character of all answered prayer. In other words, that God says or does anything at all in response to our petitions is sheer, undiluted grace. Resolute continuation in prayer, watchful perseverance, is often the best way for us to learn this invaluable lesson.

Second, steadfast endurance in coming again and again to the throne of grace is God's way of cultivating in us a sense of absolute and utter dependence upon him. We are by nature self-reliant, self-sufficient folk. If God were instantly and at all times to answer our every prayer, we would gradually lose our sense of urgency. Truth be told, most of us would soon lose sight of the fact that it is God alone who is the source of all good. By suspending his response, God is saying to each of us: "Just how desperate are you? How conscious are you that I am your only source, your sole and all-sufficient supply?"

Third, persistent praying puts us in that frame of mind and spirit in which we may properly receive what it is that God desires to give. In other words, it isn't so much that God is reluctant to give, but that we lack preparation to receive. Try to envision what a mess your life would have been if your parents granted you everything you asked for as a child! God often delays his answers because, quite simply, we are in no shape to receive them. Few of us are willing to admit that, but deep down we know it's true.

Fourth, steadfast, watchful continuation in prayer helps us differentiate between impetuous, ill-conceived, selfish desires, and sincere, deep-seated, Christ-exalting ones. Persistence in prayer thus enables us to weed out improper petitions.

Fifth, endurance at the throne of grace purifies the content of our petitions. By repeating our prayers we are forced to think and rethink what we are saying. We are compelled to evaluate our motivation and aim for asking God for something in particular. It's a bit like how I read, reread, and read yet again each of these meditations. It helps me identify mistakes, locate typographical errors, and rephrase something that otherwise might be false or misleading. I can almost envision God saying in response to my first articulation of a prayer, "Sam, are you sure you want me to answer that one? Think about it. Contemplate the long-term consequences of a yes. Then come back and ask me again in different terms, with a purified purpose."

Sixth, perseverance cultivates patience. By withholding an immediate response, we learn how to wait on God. Waiting on the Lord is far from a passive posture. It's an active, expectant, persistent pressing in to the heart and purposes of a loving God. How might we ever learn to do this were it not for steadfastness in prayer?

Seventh, oftentimes God wants to give, but not now. The answer will come in better circumstances, at a more opportune moment. By delaying his response, a greater and better and more God-glorifying end is secured than by an immediate answer.

Finally, even if none of the reasons given above makes sense to you, persevere anyway! God isn't asking you to understand; he's asking you to be faithful.

# 89

# Pray Thankfully!

## Colossians 4:2

Continue steadfastly in prayer, being watchful in it with thanksgiving.

There's always a possibility that someone reading this passage might walk away with the idea that prayer is an anxious, troublesome, fearful endeavor. Paul's language might easily contribute to that, were it not for the final two words of the text. Let me explain.

If I were to exhort you concerning some spiritual activity and insisted, perhaps with great urgency, that you "continue steadfastly" in it and that you remain alert and watchful, you might be inclined to worry, perhaps wringing your hands, biting your nails, and pacing nervously back and forth in doubt of the ultimate outcome. Now let's be clear about one thing: prayer is serious business. James put it pointedly: "You do not have, because you do not ask" (James 4:2). If we fail to pray, we most likely will not receive. It is utterly presumptuous to think that God will do for us apart from prayer what he has promised to do for us only through prayer.

But this reality must be held in delicate balance with the equally biblical truth that God is sovereign: nothing slips his mind or through his fingers. He will accomplish all his purposes. He "works all things according to the counsel of his will" (Eph. 1:11).

This is the point, I believe, of Paul's insistence that when we pray, and we should pray always and alertly, we should do so "with thanksgiving" (Col. 4:2b). Why does he insist on this? And more important still, how do we do it? How does one pray thankfully?

First, I believe Paul includes this qualifying phrase because he wants to instill confidence in us rather than fear and uncertainty as we pray. It's his way of saying, "Yes, by all means be faithful and fervent in your prayers. But know this: God is always and ever on his throne. The battle in which you fight is ultimately his, on your behalf. Let gratitude for what God has done and will do permeate your petitions. In this way you will never lose hope or fall into despair or live in fear that he has abandoned you in your hour of need."

But second, and most important, how do we do this? What does it mean to pray "with thanksgiving"? Here are a few thoughts.

First, pray with gratitude that God is actually there, alive and alert and never asleep. We do not speak into a vacuum or to a God who is preoccupied with other, allegedly more important matters.

Second, pray with gratitude that God not only lives and loves but also actually listens to what we say. He hears us! "Therefore the LORD waits to be gracious to you, and therefore he exalts himself to show mercy to you.... He will surely be gracious to you at the sound of your cry. As soon as he hears it, he answers you" (Isa. 30:18–19). As you pray, therefore, thank God that he loves to listen and to be gracious.

Third, pray with gratitude that the God who lives, loves, and listens is also more than able to do above and beyond all we ask or think (cf. Eph. 3:20). I'm so thankful that the God to whom I pray isn't a wimp or a weakling, but an omnipotent and infinitely wise Father who delights in giving good things to those who ask (Luke 11:13).

Fourth, pray thanking God that he has chosen to include you in the process. God could have ordained that all his will be accomplished independently of our participation. But he didn't. He has chosen to achieve his ultimate ends through means, the latter being primarily our prayers.

Fifth, pray thanking God for all the ways he is changing you as you pray. Wholehearted and humble intercession transforms the intercessor. Our ideas of God are elevated. Our awareness of personal dependency is intensified. The magnitude of God's power and providence is manifest in ways that we otherwise might never behold. Our dreams and hopes and desires are cleansed and purified as we humbly submit to his will and crucify our own.

Sixth, pray thanking God that what you are asking him to graciously do in the lives of others he has already done in yours. If we are not grateful for the salvation and healing and mercy granted us, how can we possibly be fervent and diligent in asking that God do the same for others?

Seventh, and finally, pray with gratitude to God not simply for what he has done but for what he will do. Thank him in advance for what he will do in response to your requests. Without being triumphalistic or sinfully presumptuous, we should pray with expectancy that whatever we ask, according to his will, God will do. Thank you, Lord!

The bottom line is this: it's hard to be fearful when you are immersed in gratitude. Thankfulness turns the human soul toward heaven and away from self. Thankfulness, by its very nature, requires that we fix our focus on the fact *that* God *is* and *who* God is and *what* God has done and will do. Thankful prayer is necessarily theocentric.

Do you recall the incident in 2 Chronicles 20 where Jehoshaphat and the kingdom of Judah came under siege by the Moabites and Ammonites? After their prayer seeking God's assistance, the prophet Jahaziel came to them with a bizarre word of counsel. "He appointed those who were to sing to the Lord and praise him in holy attire, as they went before the army, [to] say, 'Give thanks to the Lord, for his steadfast love endures forever'" (2 Chron. 20:21).

He instructs them to be thankful on the front end of the battle, before the enemy is ever engaged. Let the reality of God's steadfast love fill your heart, he told them. Praise him for who he is. Rest peacefully in what he will do. "Stand firm," he said, "hold your position, and see the salvation of the Lord on your behalf" (2 Chron. 20:17).

Thus, "when Paul says our praying is to be done with thanksgiving, he means that we should keep our eyes on the victory of God. We do not fight as losers or even as those who are uncertain. We know God will win. And if we have eyes to see, we will recognize the path of his power again and again."[2]

# 90

# Just Do It!

## Colossians 4:3–4

Continue steadfastly in prayer, being watchful in it with thanksgiving. **At the same time, pray also for us, that God may open to us a door for the word, to declare the mystery of Christ, on account of which I am in prison—that I may make it clear, which is how I ought to speak.**

Now, wait just a minute. We all agree that God loves lost souls and wants them to hear the gospel of salvation in his Son. So why does he suspend the opening of an evangelistic door on the prayers of the Colossians? I'm tempted to say, in the words of the Nike commercial: "God, 'just do it!'" Or, perhaps more reverently, "God, why don't you directly open these doors rather than telling Paul to tell us to ask you to do so? What's the point of our asking you to do what you've already revealed is in your heart to accomplish? As I said, Lord, 'just do it!'"

I suspect God's response to me would be: "No, Sam. That's not how I operate. Yes, of course, I could 'just do it' directly and instantaneously, without your involvement or anyone else's. But I prefer to do it when you ask me to. In fact, in most instances I won't do it unless you ask me to."

Here's another question that comes to mind. Why does Paul encourage the Colossians to pray for him? What's the point of his asking them to ask God to open a door for the Word? Why does he urge them to pray that God would give him clarity of speech?

Isn't it enough that he ask God himself? I'm assuming he did, but he evidently believed that it would greatly help his cause if others joined him in beseeching God for this blessing. Does this imply that God is more inclined to say yes to our requests if more people are united in asking him for them? That seems odd.

Or is it primarily to aid his cause that Paul enlists the prayers of others on his behalf? Could it possibly be that for the sake of God's greater glory he makes this request of the Colossians? I'll return to that momentarily.

Let's be clear about one thing. I didn't ask these questions because I intend to solve the tension between divine sovereignty and human responsibility. I couldn't solve it even if I wanted to, and how prayer factors into the equation is ultimately something beyond my intellectual ken.

Rather, I'm concerned about the nature of prayer. Or, more accurately, I'm concerned about the purpose of prayer. Why has God chosen to incorporate it into the way he governs the world and accomplishes his purposes?

One thing we know: God loves to be asked, and there's good reason for it. Consider Psalm 50:12, one of the most sarcastic verses in Scripture. God says to the Israelites: "If I were hungry, I would not tell you, for the world and its fullness are mine," which is to say, if God were hungry (which, of course, he's not), he wouldn't need the Israelites to provide him with a meal. "Every beast of the forest is mine," says the Lord, "[not to mention] the cattle on a thousand hills" (Ps. 50:10).

So, if God doesn't need us or our prayers, why does he create us and then command us to ask him for things? That's a pretty profound question, but it comes with a fairly simple answer.

In Psalm 50:15 God says again, "Call upon me in the day of trouble; I will deliver you, and you shall glorify me." When you're in trouble, says God, when you have needs and problems and trials and obstacles to overcome, pray to me and ask that I intervene and make provision. If you do, I'll deliver you. And in your obvious dependence upon me I will be glorified. We both win. You get delivered. I get glorified. You receive a blessing. And people and angels and demons see that I'm the all-sufficient supply, the infinitely resourceful God, the one being in the universe who exists to overflow in abundant goodness to weak and needy people like you!

It's amazing how asking a few questions about the nature and purpose of prayer drives us directly into the reason why God created the universe. God didn't create us because he was needy or lacking in some profound way. We don't supply God with anything. "The God who made the world and everything in it, being Lord of heaven and earth, does not live in temples made by man, nor is he served by human hands, as though he needed anything, since he himself gives to all mankind life and breath and everything" (Acts 17:24–25).

So, that being true, why did he make it all? He made it all so that in its (our) utter and absolute dependence on him for everything, his glory as God might be seen and savored. Our need magnifies his supply. Our lack draws attention to his abundance. God honors and glorifies himself by overflowing in bountiful blessings to those who otherwise deserve only death. And how do we get these blessings? By praying for them! God suspends his work on our prayers not because he can't do it alone but because our prayers highlight our dependence and his supply. We are humbled as dependent and he is exalted as depended upon.

Not only does he get the glory for being depended upon but we get the gladness for being dependent. Yes, please read that again. There is no greater joy than getting what God gives (and he is himself, of course, the greatest gift). And there is no greater glory than for God to be giving.

Jesus commanded his disciples to pray, and here's why: "Whatever you ask in my name, this will I do, that the Father may be glorified in the Son" (John 14:13). Although there are undoubtedly other reasons why God chose to incorporate our prayers in the accomplishment of his purposes, his glory is preeminent.

One more thing: earlier I asked why Paul felt it important to enlist the prayers of the Colossians on his behalf. It's not because God is stingy and Paul thought that a multitude of intercessors might have greater success in prevailing on God's otherwise reluctant heart than would he alone. Once again, it's all about God's glory. In 2 Corinthians 1:11 Paul wrote, "You also must help us by prayer, so that many will give thanks on our behalf for the blessing granted us through the prayers of many."

Note carefully why it's important that the Corinthians (like the Colossians) pray for him. It is so that "many will give thanks" for the "blessing" that God grants to him in response to their prayers. God's glory is more readily seen and known and savored when many rise up in unified gratitude for what he has done than if only one or a few do. So, when we pray for one another we get gladness in receiving what God gives and God gets glory for giving what we get.

# 91

# Open Doors for the Gospel

## Colossians 4:3–4

Continue steadfastly in prayer, being watchful in it with thanksgiving. **At the same time, pray also for us, that God may open to us a door for the word, to declare the mystery of Christ, on account of which I am in prison—that I may make it clear, which is how I ought to speak.**

Political correctness notwithstanding, Christianity is an evangelistic religion. Its aim is to proclaim the good news that there is eternal life in only one: Jesus Christ. Its aim, by the grace of God, is to bring about the deliverance of men and women out of the domain of darkness into the kingdom of light. There are some things, no doubt, for which we as Christians ought to apologize, but declaring that faith in Jesus Christ alone is essential for eternal life isn't one of them. We should never hesitate to proclaim the "mystery of Christ" or shrink back from seeking the conversion of every soul.

Here in Colossians 4:3–4 Paul solicits the prayers of these believers, not for his own health or freedom or prosperity but for the opportunity and clarity to proclaim Jesus as Lord to lost and dying people. There are two elements in Paul's request that call for our attention.

First, he asks them to ask God to open "a door for the word" that he might proclaim "the mystery of Christ" (v. 3). This isn't the first time he's used this imagery for evangelistic opportunities (see also Acts 14:27; 1 Cor. 16:8–9; 2 Cor. 2:12).

The "door," evidently, is closed. This may suggest political opposition; social, cultural, and educational barriers to sharing the faith; adverse weather that hinders travel; or any number of factors that make evangelism difficult from a human perspective. It may be that Paul is asking God to grant him favor with those who have the authority to give him access to certain arenas of activity or platforms from which he might declare his message. In any case, Paul believed that God is sovereign over all such circumstances and that he can remove obstacles and overcome resistance and restrain the enemies of the faith when asked to do so by his people.

That an apostle, no less, would ask ordinary Christians like these Colossians to pray for his evangelistic success is stunning. Paul refused to trust in his skill or eloquence or theological knowledge alone. He needed the intercessory support of other believers. It's almost as if he's saying, "I'm helpless if you don't ask God to help me." Amazing!

And what might Paul do should the door be opened? He has one goal, one solitary purpose: to proclaim the mystery of Christ. The word *mystery* doesn't mean what it does in a P. D. James novel or in a Sudoku puzzle. Paul typically uses this word when he has in mind a truth formerly hidden but now made known in Jesus Christ.

The mystery of Christ is the revelation of what God has done in and through his Son to make possible atonement for sin and its forgiveness. That the Word should become flesh (John 1:14) is a mystery now made known for our salvation. That God was in Christ reconciling the world to himself (2 Cor. 5:19) is a mystery now revealed for our justification. That faith alone in a crucified Messiah is the power of God unto salvation is a mystery now made known for our eternal welfare.

Where Christ is not proclaimed, the gospel is not known. No matter how psychologically soothing a sermon may be, if the mystery of Christ is not center stage, the gospel has not been preached. The focus of our message is not self-esteem, social justice, the plight of the poor, or world peace (as important as those issues are in their own right), but Jesus Christ crucified and risen for the salvation of lost souls.

Paul's second request is that they ask God to enable him to proclaim this mystery with clarity (v. 4). "Pray that God will work in me," says Paul, "that I might have the words to speak in the most persuasive manner and at the most appropriate time. Ask God to operate in my heart and mind and soul so that my message will ring true and will reverberate with passion and conviction and courage."

Stunning, isn't it, that a man of Paul's spiritual caliber and gifting felt so desperately dependent on the prayers of others for his effectiveness in ministry! He made a similar plea to the Roman church, appealing to them to strive together with him in their prayers to God on his behalf, that he might be delivered from the unbelievers in Judea and that his service for Jerusalem may be acceptable to the saints (Rom. 15:30–31).

His request of the Colossians raises an interesting question: What precisely might serve to inhibit or hinder his clarity of speech or prevent him from proclaiming the gospel in the way he desired? It may be that he anticipated trick questions from a hostile crowd and needed the assistance of the Spirit to see through their deception and speak truth into the fog of error. It may be that he sensed the importance of using just the right illustration or parable or analogy to make a point that would penetrate a closed and calloused heart with the truth that brings light and life. Paul, no doubt, felt confused at times and needed the quickening ministry of the Spirit in his mind. "Pray that God would clear my head of intellectual cobwebs and overcome any sluggishness of speech that would be unworthy of the gospel I proclaim. Pray that the Father would fill me with the Spirit of boldness and confidence and drive from me all fear of man and concern for my own reputation or physical safety."

If he felt this burden, how much more you and I! Have you committed to praying consistently for your pastor each time he preaches? Have you interceded for that Sunday school teacher who tells the story of Jesus to indifferent and mocking junior high students? Have you petitioned God for yourself as you prepare to share your testimony with an unsaved neighbor? We are all desperately in need of such anointing and spiritual support from on high every time we open our mouths to speak of Christ.

"O, grant us open doors, Father, that we may speak boldly and clearly and joyfully of your Son and all that you have done for sinners in and through him! Work in us by your Spirit that we might have just the right story, the most telling illustration, the most persuasive phrasing as we declare the mystery of Christ Jesus! Amen."

# 92

# Human Setbacks or Divine Setups?

## Colossians 4:3–4

Continue steadfastly in prayer, being watchful in it with thanksgiving. **At the same time, pray also for us, that God may open to us a door for the word, to declare the mystery of Christ, on account of which I am in prison—that I may make it clear, which is how I ought to speak.**

Perhaps the most revealing test of spirituality is our response to undeserved adversity. If we suffer because we've sinned, there's nothing particularly special in yielding to it without complaint. We typically find the strength to endure with the reminder that the fault lies within. It may hurt, but there's no one to blame but ourselves.

But if one suffers unjustly and is able to avoid bitterness or resentment, that's another thing altogether. The apostle Peter had this in mind in his counsel to servants who labored under oppressive and cruel masters. "What credit is it," asks Peter, "if, when you sin and are beaten for it, you endure? But if when you do good and suffer for it you endure, this is a gracious thing in the sight of God" (1 Pet. 2:20).

This is what makes Paul's prayer request in Colossians 4:3–4 so incredibly important and instructive for us. It also reveals the depths of his maturity and his unshakable confidence in the providence and goodness of God. Tucked away in this passage in such a way that it probably goes unnoticed by many is a brief statement by Paul that we need to consider. Here is the text. See if you can identify what I have in mind: "At the same time, pray also for us, that God may open to us a door for the word, to declare the mystery of Christ, on account of which I am in prison—that I may make it clear, which is how I ought to speak" (Col. 4:3–4).

It's the phrase "on account of which I am in prison." Paul is clearly referring to "the mystery of Christ," which is to say, the gospel, as the reason for his incarceration. The apostle isn't in prison for embezzling church funds or for fomenting rebellion against the civil authorities. Neither is he there for sins of the flesh, whether lust or greed or pride or even blasphemy. He's there for one reason: he faithfully and fearlessly proclaimed the mystery of Christ to a lost and dying world.

His legs are in chains because he loved Jesus too much to keep silent. His freedom has been curtailed, his privileges stripped, his reputation destroyed because he is obsessed with the glory of Christ and refused to keep it to himself. Had Paul been arrested because of some overt criminal act, I suspect he would hardly have mentioned his imprisonment to the Colossians. If God had orchestrated his imprisonment as discipline for repeated sexual misconduct or as a way of bringing humility into his otherwise arrogant and prideful heart, that would be one thing. But Paul is in jail because of his determination to proclaim the person and work of Christ to lost souls.

Let's note a few important lessons from this.

First, contrary to what you may have been told, God doesn't promise to protect us from painful and unjust experiences if we will but remain faithful and obedient. Paul couldn't have been more to the point: "It is precisely because I was diligent to obey the call to preach the gospel that I now suffer this horrid and distressing imprisonment." What God does promise is that while we languish in prison, he will never leave us nor forsake us. The declaration on which we can rest assured is that notwithstanding tribulation and distress and persecution and famine and nakedness and danger and sword we will never suffer separation from the love of God in Christ Jesus our Lord (Rom. 8:35, 39).

Second, we need to learn from Paul's reaction to his plight. There's no indication here of self-pity or bitterness or anger with God for having permitted this to occur. The last thing Paul would have said was, "Why me, Lord?" which, I'm sad to say, are usually the first words out of my mouth when things don't go my way.

Had I (you?) been imprisoned in this way, I fear my reaction would have been: "God has forgotten me," or "I must have sinned horribly to deserve this," or "I guess God has rescinded my calling and withdrawn his anointing from my life," or "God hates me," or "Satan has really won a victory in all this."

Paul's perspective is perhaps best seen in Philippians 1:12–18 where he again makes reference to his imprisonment for preaching the gospel. He clearly looks on his situation as a divinely orchestrated setup to elevate the gospel into places where it otherwise might never have reached. The Philippians probably thought his imprisonment was a hindrance to the spread of the mystery of Christ, a strategic setback, a defeat for the kingdom of our Lord. Not Paul! What has happened to me, he wrote, "has really served to advance the gospel, so that it has become known throughout the whole imperial guard and to all the rest that my imprisonment is for Christ" (Phil. 1:12–13). More than that, "most of the brothers, having become confident in the Lord by my imprisonment, are much more bold to speak the word without fear" (Phil. 1:14).

In other words, adverse events that from a human perspective seem to be obstacles of defeat are by divine providence transformed into instruments of victory. Or again, human setbacks are gloriously changed into divine setups. We see this often in Scripture, whether in Joseph's being sold into slavery or the nation Israel's being hemmed in at the Red Sea or even Jesus' being nailed to a Roman gibbet.

Third, few, if any, who are reading this have yet to suffer to the extent that Paul did. But it may well be that you have endured other forms of unjust treatment for no other reason than that you love Jesus and are committed to the proclamation of the gospel. Many of you are in a position to say, by God's grace, "Pray that I will have additional opportunities to share the good news of the gospel, on account of which I have been denied promotion at work," or "on account of which I have been mocked by my colleagues," or "on account of which I have been ostracized and made to feel like a leper," or "on account of which

I have lost lucrative business deals," or "on account of which I have said no to certain pleasurable activities with friends," or "on account of which I have been slandered by those I once trusted."

Fourth, and finally, have you thanked God today, as Paul no doubt did on numerous occasions, for the *gift* of suffering? No, I haven't taken leave of my senses, for "it has been granted to you that for the sake of Christ you should not only believe in him but also suffer for his sake" (Phil. 1:29). I can't account for Paul's perspective in Colossians 4 apart from this statement in Philippians 1. Suffering, he says (without stuttering), is as much a gift of God as believing in Christ is!

Something was obviously more important to the apostle than physical comfort and freedom of movement. Something mattered more than convenience and ease and personal peace or security. That "something" was the advance and exaltation of the "mystery of Christ" (Col. 4:3). Have we sufficiently tasted of the sweetness of this glorious truth that undeserved adversity is embraced as opportunity rather than oppression?

# 93

# "Salty" Speech and the Salvation of Souls

## Colossians 4:5–6

> Conduct yourselves wisely toward outsiders, making the best use of the time. Let your speech always be gracious, seasoned with salt, so that you may know how you ought to answer each person.

Christians have often jokingly said that the three least appealing responsibilities they face are fasting, praying, and sharing their faith with nonbelievers. Sadly, though, it's not just a joke. It's a reality that has severely crippled the ministry of the body of Christ. Few have incorporated regular fasting into their spiritual diet (pun intended). Perhaps a few more actually pray on a regular basis, hopefully in accord with Paul's exhortation in Colossians 4:2–4. But evangelism? Now that's another story.

If they were totally honest, I suspect most Christians would say they'd happily skip a meal and spend it praying rather than have to talk to a non-Christian about Jesus. You may be wondering why I even bring up the topic at this point in our meditations through Colossians. Yes, all acknowledge that Paul requested their prayers on behalf of his own evangelistic efforts (Col. 4:2–4), but few recognize that when he turns again in verses 5 and 6 to instruct the Colossians he has *their* (and our) evangelistic efforts in mind.

Let's look more closely at these two verses. I'm convinced he is talking about evangelistic witness, and for three reasons. First, as noted, evangelism is on his mind in the immediately preceding context (see vv. 2–4). Second, he wants all of us to be fully equipped to "answer each person," those he calls "outsiders" (undoubtedly a reference to those outside the church, i.e., non-Christians). And third, the word translated "speech" in verse 6 is the same Greek word (*logos*) used in verse 3 where he asks that God open a door for the "word," i.e., that he be granted opportunities to preach the "word" of the gospel, the mystery of Christ.

There are five important points in these two verses about sharing our faith with others. Let's look at each in turn.

First, we are exhorted to conduct ourselves wisely toward outsiders. I think at least two things are in view here. I'm immediately reminded of our Lord's words in the Sermon on the Mount: "Do not give dogs what is holy, and do not throw your pearls before pigs, lest they trample them underfoot and turn to attack you" (Matt. 7:6). Wisdom requires that we be discerning as to when we speak and to whom. Sometimes we need to be bold and forthright, while on other occasions, because of the calloused and hostile posture of our audience, we need to keep our mouths shut.

The other point of emphasis in Paul's use of the word *wisdom* has been ably summarized by John Piper. I can do no better than quote him directly: "Wisdom is knowing what to do for the glory of God when the rule book runs out. It's knowing how to become all things to all men without compromising holiness and truth. It is creativity and tact and thoughtfulness. It's having a feel for the moment, and having an eye for what people need and want."[3]

Second, we mustn't lose sight of the urgency of our task. The ESV renders this, "making the best use of the time," while older translations retain the more literal translation, "redeeming the time" (KJV). Commentators do a good job of highlighting Paul's emphasis. Peter O'Brien renders it, "snapping up every opportunity that comes."[4] Murray Harris is even more to the point: "In the open market where the commodity of 'kairos' [time] is on sale, Christians are to make a 'timely' purchase for themselves. In other words, they are to seize eagerly and use wisely every opportunity afforded them by time to promote the kingdom of God."[5]

Don't waste any opportunity that comes your way or squander the chance to walk boldly through an open door into the heart of an unbeliever! Every encounter has the potential to be soul-saving. Don't let fear or hesitation or lack of preparation steal that moment.

Third, our witness must always be "gracious" (v. 6), which is to say, as charming as possible without crossing the line into compromise. Be accommodating and kind, says Paul, but not at the expense of truth.

What matters is not simply the content but the manner or spirit in which you speak of Christ to others. We are to be both pointed and pleasant in our witness. Sadly, many embrace one to the exclusion of the other, finding it difficult to embrace both in delicate balance. Either they care for nothing but the truth, regardless of how it is conveyed, or they are so afraid of sounding offensive or pushy that they end up diluting the truth and fail to articulate the realities of sin, death, and hell.

Fourth, our proclamation of the mystery of Christ must be "seasoned with salt" (v. 6). Let there be a pungency to our preaching, a flavor worthy to savor. There's no virtue in being dull or insipid or lukewarm in the presentation of the gospel.

My former professor at Dallas Theological Seminary Howard Hendricks was often heard to say: "According to the old adage, you can lead a horse to water, but you can't make him drink. That's true, but you can feed him salt!" Do you talk of Jesus in a way that makes people's mouths water? Do your words and manner create the opportunity for a spiritual thirst to emerge?

The psalmist said, "Oh, taste and see that the LORD is good!" (Ps. 34:8a). Do people see and sense the sweetness of the Savior when we speak of him? He is altogether lovely and should not be made known in an unlovely or unappealing manner. Jesus tastes good! Don't spoil the flavor by sinful additives and sour dispositions.

Fifth, and finally, we must be diligent to answer "each person" (v. 6). He doesn't mean that we should speak the same way to "everyone," but that we ought to speak appropriately to "each separate person" as he or she has need. We must supply perceptive and discerning answers in accordance with the unique circumstance of each individual. Not everyone hears the gospel the same way. Some encounter Christ with probing intellectual objections, while others are struggling with deeply entrenched sinful habits.

Evangelism should never be monolithic, as if one mode or manner of presentation is suitable for all souls. Yes, each is in need of a savior from sin. Of course, there is but one Savior and his name is Jesus. But each person is also at a different stage of life, facing a unique set of trials and troubles, each with varying degrees of understanding of who Jesus is and what he has accomplished. In sum, be adept to adapt, and pray that the Spirit would awaken all hearts to see and celebrate the mystery of Christ!

# 94

# When Christians Clash (1)

## Colossians 4:10, 14

**Aristarchus my fellow prisoner greets you, and Mark the cousin of Barnabas (concerning whom you have received instructions—if he comes to you, welcome him),** and Jesus who is called Justus. These are the only men of the circumcision among my fellow workers for the kingdom of God, and they have been a comfort to me. Epaphras, who is one of you, a servant of Christ Jesus, greets you, always struggling on your behalf in his prayers, that you may stand mature and fully assured in all the will of God. For I bear him witness that he has worked hard for you and for those in Laodicea and in Hierapolis. **Luke the beloved physician greets you, as does Demas.**

What are we to do when Christians clash? I'm not thinking of momentary spats or minor disagreements, but of significant divisions and conflict grounded in equally sincere convictions about what is right and wise. If you've been a Christian for any period of time you've no doubt seen it or, sadly, been embroiled in one of your own.

Once again, one of the admirable things about the Bible is its often brutal honesty, its refusal to gloss over the glitches in believers' lives. There are a number of examples I could cite, but none more pointed than the breakdown between Paul, Barnabas, and Mark, and their subsequent reconciliation. The latter two are mentioned in Colossians 4:10. I should also throw in a certain Demas, whose name appears in verse 14.

These men, together with Tychicus (vv. 7–8), Onesimus (v. 9), Aristarchus (v. 10), Justus (v. 11), Epaphras (vv. 12–13), Luke (v. 14), Archippus (v. 17), and one lady named Nympha (v. 15), are all included in Paul's traditional closing list of those to and from whom he sends his greetings.

I will have occasion in subsequent meditations to say a brief word about a few of these individuals, but I want to focus in detail on the rocky relationship and the glorious reconciliation that occurred with Paul, Barnabas, and Mark. I'll include the defection from Paul (and the faith?) of Demas and contrast this with the way in which Mark proved his faithfulness following a momentary lapse in judgment. There are countless practical lessons we can learn from these men and their struggles. So let's begin.

If we are going to understand and learn from this "clash of Christians," we need to move outside of Colossians and take note of a story that is recorded for us in Acts 15. Our principal characters are Paul (who needs no comment), Barnabas, and Mark.

Barnabas was the kind of man whom you would want as a best friend. No matter how bad things got, no matter how low and lousy you might feel, no matter how badly you may have failed, when your world stinks, Barnabas was the sort who brings a sweet aroma to life. You could always count on his being there. He wouldn't have closed an eye to your sin. In fact, he would have rebuked you if needed, but you'd know it's because he really cared.

Much is said of Barnabas in the New Testament, all of which is worthy of imitation. He is described as generous in Acts 4:36–37 (if you're in financial stress, he'd give you what he had, even if it wasn't much). He had an uncanny knack for encouraging others when they were in distress. "Barnabas," as most of you know, actually means "Son of Encouragement," as Acts 4:36 and 11:23 bear witness (cf. Acts 9:27). He was a "good" man (Acts 11:24); what a brief but glorious epitaph! He was "filled with the Spirit" and "full of faith" (Acts 11:24), i.e., rock solid and spiritually steady, no matter the circumstance, always looking confidently to the trustworthiness and sufficiency of Jesus. He was a teacher, prophet, evangelist, and apostle (Acts 11:26; 13:1; 14:14), obviously quite gifted! Perhaps best of all, he could be counted on, which is to say, he was reliable (see Acts 11:29–30; 12:25).

## Colossians 4:10, 14

Our third character is Mark, called "John Mark" (it was common to have two names, one acceptable to Greeks and Romans and the other Jewish). He lived in Jerusalem with his mother, Mary, in his whose home prayer meetings were regularly held (Acts 12:12). We know he was the cousin of Barnabas, as Paul indicates in Colossians 4:10, and was selected by Paul (no doubt on Barnabas's recommendation) to accompany them on their missionary journeys (Acts 12:25).

The problem, the "clash," if you will, was precipitated by something recorded for us in Acts 13:13–14 during Paul's second missionary journey. There we read that "Paul and his companions set sail from Paphos and came to Perga in Pamphylia. And John [Mark] left them and returned to Jerusalem, but they went on from Perga and came to Antioch in Pisidia." Luke doesn't tell us at this point why John Mark left them, nor does he suggest at this stage that his decision was wrong or sinful.

Why did Mark leave? There are any number of possibilities. For example, he may have been homesick. Perhaps he missed his mother, their spacious home in Jerusalem, and the comfort provided by the servants present there.

Others believe that he had come to resent Paul for eclipsing his cousin Barnabas in importance and fame. Paul was now the acknowledged leader of the group. Was it familial jealousy that drove this young man?

The explanation could be as simple as physical exhaustion. Mark may not have been accustomed to the rigors of travel, or perhaps he was a bit lazy, at least by Paul's standards. Was he having second thoughts about his calling as a missionary ("Did I really hear God?")? Was he discouraged ("This isn't what I had in mind at all!")?

When Paul reached the cities of south Galatia he was quite ill (see Gal. 4:13–15). He may have contracted malarial fever, which could be reduced by leaving the climate of the low-lying coastal plain and going to the coolness of the Taurus Plateau some 3,500 feet above sea level. A few have argued that perhaps Mark thought Paul was foolish in making the decision to go north over the mountains and decided it was unwise to accompany him.

There is also the possibility that as a loyal member of the church in Jerusalem he disagreed with Paul's policy of evangelizing Gentiles and granting them equal status in the church. Some suggest it was

Mark who provoked the Judaizers in Jerusalem into opposing Paul (cf. Acts 15:1ff), but we have no explicit evidence to support this.

Other possible explanations are his fear of bandits, thieves, and muggers who infested the Taurus Mountains into which Paul insisted they go (cf. 2 Cor. 11:26), or perhaps his fear of persecution (cf. Acts 14:19).

Whatever the reason for Mark's refusal to continue with Paul and Barnabas, whatever excuse he used to make a hasty retreat to Jerusalem and the comforts of home, Paul took it as a sign of weakness and immaturity and unreliability. So did Barnabas, I suspect, although later they would differ greatly on how best to deal with the problem.

Following the Jerusalem Council (Acts 15), Paul said to Barnabas, "Let us return and visit the brothers in every city where we proclaimed the word of the Lord, and see how they are" (Acts 15:36). Barnabas wanted Mark to come along, "but Paul thought best not to take with them one who had withdrawn from them in Pamphylia and had not gone with them to the work" (Acts 15:37–38).

Note well what happened next: "And there arose a sharp disagreement, so that they separated from each other. Barnabas took Mark with him and sailed away to Cyprus, but Paul chose Silas and departed, having been commended by the brothers to the grace of the Lord" (Acts 15:39–40). It testifies to the historical reliability of Acts that Luke makes no effort to cover up this dispute. He's not afraid to face reality or point a finger at warts on the face of the church.

Barnabas would not have disputed the fact that Mark blew it badly when he deserted them in Cyprus. Sin is sin. He no doubt agreed with Paul that Mark failed miserably on his first outing, but he also believed Mark had sincerely repented and should be welcomed back and given a second chance.

There's no reason to think Paul doubted Mark's sincerity in repenting. But the great apostle could not afford to risk the lives of others and the success of the mission on a man who, in his opinion, had yet to prove himself reliable and trustworthy in the heat of battle. Perhaps Paul said to Barnabas (using modern lingo): "When the going gets tough, the tough get going; but, Barnabas, don't you remember Cyprus? When the going got tough there, Mark turned tail and ran away. It's not that I don't love the young man, but too much is at stake to trust him this early in his recovery."

Who was right, Paul or Barnabas or both? Paul believed that Mark needed to prove his reliability before being entrusted with such an awesome responsibility. That's probably true. But Barnabas believed he also needed encouragement and love and acceptance. Again, no argument there. But with neither man willing to concede, the split was unavoidable.

So what ultimately happened with Mark? How did he end up with Paul during his imprisonment in Rome? And how is it that Paul now commends him to the church in Colossae (Col. 4:10)? And what lessons can we learn from it all? To be continued . . .

# 95

# When Christians Clash (2)

## Colossians 4:10, 14

**Aristarchus my fellow prisoner greets you, and Mark the cousin of Barnabas (concerning whom you have received instructions—if he comes to you, welcome him),** and Jesus who is called Justus. These are the only men of the circumcision among my fellow workers for the kingdom of God, and they have been a comfort to me. Epaphras, who is one of you, a servant of Christ Jesus, greets you, always struggling on your behalf in his prayers, that you may stand mature and fully assured in all the will of God. For I bear him witness that he has worked hard for you and for those in Laodicea and in Hierapolis. **Luke the beloved physician greets you, as does Demas.**

Luke describes the incident between Paul and Barnabas as a "sharp disagreement" (Acts 15:39). I don't know, but it may have sounded something like this:

"Paul! You're being unreasonable. I know you're a man of conviction, but for heaven's sake ease up a bit."

"I may be unreasonable in your estimation, Barnabas, but you are showing a distinct lack of wisdom. Don't let the fact that he's your cousin blind you to his failures. We need to think first and foremost about the welfare of this ministry God has entrusted to us."

"I am thinking of the ministry. But Mark is a sensitive and loving young man. Your inflexibility could crush his spirit. Must you be so harsh?"

## Colossians 4:10, 14

"Must you be so soft? I love Mark. Really, I do. But you're letting your compassion override your convictions."

"And you're letting your principles override your pity."

In any case, the split must have been painful for everyone involved. I suspect even Mark felt guilty for being the cause of a separation between these two friends and coworkers. But let's learn from what happened. There are five valuable lessons we can ill-afford to ignore.

First, we mustn't forget that Paul and Barnabas, not just Mark, were also human and prone to sin. I can't get over the fact that two apostles, that's right, apostles (!), are engaged in a verbal brawl. I'm not in the least suggesting this justifies such behavior in us or that what occurred wasn't grievous to the heart of God. But it reminds us that no one in this life achieves perfection or rises above the promptings of the flesh. These two men had worked miracles by the Spirit of God. They had laid hands on the sick and healed them. They both prayed in tongues (at least Paul did). They both loved Jesus. Yet here they are shouting angrily at each other.

If you had witnessed this clash, what conclusions would you have drawn? Or let's bring it into the twenty-first century. If you were a new Christian visiting a local church for the first time, and you happened upon such an argument in the parking lot or even the foyer of the church, what might you think?

Perhaps: "These men obviously can't be Christians."

Or perhaps: "I won't believe anything either of them teaches. They are obviously disqualified from instructing others when they can't get along with each other."

Or maybe: "Who appointed these guys to be missionaries? Someone needs to re-evaluate the screening process!"

Or again: "I'll bet you God never blesses or anoints either of them again. No more signs and wonders through their hands!"

Or lastly: "Hypocrites! The church is full of them. I'll never again darken the door of this place as long as people like that are around."

If nothing else, we learn from this not to judge too quickly or draw decisive conclusions about the goodness of people from a singular incident.

Second, is there anything we can learn from Paul's position? I think his decision reminds us that we don't entrust the young and immature with major tasks (cf. 1 Timothy 3:10). We don't push people into ministry or positions of leadership and authority who may not be capable of bearing the burden or dealing with the pressure. A proven track record and proven character are indispensable.

Can we learn something important from Barnabas? Certainly. We learn that even those who fail are not to be abandoned and forever spurned. They are to be lovingly rebuked and corrected and then encouraged until conviction grips their hearts and repentance is forthcoming. We learn that failure such as this is not grounds for permanent exclusion from ministry. More on this later.

Third, observe how God providentially brought good out of this tragic turn of events. With Paul and Barnabas splitting up and going their separate ways, two missionary teams instead of one are unleashed on the unbelieving world. Paul took Silas with him, while Barnabas took Mark. We must never justify our failures or sins by appealing to the overriding role of divine providence, but it is reassuring to know that God can redeem for his glory even the most petty as well as substantive clashes among his children.

Fourth, there are important lessons to learn from the experience of Mark himself. It would appear that although Mark abandoned them, he had returned on his own initiative. This was a courageous and humbling act on his part, demonstrative of the reality of his repentance.

Note also that Mark was not only received back by Paul, but was restored to ministry as well. In Colossians 4:10 Paul sends the church greetings from Mark and adds this comment: "concerning whom you have received instructions—if he comes to you, welcome him." Evidently Mark's restoration had not been fully acknowledged by all. I suspect that some in Colossae were suspicious of him, which is why Paul insists that they receive him warmly and wholeheartedly.

If that weren't enough to restore confidence in Mark, Paul explicitly calls him his "fellow worker" in Philemon 24. Better still is what Paul wrote to Timothy in his second epistle. Remember, at the time of that letter Paul was in prison in Rome, perhaps only weeks, at most months, away from execution. Virtually everyone had either abandoned him or left for other ministry opportunities (see 2 Tim. 4:9–10). "Luke alone is with me" (2 Tim. 4:11a), wrote Paul.

It's a bit depressing, isn't it? Paul is at the end of his life. His ministry is near over. Of all the people he could have asked to come and support and encourage him, guess whom he mentions? "Get Mark and bring him with you, for he is very useful to me for ministry" (2 Tim. 4:11b). Mark? Useful? For ministry? Indeed! Isn't God's grace amazing?

Fifth, how was Mark restored to ministry? I suspect there were at least three human contributors through whom the Spirit worked. First was Barnabas and his constant encouragement and friendship. Second was Peter, Mark's spiritual father (1 Pet. 5:13). Peter knew a bit about failure himself! He knew the joy of restoration as well. No doubt his advice and prayers and support proved invaluable to Mark on his journey back. Finally, Paul's principles, his rebuke, and the discipline on which he insisted must also have played a role. "Better is open rebuke than hidden love. Faithful are the wounds of a friend; profuse are the kisses of an enemy" (Prov. 27:5–6). I suspect Mark would have been the first to say that all three men were indispensable to him.

# 96
# When Christians Clash (3)

### Colossians 4:10, 14

Aristarchus my fellow prisoner greets you, and Mark the cousin of Barnabas (concerning whom you have received instructions—if he comes to you, welcome him), and Jesus who is called Justus. These are the only men of the circumcision among my fellow workers for the kingdom of God, and they have been a comfort to me. Epaphras, who is one of you, a servant of Christ Jesus, greets you, always struggling on your behalf in his prayers, that you may stand mature and fully assured in all the will of God. For I bear him witness that he has worked hard for you and for those in Laodicea and in Hierapolis. **Luke the beloved physician greets you, as does Demas.**

We've learned much from the clash of Paul and Barnabas over Mark. But there's one more lesson to note. It comes by way of a painful contrast.

Among those listed in the concluding paragraph of Colossians is a man named Demas (Col. 4:14). He, too, was with Paul in Rome, faithfully serving the apostle alongside of Mark, Luke, Epaphras, and others. But not for long.

Is there a more painful experience than being abandoned by a friend? One struggles to find words adequate for the distress that is felt when a close, trusted companion and fellow-worker (see Philem. 24) walks away.

It's important to remember that this was Paul's first Roman imprisonment when conditions were not so threatening. But things were to change. When Paul wrote again from prison in Rome, his life was in the balance. Here are his words to his spiritual son, Timothy: "Do your best to come to me soon. For Demas, in love with this present world, has deserted me and gone to Thessalonica" (2 Tim. 4:9–10). Ouch! Double ouch!!

Was Demas a "convenient" Christian, one who was happy to follow Jesus and assist the apostle so long as it was rewarding and safe? We can't be sure, but it's clear that Demas wanted nothing to do with Paul. The verb translated "deserted" in 2 Timothy 4:10 implies not simply that Demas had left but had left him in the lurch, had abandoned and forsaken him.

Paul would have recalled the wisdom of Solomon: "Trusting in a treacherous man in time of trouble is like a bad tooth or a foot that slips" (Prov. 25:19). Nothing hurts quite like the disloyalty and betrayal of someone trusted. It's like a decaying, rotten tooth and a palsied, disjointed foot. Not only are they functionally useless (for chewing and walking), they hurt!

For some of you, no doubt, your experience with this sort of person has made you hesitant to trust another. Perhaps you've closed your heart to starting new friendships or found yourself keeping folk at arm's length. But Paul didn't let the betrayal and abandonment of Demas and others scare him off or sour him to friendship altogether. He didn't say, "Oh, Timothy, how do I know you won't abandon me like Demas did?" There's an important lesson in that.

Demas abandoned Paul in his hour of need because he had fallen "in love with this present world" (2 Tim. 4:10a). He preferred material prosperity to spiritual blessings. Comfort and wealth and safety meant more to him than the advance of the gospel and the welfare of the apostle.

What lessons might we learn from the contrast between Demas and Mark?

First, when you look for the first time at these two men, Demas appeared faithful and loyal while Mark gave every indication of cowardice and weakness. But as time passed, their situations reversed. Demas proved himself to be disloyal and unreliable, and Mark grew into the sort of trusted friend whom Paul wanted at his side in his final days on earth.

Don't be hasty in making snap judgments about people. Initially, Paul thought Demas would never leave and Mark would never be of use. Now, Demas has left and Mark is back. We're reminded by this that more important than how you start a race is how you finish. It's been said before and I'll say it again: the Christian life is a marathon, not a sprint! So let's be careful and not place excessive responsibility on those who do well at first, nor give up entirely on those who appear to have slipped at the starting line.

Second, some say Mark was not a Christian when he abandoned Paul and Barnabas but converted later on. They also argue that Demas was a Christian but lost his salvation when he deserted Paul for love of the world. But this is based on the assumption that a true believer is incapable of the sin of fear or cowardice. Cowardice was Mark's transgression; Peter's too! It also assumes that someone who is born again cannot fall into the grip of materialism and self-protection, which may well have been Demas's struggle.

I suspect, but can't prove, that Demas was a Christian with whom God dealt no differently from how he dealt with Mark. He would have come under the conviction of the Spirit and felt the call to repentance. Short of his restoration, divine discipline would have ensued. Was he restored? We don't know. There are other instances in Scripture where discipline is temporally (but not spiritually) fatal (cf. Acts 5:1–11; 1 Cor. 11:30–32). In the case of Demas, the Bible is silent, and we must be content with that.

Third, and finally, Barnabas received Mark back. Peter received Mark back. Paul received Mark back. The church as a whole received Mark back. But what about God? God used him to write the Gospel of his Son! This miserable failure who initially proved so unreliable was received and restored by God to fulfill a task of awesome and eternal significance. As I said before, isn't grace amazing?

# 97

# Superstar-less Christianity

## Colossians 4:7–17

Tychicus will tell you all about my activities. He is a beloved brother and faithful minister and fellow servant in the Lord. I have sent him to you for this very purpose, that you may know how we are and that he may encourage your hearts, and with him Onesimus, our faithful and beloved brother, who is one of you. They will tell you of everything that has taken place here. Aristarchus my fellow prisoner greets you, and Mark the cousin of Barnabas (concerning whom you have received instructions—if he comes to you, welcome him), and Jesus who is called Justus. These are the only men of the circumcision among my fellow workers for the kingdom of God, and they have been a comfort to me. Epaphras, who is one of you, a servant of Christ Jesus, greets you, always struggling on your behalf in his prayers, that you may stand mature and fully assured in all the will of God. For I bear him witness that he has worked hard for you and for those in Laodicea and in Hierapolis. Luke the beloved physician greets you, as does Demas. Give my greetings to the brothers at Laodicea, and to Nympha and the church in her house. And when this letter has been read among you, have it also read in the church of the Laodiceans; and see that you also read the letter from Laodicea. And say to Archippus, "See that you fulfill the ministry that you have received in the Lord."

There's a sickness in our society that has infiltrated and infected the church. I have in mind our modern obsession with superstars. Whether they be Hollywood actors, Wall Street moguls, or overpaid, egotistical athletes, they seem to fill our newspapers and dominate our headlines and have become, tragically in most cases, role models for our children.

The church is by no means immune to this infatuation with celebrity. Mega-church pastors, health-and-wealth advocates, and bestselling authors are promoted and praised as if they are in better standing with the Lord than the faithful but unacknowledged housewife or the quiet pastor who tends a flock of less than a hundred folk in rural Alabama.

I think Paul would have been disgusted with it all. In fact, I know it. One need only read 2 Corinthians (especially chapter 11) to observe his disdain for those who fancied themselves "super-apostles" (2 Cor. 11:5). It's also evident from his commendations at the close of most of his letters. The kind of folk that most impressed him didn't necessarily hold ecclesiastical office or write books or have their names bandied about among gossipers.

The people who impressed Paul were the likes of Tychicus, Onesimus, Aristarchus, Justus, Epaphras, Luke (okay, there's one famous name), and Archippus. And the things Paul noted concerning them would hardly get their names on the evening news or generate enough money to subsidize a program on TBN.

Take Tychicus, for example, Paul's special envoy to the churches of provincial Asia. Before I mentioned him here, had you ever heard his name? God had! He's described here as "a beloved brother and faithful minister and fellow servant in the Lord" (Col. 4:7; see the meditation on Col. 1:7–8 for an explanation of these terms), a man with the gift of encouragement (Col. 4:8) who was trusted implicitly by the apostle Paul given the fact that he most likely delivered the Colossian and Ephesian epistles each to its respective congregation.

Then there's Onesimus, another "faithful and beloved brother" (Col. 4:9). That wouldn't be noteworthy to most people were it not for the fact that this is probably the same Onesimus mentioned in Paul's letter to Philemon. Yes, the slave Onesimus. Here's a man with no possessions, no rights, no inheritance under Roman law, of no regard to the vast majority of people in his day, a man nevertheless whom Paul loves and describes as his spiritual son (Philem. 10), a man who diligently served Paul during his imprisonment and for whom Paul now willingly stands surety (Philem. 11, 17–19).

Aristarchus, a Thessalonian who traveled with Paul on several occasions (cf. Acts 19:29; 20:4), was incarcerated with the apostle, probably for the same offence: fearlessly proclaiming the mystery of Christ (Col. 4:3). How would you like to be known to history for only one thing: loving Jesus so much that you willingly spent time behind bars? I suspect Aristarchus wouldn't object.

Justus is included among only three Jews who are said to have assisted Paul as "fellow workers for the kingdom of God" (Col. 4:11). But Paul is quick to point out that Justus, together with Aristarchus and Mark, were "a comfort" to him. Although Paul was courageous and willing to endure whatever suffering came his way, he was susceptible to discouragement and depression and disillusionment like the rest of us. These men comforted him! They spoke truth to his soul. They reminded him daily of God's faithfulness and goodness and the heavenly reward that lay ahead. Such people Paul praises.

I've already discussed Epaphras at some length (see my comments on 1:7–8), so we move to Luke and Archippus. The author of the third Gospel and the book of Acts is here referred to as "the beloved physician" (4:14). Was he Paul's personal doctor or is this mentioned only because "Luke's profession was an unusual one"?[6] We don't know.

As for Archippus, he is evidently in Colossae and is the focus of this exhortation: "See that you fulfill the ministry that you have received in the Lord" (Col. 4:17). He's mentioned again in Philemon 2 and described as "our fellow soldier." Some speculate that he was the son of Philemon, a reasonable deduction. What was his "ministry"? Was he a deacon in the church, perhaps an elder, or an evangelist in the surrounding community? We don't know, but to be singled out as the only Colossian to receive a personal exhortation from Paul indicates he had some degree of authority in the church. We can only hope he heeded the word!

Well, there you have it. Not exactly a spiritual Hall of Fame: no one like Moses or David or Daniel, but not for that reason any less precious to the Lord Jesus. I quoted Paul's words to the Philippians in an earlier lesson, but they apply here again with equal force: "Honor such men" (Phil. 2:29).

Don't be caught up in the feigned adulation of superficial and self-indulgent folk, whether they be in Hollywood or the church down the street. Seek out and support "beloved brothers and sisters" who are "faithful ministers" and "fellow servants" of the Lord Jesus and "fellow workers for the kingdom" who expend themselves and intercede for the saints. These are the true superstars!

# 98

# Women on the Front Lines

## *Colossians 4:15*

> Give my greetings to the brothers at Laodicea, and to Nympha and the church in her house.

We must never minimize or overlook the incredible influence in the early church of a number of courageous and faithful women. Where does one begin to list them all? I suppose we'd have to give preeminent notice to Mary, the mother of Jesus, whose remarkable faith and submission to God's will is an example for all people, male and female, of all ages (cf. Luke 1:38).

One thinks also of Elizabeth, Mary's cousin, the mother of John the Baptist. Mary and Martha, sisters of Lazarus, also played a vital role in the early ministry of Jesus, as did Mary Magdalene (no, that's *not* because she was the wife of Jesus and bore his child!).

The book of Acts is full of powerful and passionate women who put their lives and livelihood on the line for the kingdom of God. Yet another Mary, the mother of Mark, opened her home as a base for prayer and fellowship (Acts 12:12). Lydia's conversion is well known, but not as many are aware that she opened her home to Paul and Silas, which may well have been the original house church in the city of Philippi (Acts 16:15, 40).

Priscilla, wife of Aquila, was evidently well educated and was used of the Lord together with her husband to explain to Apollos "the way of God more accurately" (Acts 18:26). In fact, they also opened their home to serve as the base for a local church (1 Cor. 16:19). The four unmarried daughters of Philip the evangelist ministered faithfully in the gift of prophecy (Acts 21:9). The apostle Paul had such great trust in Phoebe, "a servant of the church in Cenchreae" (Rom. 16:1), that it was she to whom he probably entrusted delivery of his letter to the Romans. Euodia and Syntyche "labored side by side" with Paul in the work of the gospel (Phil. 4:2) and I'm sure there were others who shared this great honor. These are but a few of the many who could be mentioned.

I raise this point because we encounter yet another faithful servant of the Lord in this epistle. In Colossians 4:15 Paul sends his greetings to "the brothers at Laodicea and to Nympha and the church in her house." There is a measure of ambiguity as to whether the name is masculine or feminine, but the weight of textual evidence supports the possessive pronoun *her* rather than *his* in the subsequent phrase.

As you probably know (if not, you should), so-called house-churches are mentioned on several occasions in the New Testament. Christians didn't congregate in larger, public facilities until late into the third century (at the earliest). In some smaller towns the entire body of Christ would have gathered in one person's home, while in larger cities several house-churches would have existed.

In addition to the congregation that met in Nympha's house in Laodicea (which was located some ten miles to the west of Colossae), Philemon's house was the meeting place for a (the?) congregation in Colossae (Philem. 2). Evidently the house of Gaius was large enough to host, at least on occasion, "the whole church" (Rom. 16:23; cf. 1 Cor. 14:23) in the city of Corinth. In all likelihood there were smaller groups of Christians that also met throughout that city. Priscilla and Aquila customarily hosted a church in their home wherever they lived, whether in Ephesus (see 1 Cor. 16:19) or in Rome (see Rom. 16:5).

Let me conclude with two observations. First, this text in Colossians 4:15, together with the others noted, reminds us of the nature of the church and how far removed we are from its original meaning. Use the word *church* today and the vast majority in our society, both Christian and non-Christian, immediately think of a building, a physical structure of some sort, whether in a strip mall or one of the more massive mega-churches that dot the American landscape with increasing frequency.

My point is simply that the church is people, an assembly of gathered believers in the Lord Jesus Christ. Whether they meet in a cave (to avoid arrest) or on a hillside (to enjoy the beauty of God's creation) or in a home (for lack of money to meet elsewhere) or in a ten-thousand-seat auditorium, the church is the body of Christ. In Nympha's house, a living, vibrant, spiritual organism (not organization) gathered and thrived and worshiped and prayed and studied God's Word.

Walk through Nympha's house and observe the absence of electricity, amplified sound system, Power Point, indoor plumbing, robed choirs, offering plates, Sunday school classrooms, air-conditioning, padded pews, pipe organs, pianos, carpeted hallways, computers, printed bulletins, or any of the paraphernalia we typically associate with normal church life, but you would assuredly encounter a genuine, God-fearing, Christ-exalting *church*!

I'm not in the least surprised by the growth and popularity of the so-called house-church movement today. There is a simplicity and spiritual authenticity that often is found in such gatherings that is sorely missed in what *can be* the impersonal and sterile environment of a mega-church (I emphasize the words "can be," acknowledging that some large congregations do well in welcoming the stranger and facilitating every-member ministry). So long as these house churches embrace the biblical guidelines for a local congregation (plurality of elders, teaching of the Scriptures, observance of the sacraments, discipline of its members, etc.), one can hardly object to their existence. Indeed, we should thank God for them!

Second, and finally, I also thank God for women such as Nympha and others like her in the history of the church. The fact that Nympha's name stands alone probably indicates that she was either single or a widow. In any case it is testimony to her courage, her capacity to bear an immense spiritual and physical burden, and especially her willingness to subject herself to persecution and slander. A recognition of the biblical principle of male headship in church leadership and in marriage should in no way undermine the spiritual gifting of women or inhibit their contribution to the expansion of God's kingdom. "Thank you, Lord, for Nympha and others like her!"

# 99

# The Public Reading of "Lost" Scripture

## Colossians 4:16

And when this letter has been read among you, have it also read in the church of the Laodiceans; and see that you also read the letter from Laodicea.

It wasn't until the year 2000, when I joined an Anglican church in Wheaton, Illinois, that I was exposed on a consistent basis to the public reading of Scripture. In the churches where I had formerly been a member or had served on the pastoral staff (Southern Baptist, independent Bible church, Vineyard), the only biblical text read aloud was the one on which the sermon was based.

Not being accustomed to anything remotely liturgical, it took some getting used to. But soon I grew to appreciate the power of the public reading of the written Word. First came the Old Testament text, then a psalm, followed by a paragraph from the Epistles, all of which concluded with a reading from the Gospels. I fear that in many churches, especially those which resist all things liturgical, a glorious experience is being missed. Every church need not follow the same procedure, but we would do well to give place, in some form or other, to the public reading of the Word.

In his concluding comments to the church at Colossae, Paul writes: "And when this letter has been read among you, have it also read in the church of the Laodiceans; and see that you also read the letter from Laodicea" (Col. 4:16).

This may not strike us today as a momentous occasion, given our reliance upon the printed page and the wonderful blessing of a Bible (or several, and in multiple translations) for each person. But in the first century the reception of an apostolic letter and its public reading was a glorious event. I fear that were a pastor in our day to announce that he planned on reading all four chapters of Colossians to his congregation, many would wince, some would sleep, most would be distracted, and not a few would simply get up and leave. How tragic.

I recently attended the funeral service of my aunt in Ponca City, Oklahoma. It was most unusual and, for that reason, quite edifying. Before her death she had instructed the presiding pastor to read just the Sermon on the Mount. She wanted no obituary to be read, no eulogy to be spoken. Just the Scriptures. It just so happened that her pastor had memorized the sermon (Matthew 5–7). Thus the entire service, aside from our singing of hymns, consisted of his reciting, dramatically and powerfully, the Sermon on the Mount.

The public reading of God's Word was a common practice in the synagogue (Luke 4:16; Acts 13:15, 27; 15:21; 2 Cor. 3:14–15) and was taken over in the early church as well. In his first epistle to the Thessalonians Paul wrote, rather forcefully: "I put you under oath before the Lord to have this letter read to all the brothers" (5:27). And again, in writing to his spiritual son Timothy, he exhorts: "Until I come, devote yourself to the public reading of Scripture, to exhortation, to teaching" (1 Tim. 4:13).

Perhaps someone will argue that it is less effective as a means of communication and instruction to read aloud in a congregational gathering than it is to read the printed page privately. That may be true. But there is also something powerful, perhaps even sacramental, in the corporate hearing of the inspired text. All of God's people are brought under the authority of the Word. All are called to hear, heed, and obey. This also bears powerful witness to any unbelievers present of the foundational function of Scripture in the life of God's people.

That Paul regarded this as crucial for the life of all Christians, and not simply this one congregation, is seen in his request that the

Colossians take steps to have the letter read publicly in the church at Laodicea. In addition, they are to read publicly "the letter from Laodicea" (4:16). Clearly the two letters were sufficiently different, each with its own distinct points of emphasis, that Paul thought it wise and helpful for both letters to be read in each congregation.

This raises a huge and important question: What is this letter from Laodicea? Some believe it was a letter written to Paul by the Laodicean church, or perhaps by its leadership, or even one of its members. But it is more likely that Paul means they are to get hold of a letter from him, currently in the possession of the Laodiceans, which had been written to that neighboring church. But what letter might this be?

There is a long-standing belief that Paul is referring to his canonical letter to the Ephesians. A number of scholars believe that this was a general epistle sent not only to the Ephesian church but to all the many Gentile congregations in southwestern Asia Minor. Others have pointed out that the words "in Ephesus" (Eph. 1:1) may not have been part of the original text of this document. In any case, most acknowledge that the epistle was initially sent to Ephesus, since it was the center for communication and commerce throughout the province. Paul's intent, apparently, was that it be circulated among the many house churches in Ephesus and its environs. It would make perfectly good sense, then, for him to encourage the Colossians to have it read in their midst as well.

There is one seemingly insurmountable problem with this theory: the epistle to the Ephesians was most likely written *after* Colossians. I suppose someone could argue that Paul wrote Colossians 4:16 in view of his intent to write a more general epistle to the church at Ephesus, but this seems a bit far-fetched.

Another theory is that it was Paul's letter to Philemon, but this was a distinctly personal and private letter. Also, Philemon lived in Colossae, not Laodicea.

I'm persuaded that Paul is referencing a letter that he himself wrote to the Laodiceans, one that obviously did not survive for inclusion in the canon of Scripture. What happened to it? We don't know, but it's possible that it was destroyed in the massive earthquake that hit the region in A.D. 61. But that's only speculation.

You shouldn't be bothered by this, given the fact that Paul most likely wrote four letters to the Corinthian church, only two of which are included in our canon (see 1 Cor. 5:9–11, a reference to the letter written in A.D. 54, now lost; and 2 Cor. 2:4, 9, references to the letter written in the summer of A.D. 55, often called the "severe" or "tearful" letter, also now lost).

There are some questions, though, that we can't avoid. Were these "lost" letters as inspired and infallible as those which were included in the canon? Yes, I believe so, especially given the fact that Paul's instructions in Colossians 4:16 envision the church hearing and heeding the content of both letters. Likewise, there's no indication in 1 Corinthians 5:9–11 and 2 Corinthians 2:4, 9 that he viewed these lost documents as possessing a lesser moral authority than the canonical Corinthian correspondence. I can only conclude that the Colossian Christians and the Corinthians, as well as all others who had access to these lost epistles, were as morally obligated to believe and obey what Paul wrote in them as they were what he wrote in the epistles that eventually made their way into the biblical canon.

Why, then, didn't God preserve these and other apostolic writings for the church of subsequent generations? Evidently, once these letters served their divinely designed function for the early church, God sovereignly arranged for their disappearance or destruction. In his infinite and gracious wisdom he determined that the content of those epistles was not essential for the life and faith of the church beyond the first century. Ultimately we must trust in divine providence and believe that God has preserved for us everything that is necessary for a life of truth and godliness.

Finally, if these so-called lost letters were suddenly found, perhaps similar to the discovery of the Dead Sea Scrolls, should they be included in our canon of Scripture? It's a moot point, for I'm convinced they won't be found. If God deemed them essential for the life of the church in the twenty-first century (indeed, for the life of the church in the entire post-apostolic period), he would certainly have preserved them and providentially orchestrated their inclusion in the canon along with those documents that now constitute what we regard as Scripture. Therefore, I'll leave it to others to speculate on what the universal body of Christ should or would do if I happen to be proven wrong.

In the meantime, let's all agree to diligently read and heed the Scripture we have and not waste time wondering about those apostolic writings that God obviously did not intend for us to possess.

# 100

# Remember My Chains

## Colossians 4:18

I, Paul, write this greeting with my own hand. Remember my chains. Grace be with you.

With these three terse comments, Paul brings his letter to the Colossians to a close. And with them we come to the one hundredth and last of our meditations on what he has said.

Paul's custom was to dictate his letters to an amanuensis or secretary, perhaps in this case Tychicus (see Rom. 16:22 where Tertius identifies himself as the one who "wrote this letter"). But now the apostle himself takes pen in hand to write these concluding words (for other instances of the same, see 1 Cor. 16:21; Gal. 6:11; Philem. 19).

What's his purpose in doing so? The answer may be found in the conclusion to his second letter to the Thessalonians. There he writes, "I, Paul, write this greeting with my own hand. This is the sign of genuineness in every letter of mine; it is the way I write" (3:17).

Evidently there was the ever-present threat of forged letters circulating in Paul's name that claimed to have been written by him (cf. 2 Thess. 2:2). The apostle is jealous to guard the truth of what God has revealed and will not tolerate anyone passing himself off under false pretenses and potentially leading the sheep astray. Such is the heart of a good shepherd.

But why call on them to remember his chains? Certainly he's not asking for pity. The last thing he wanted was for them to shift their focus from the sufficiency of Christ to the suffering of his servant. Still, it was important that they (and we) not forget where devotion to Jesus will often lead: to suffering, to loss of freedom, to oppression and the end of convenience and comfort, but never to despair!

I suspect that this request is his way of asking for their continued intercession on his behalf. He doesn't explicitly ask that they pray for his release, but I'm certain he would have welcomed the opportunity to move about freely yet again and share the gospel in those regions where it had not been heard. In any case, he rejoices in his suffering (Col. 1:24) and is faithful to redeem even this season of incarceration for the sake of the mystery of Christ (see Phil. 1:12–18).

Make no mistake: the chains were real, not figurative. Could the fact that Paul hand-wrote only this one final verse be an indication that his hands were shackled and chafed, making any attempt to write particularly painful?

His words here remind me of his exhortation to young Timothy: "Do not be ashamed of the testimony about our Lord, nor of me his prisoner, but share in suffering for the gospel by the power of God" (2 Tim. 1:8). And again, he commends Onesiphorus because "he often refreshed me and was not ashamed of my chains" (2 Tim. 1:16).

Perhaps Paul was concerned lest the Colossians recoil in their commitment to him and above all to Christ because of the embarrassment his imprisonment might evoke. Few people talk openly (and proudly) about a friend or family member who is in jail! It's not a suitable topic for dinner parties or coffee at Starbucks.

Paul knew the pressures they faced, the fear of rejection they felt, together with the appeal of riches and personal comfort that assaulted them on a daily basis. But they must resist the temptation to think that imprisonment for Christ's sake is a disgrace. "Remember my chains! Rejoice in them! Redeem the pain they inflict for the greater glory of our Lord!"

And may the "grace [of God] be with you!" Let me remind you of Paul's inaugural blessing in Colossians 1:2: "Grace to you and peace from God our Father." To make sense of what would otherwise appear as a simple, standard greeting, I cited earlier the words of John Piper. I can do no better than to quote him again, and thus bring our meditations in this marvelous epistle to an end. At the beginning of his letters, writes Piper:

Paul has in mind that the letter itself is a channel of God's grace *to* the readers. Grace is about to flow "from God" through Paul's writing *to* the Christians. So he says, "Grace *to* you." That is, grace is now active and is about to flow from God through my inspired writing *to* you as you read—"grace [be] *to* you." But as the end of the letter approaches, Paul realizes that the reading is almost finished and the question rises, "What becomes of the grace that has been flowing to the readers through the reading of the inspired letter?" He answers with a blessing at the end of every letter: "Grace [be] *with* you." *With* you as you put the letter away and leave the church. *With* you as you go home to deal with a sick child and an unaffectionate spouse. *With* you as you go to work and face the temptations of anger and dishonesty and lust. *With* you as you muster courage to speak up for Christ over lunch.... [Thus] we learn that grace is ready to flow *to* us every time we take up the inspired Scriptures to read them. And we learn that grace will abide *with* us when we lay the Bible down and go about our daily living.[7]

Grace be *with* you!

# Notes

**Part One: Colossians 1:1–29**

1. Jonathan Edwards, "The Importance and Advantage of a Thorough Knowledge of Divine Truth," in *Sermons and Discourses 1739–1742*, ed. Harry S. Stout and Nathan O. Hatch (New Haven, CT: Yale University Press, 2003), 101.
2. *Webster's New Collegiate Dictionary* (Springfield, MA: G. & C. Merriam, 1979): s.v. "assiduous."
3. Klyne Snodgrass, *Ephesians: The NIV Application Commentary* (Grand Rapids, MI: Zondervan, 1996), 40.
4. H. C. G. Moule, *Colossians Studies* (London: Hodder & Stoughton, 1898), 28.
5. John Piper, *Future Grace* (Sisters, OR: Multnomah, 1995), 66–67.
6. John Calvin, *Sermons on the Epistle to the Ephesians* (Carlisle: Banner of Truth, 1973), 83.
7. Cited in G. H. Pike, *The Life and Work of Charles Haddon Spurgeon* (London: Cassell & Co., n.d.), 6:337.
8. Cited in Arnold Dallimore, *Spurgeon* (Chicago: Moody, 1984), 184.
9. Ibid., 183.
10. *One Thing: Developing a Passion for the Beauty of God* (Ross-Shire: Christian Focus, 2004).
11. John Piper, "The Fruit of Hope: Love," a sermon on Colossians 1:3–8 (July 13, 1986), http://www.desiringgod.org.
12. Ibid.
13. Ibid.
14. These can be found at http://www.samstorms.com in the Theological Studies section under "Miscellaneous Topics."
15. James D. G. Dunn, *The Epistles to the Colossians and Philemon: A Commentary on the Greek Text* (Grand Rapids, MI: Eerdmans, 1996), 65.
16. Lloyd John Ogilvie, *Praying with Power* (Ventura, CA: Regal, 1983), 63.
17. See "Book Reviews" at http://www.samstorms.com, Recommended section.
18. James D. G. Dunn, *The Epistles to the Colossians and Philemon*, 72.
19. Peter T. O'Brien, *Colossians, Philemon*, Word Biblical Commentary (Waco: Word, 1982), 22.
20. Ibid., 24.

21. John Piper, *God Is the Gospel: Meditations on God's Love as the Gift of Himself* (Wheaton, IL: Crossway Books, 2005), 13.

22. Ibid., 15.

23. Sam Storms, *The Singing God: Discover the Joy of Being Enjoyed by God* (Lake Mary, FL: Creation, 1998).

24. Jerry Bridges, *Transforming Grace* (Colorado Springs, CO: NavPress, 1988), 40.

25. Charles H. Spurgeon, *The Treasury of David* (Peabody, MA: Hendrickson, n.d.), 1b:82.

26. J. B. Lightfoot, *Saint Paul's Epistles to the Colossians and to Philemon* (1879; repr., Grand Rapids, MI: Zondervan, 1976), 157.

27. Peter T. O'Brien, *Colossians, Philemon*, 53.

28. James D. G. Dunn, *The Epistles to the Colossians and Philemon*, 101.

29. Peter T. O'Brien, *Colossians, Philemon*, 265.

30. *The Dallas Morning News*, March 4, 2006, 3H.

31. John Murray, "The Reconciliation," in *Collected Writings of John Murray* (Carlisle: Banner of Truth, 1982), 4:99–100.

32. John Eadie, *A Commentary on the Greek Text of the Epistle of Paul to the Colossians* (Grand Rapids, MI: Kregel, n.d.), 22–23.

33. For a fuller discussion you can check out my web site (http://www.samstorms.com) in the Theological Studies section under "Eternal Security."

34. See my web site (http://www.SamStorms.com) for an extensive discussion of this position and what I believe is a biblical response to it.

35. John Piper, *Desiring God: Meditations of a Christian Hedonist* (Sisters, OR: Multnomah, 2003), 268.

36. Ibid., 269.

37. Ibid., 269–70.

38. Murray J. Harris, *Exegetical Guide to the Greek New Testament: Colossians and Philemon* (Grand Rapids, MI: Eerdmans, 1991), 72.

39. J. I. Packer, *Keep in Step with the Spirit* (Old Tappan, NJ: Revell, 1984), 156.

## Part Two: Colossians 2:1–23

1. Jonathan Edwards, *The Life of David Brainerd*, ed. Norman Pettit (New Haven, CT: Yale University Press, 1985), 7:162.

2. Ibid.

3. Ibid., 260.

4. Cited in Charles Spurgeon, *Lectures to My Students* (Grand Rapids, MI: Zondervan, 1975), 48.

5. Cited in Donald G. Bloesch, *The Struggle of Prayer* (San Francisco: Harper & Row, 1980), 79.

6. James Henley Thornwell, *The Collected Writings of James Henley Thornwell*, vol. 2 (1875; repr., London: Banner of Truth, 1974), 442–43.

7. C. E. B. Cranfield, *A Critical and Exegetical Commentary on the Epistle to the Romans* (Edinburgh: T. & T. Clark, 1979), 2:777.

8. Peter T. O'Brien, *Colossians, Philemon*, Word Biblical Commentary (Waco: Word, 1982), 117.

9. John Piper, "Buried and Raised in Baptism through Faith," a sermon on Colossians 2:8–15 (May 11, 1997), http://www.desiringgod.org.

10. John R. W. Stott, *The Message of Ephesians: God's New Society* (Downers Grove, IL: InterVarsity, 1979), 72.

11. Quoted in John Gerstner, *A Predestination Primer* (Winona Lake, IN: Alpha, 1979), 20.

12. J. B. Lightfoot, *Saint Paul's Epistles to the Colossians and to Philemon* (1879; repr., Grand Rapids, MI: Zondervan, 1976), 150.

13. F. F. Bruce, *The Epistles to the Colossians, to Philemon, and to the Ephesians* (Grand Rapids, MI: Eerdmans, 1984).

14. John Calvin, *The Epistles of Paul the Apostle to the Galatians, Ephesians, Philippians and Colossians*, trans. T. H. L. Parker (Grand Rapids, MI: Eerdmans, 1972), 336.

15. F. F. Bruce, *The Epistles to the Colossians, to Philemon, and to the Ephesians*, 117.

16. See chap. 8, "What to Eat When You're on a Fast," in my book *Pleasures Evermore: The Life-Changing Power of Enjoying God* (Colorado Springs, CO: NavPress, 2000).

17. David E. Garland, *Colossians and Philemon: The NIV Application Commentary* (Grand Rapids, MI: Zondervan, 1998), 177.

18. David E. Garland, *Colossians and Philemon*, 188.

**Part Three: Colossians 3:1–25**

1. David E. Garland, *Colossians and Philemon: The NIV Application Commentary* (Grand Rapids, MI: Zondervan, 1998), 222.

2. Peter T. O'Brien, *Colossians, Philemon*, Word Biblical Commentary (Waco: Word, 1982), 165.

3. John Piper, "All Things Are from God, through God, and to God. The Glory Is All His," a sermon on Romans 11:33–36 (March 28, 2004), http://www.desiringgod.org.

4. John Stott, *The Gospel & the End of Time: The Message of 1 & 2 Thessalonians* (Downers Grove, IL: InterVarsity, 1991), 149.

5. John Owen, "Of the Mortification of Sin in Believers," in *The Works of John Owen*, vol. 6 (Carlisle: Banner of Truth, 1974), 9.

6. *Webster's New Collegiate Dictionary* (Springfield: G. & C. Merriam, 1979): s.v. "reckless."

7. F. F. Bruce, *The Epistles to the Colossians, to Philemon, and to the Ephesians* (Grand Rapids, MI: Eerdmans, 1984), 266.

8. David E. Garland, *Colossians and Philemon: The NIV Application Commentary* (Grand Rapids, MI: Zondervan, 1998), 224.

9. Peter T. O'Brien, *Colossians, Philemon*, 178.

10. John Piper, *Future Grace* (Sisters, OR: Multnomah, 1995), 221.

11. Ibid.

## Notes

12. Ibid.
13. Joel B. Green and Mark D. Baker, *Recovering the Scandal of the Cross: Atonement in New Testament & Contemporary Contexts* (Downers Grove, IL: InterVarsity, 2000).
14. Ibid., 56.
15. Ibid., 63.
16. Ibid., 53.
17. Ibid., 55.
18. Ibid., 54.
19. J. I. Packer, *Knowing God* (1973; repr., Downers Grove, IL: InterVarsity, 1993), 151.
20. Leon Morris, *The Apostolic Preaching of the Cross* (Grand Rapids, MI: Eerdmans, 1972), 185.
21. C. E. B. Cranfield, *A Critical and Exegetical Commentary on the Epistle to the Romans* (Edinburgh: T. & T. Clark, 1979), 1:111.
22. Peter T. O'Brien, *Colossians, Philemon*, 188.
23. See Daniel B. Wallace, *Greek Grammar beyond the Basics: An Exegetical Syntax of the New Testament* (Grand Rapids, MI: Zondervan, 1996), 491–92.
24. Ernest Best, *A Critical and Exegetical Commentary on Ephesians* (Edinburgh: T & T Clark, 1998), 450.
25. Peter T. O'Brien, *Colossians, Philemon*, 188.
26. John Stott, *The Gospel & the End of Time*, 185.
27. Peter T. O'Brien, *Colossians, Philemon*, 190–91.
28. Ibid., 191.
29. Andrew T. Lincoln, *Ephesians*, Word Biblical Commentary (Dallas: Word, 1990), 285–86.
30. David E. Garland, *Colossians and Philemon*, 206.
31. C. F. D. Moule, *Colossians Studies*, 120.
32. Murray J. Harris, *Exegetical Guide to the Greek New Testament: Colossians and Philemon* (Grand Rapids, MI: Eerdmans, 1991), 153.
33. Ibid.
34. Ibid., 155.
35. Jackie Pullinger, *Chasing the Dragon* (Ann Arbor, MI: Servant, 1980).
36. I highly recommend Dan Allender's book *Bold Love* (Colorado Springs, CO: NavPress, 1993).
37. Again, see Allender's book *Bold Love* for insights on this theme.
38. James D. G. Dunn, *The Epistles to the Colossians and Philemon: A Commentary on the Greek Text* (Grand Rapids, MI: Eerdmans, 1996), 232.
39. David E. Garland, *Colossians and Philemon*, 211–12.
40. James D. G. Dunn, *The Epistles to the Colossians and Philemon*, 232.
41. Murray J. Harris, *Exegetical Guide to the Greek New Testament: Colossians and Philemon*, 165.
42. James D. G. Dunn, *The Epistles to the Colossians and Philemon*, 239.
43. Ibid.
44. Murray J. Harris, *Exegetical Guide to the Greek New Testament: Colossians and Philemon*, 169.

45. Peter T. O'Brien, *Colossians, Philemon*, 209.
46. Warren Wiersbe, *Real Worship* (Nashville, TN: Oliver Nelson, 1986), 137.
47. Sam Storms, *The Singing God: Discover the Joy of Being Enjoyed by God* (Lake Mary, FL: Creation, 1998), 22.
48. James D. G. Dunn, *The Epistles to the Colossians and Philemon*, 240.
49. John Stott, *The Gospel & the End of Time*, 232.
50. C. F. D. Moule, *Colossians Studies*, 129.
51. John Stott, *The Gospel & the End of Time*, 235.
52. Peter T. O'Brien, *Colossians, Philemon*, 225.
53. John Eadie, *A Commentary on the Greek Text of the Epistle of Paul to the Colossians* (Grand Rapids, MI: Kregel, n.d.), 261.
54. Craig S. Keener, *Paul, Women & Wives: Marriage and Women's Ministry in the Letters of Paul* (Peabody, MA: Hendrickson, 1992), 184.
55. Wayne Grudem, *Evangelical Feminism & Biblical Truth* (Sisters, OR: Multnomah, 2004), 341.
56. Ibid., 340.

**Part Four: Colossians 4:1–18**

1. John Eadie, *A Commentary on the Greek Text of the Epistle of Paul to the Colossians* (Grand Rapids, MI: Kregel, n.d.), 266.
2. John Piper, "Walk in Wisdom toward Those Outside," a sermon on Colossians 4:2–6 (May 29, 1988), http://www.desiringgod.org.
3. Ibid.
4. Peter T. O'Brien, *Colossians, Philemon*, Word Biblical Commentary (Waco: Word, 1982), 241.
5. Murray J. Harris, *Exegetical Guide to the Greek New Testament: Colossians and Philemon*, 197.
6. Peter T. O'Brien, *Colossians, Philemon*, 256.
7. John Piper, *Future Grace* (Sisters, OR: Multnomah, 1995), 66–67.